HOW TO RETHINK MENTAL ILLNESS

The world of mental illness is typically framed around symptoms and cures, where every client is given a label. In this challenging new book, Professor Bernard Guerin provides a fresh alternative to considering these issues, based in interdisciplinary social sciences and discourse analysis rather than medical studies or cognitive metaphors.

A timely and articulate challenge to mainstream approaches, Guerin asks the reader to observe the ecological contexts for behavior rather than diagnose symptoms, to find new ways to understand and help those experiencing mental distress. This book shows the reader:

- how we attribute 'mental illness' to someone's behavior
- why we call some forms of suffering 'mental' but not others
- what Western diagnoses look like when you strip away the theory and categories
- why psychiatry and psychology appeared for the first time at the start of modernity
- the relationship between capitalism and modern ideas of 'mental illness'
- why it seems that women, the poor and people of Indigenous and non-Western backgrounds have worse 'mental health'
- how we can rethink the 'hearing of voices' more ecologically
- how self-identity has evolved historically
- how thinking arises from our social contexts rather than from inside our heads.

Offering solutions rather than theory to develop a new 'post-internal' psychology, *How to Rethink Mental Illness* will be essential reading for every mental health professional, as well as anyone who has either experienced a mental illness themselves, or helped a friend or family member who has.

Bernard Guerin is Professor of Psychology at the University of South Australia, teaching social and community behavior, and language and discourse analysis. Most of his research is now focused on working alongside communities, primarily on issues of responding to racism, mental health, mobility, sustainability of communities and attachment to country. He has worked in partnership with Indigenous Australian, Māori, Somali refugee and migrant communities. His broader goal has been to integrate social and community psychology with other social sciences into an interdisciplinary framework for practical analysis and intervention.

HOW TO RETHINK MENTAL ILLNESS

The Human Contexts behind the Labels

Bernard Guerin

FEB 08 2018

PROPERTY OF
SENECA COLLEGE
LIBRARIES
KING CAMPUS

Routledge
Taylor & Francis Group

LONDON AND NEW YORK

First published 2017
by Routledge
2 Park Square, Milton Park, Abingdon, Oxon OX14 4RN

and by Routledge
711 Third Avenue, New York, NY 10017

Routledge is an imprint of the Taylor & Francis Group, an informa business

© 2017 Bernard Guerin

The right of Bernard Guerin to be identified as the author of this work
has been asserted by him in accordance with sections 77 and 78 of the
Copyright, Designs and Patents Act 1988.

All rights reserved. No part of this book may be reprinted or reproduced or
utilised in any form or by any electronic, mechanical, or other means, now
known or hereafter invented, including photocopying and recording, or in
any information storage or retrieval system, without permission in writing
from the publishers.

Trademark notice: Product or corporate names may be trademarks or
registered trademarks, and are used only for identification and explanation
without intent to infringe.

British Library Cataloguing in Publication Data
A catalogue record for this book is available from the British Library

Library of Congress Cataloging in Publication Data
Names: Guerin, Bernard, 1957- author.
Title: How to rethink mental illness : the human contexts behind the
    labels / Bernard Guerin.
Description: New York, NY : Routledge, 2017. | Includes bibliographical
    references and index.
Identifiers: LCCN 2016044341| ISBN 9781138207295 (hbk : alk.
    paper) | ISBN 9781138207301 (pbk : alk. paper) |
    ISBN 9781315462615 (ebk)
Subjects: LCSH: Mental illness. | Thought and thinking.
Classification: LCC RC460 .G84 2017 | DDC 616.89—dc23
LC record available at https://lccn.loc.gov/2016044341

ISBN: 978-1-138-20729-5 (hbk)
ISBN: 978-1-138-20730-1 (pbk)
ISBN: 978-1-315-46261-5 (ebk)

Typeset in Bembo
by Swales & Willis Ltd, Exeter, Devon, UK

CONTENTS

TABLES

FIGURES

PREFACE

Like many others, I started studying and reading psychology (before university in fact) because I wanted to understand myself better, because I wanted to help people (naïvely), and because I wanted to be a clinical psychologist. By the time I started university I was 'into' Jung in a big way, but was then puzzled by the small amounts in my courses which seemed to be about actually under-standing people, by the huge number of theories, and by the abstractness of the new cognitive theories that had taken over psychology at that time.

I knuckled under to the conformity and went on to do a PhD in an almost completely abstract and highly theoretical area of social psychology called 'social facilitation'. I later turned that work into my first book. Despite look-ing like a model cognitive social psychologist, the conclusion of that book (rarely noticed by readers) was that the whole area was not of much use and that researchers needed to observe far more *context* in real settings for it to be of any use. A portent: "that we study the conditions in the various settings rather than the patterns of responding themselves" (p. 186). For this book, we should read: "that we study the contexts in the various life settings rather than the patterns of mental health behaviours by themselves".

My research since that early time has been trying to make the study of people's social behaviour into something more realistic of everyday lives and people's real lives. In doing this I have worked my way through every major approach to studying humans, learning in detail the other social sciences which also 'explain' social behaviour but which were ignored in social psychology—especially social anthropology and sociology—as well as learning from discourse analysis and postmodern and poststructuralist approaches, and more besides.

During a wonderfully free postdoc period, I also absorbed the behaviour analysis approach and learned much from there, especially to focus on natural observations and not to worry about a lack of theories. Theorizing just tells us that you have not observed enough and must resort to making something up to fill in the gaps from your weak observations. Of course, I had already learned from social anthropology that you must spend a lot of time with people if you want to really understand them—something foreign to most psychology researchers and their methodologies (who are currently happy to understand people with online surveys).

With this book, I have come a full circle back to my younger aim of making a contribution to a more realistic psychology, to clinical psychology, and to the suffering of people given labels of 'mental illness'. But this is nothing like I might have imagined entering university armed with both my Jung's Collected Works and my naïve good intentions.

I do not have all the answers but I argue strongly that we should not be complacent about how we think of 'mental illness'. There is so much in psychology, especially in theory and research methods, that everyone just goes along with without being critical—what I call 'professional acquiescence'. I try to focus on the observable, especially the suffering of people labelled with mental illness as part of the general pool of suffering we find in all lives, not as something special inside our heads. This forms an ecological or contextual approach focused on observing as much as we can about people and their contexts before making judgements. It also takes a 'post-internal' view of psychology (if we should still call it that) in which a person's actions, talk and thinking originate in their external social ecology, not in their head, their brain, or the more mysterious 'mind'.

Part of my later research over two or more decades, with a few great teams of researchers, was to use these longer methods and contextual observations to find out more about the 'mental health' of people with a refugee background and with Indigenous peoples. Living alongside those groups over years taught me even more about how 'mental health' symptoms are ordinary ways (perhaps gone wrong) of dealing with bad conflict situations, and also taught me how Western society *causes* a lot of the current mental health issues from the way it forces us all to live now. That is all in this book as well, although there is so much more we need to learn with the right methods.

So, this approach makes a lot of the weird stuff in talking and thinking about 'mental illness' look more like sincere attempts by ordinary people to adapt to difficult situations not of their making. It also removes the blame from the victims and forces us to observe more of someone's contexts before attempting to judge them, analyse what they do, intervene to change them, or claim that we can understand what they do, say or think.

ACKNOWLEDGEMENTS

This book is a culmination of many years, so there are too many people to thank (or even remember). But I would like to thank Mike Innes for his tacit approval during my PhD for reading widely (everything) and having discussions with me over any of the issues I was reading about, and the University of Queensland for the generous Postdoc so many years ago which gave me the privilege of again reading widely.

My key audiences for this particular material have been Rhianna, Vincent, Marcela, Kamelia, Gui, Abdirizak, Pauline, Fatuma, Natalie, Mel, Anthony, Julio, Deirdre, Bebe, Gary, and Sandra, and the many participants in research who discussed their life experiences of 'mental illness' and their ideas. I especially thank all those researchers *and participants* in the lengthy studies with Indigenous peoples and with people of refugee background. Many thanks one and all, I will not name you; you know we worked together but perhaps do not know how much I learned from you.

I wish to thank NaNoWriMo for providing a virtual space five times for me to write. Sure, I did the all the planning and the goals, and certainly all the hard work, but they provided a virtual space for me to do all that.

Finally, also many thanks to the staff at Routledge for their belief in this trilogy, especially Michael Strang, and their excellent production work.

A note on referencing and acknowledging the earlier work of others (or lack thereof)

I wish to say upfront that this book depends on the work of many researchers and authors. In all my previous books I have given hundreds of references to the work of others that has shaped my thinking. However, I know that referencing slows down a lot of readers whom I would like to take something away from this current book which might be of use to them. Many of my intended readers also do not have the privilege of being able to track down the references in any case.

For these reasons, I am being a very bad academic in this book and mostly referring to my own summary works. This current book has been intentionally written so that it can be understood without knowing those earlier books, but to academics (real ones, not me) this causes them distress because it looks like I am claiming others' ideas. I certainly do not intend this but having thousands of references interrupting the text causes distress to other readers. This time, I am balancing the distress the other way. You can find the references in my earlier books if that is still of importance. I have also used entries in the current Index taken from these earlier books so references can be found more easily and details followed up.

Obviously, where I use or rely heavily on someone's work, I cite it. But I have done my referential duty for academia many times in the past and academics can look up all the references they like and find the sources. I do not have much confidence in the current state of academia in any case. But this book is aimed at different audiences.

1

WHICH BEHAVIOURS ARE JUDGED AS 'MENTAL ILLNESS' AND WHY ARE THEY CALLED 'MENTAL'?

> People do not 'have mental illness'; people live, and have lived, in contexts that do not support healthy behaviours.

This statement is the starting and finishing point for this book. We need to rethink what is thought of as mental illness, and, by the end of the book, discover and describe the contexts that bring about the behaviours, complaints or 'symptoms' that are currently attributed to a disease, chemical or brain problem. This is not easy, and many theorists have called for this in principle but have not been able to show those contexts or environments which can replace the old models. Some practitioners have been able to work effectively in these ways to make changes, but have been unable to articulate what exactly is happening.

The basis for this book is simple in outline:

- We have been thinking about the 'psychology' of people in wrong ways for a few centuries.
- We can rethink 'psychology' in terms of external contexts—a 'post-internal' discipline.
- Mental health has not been dealt with very well for a long time.
- We can apply new ways of rethinking 'psychology' to explore new ways to rethink 'mental health'.
- A large part of 'mental health' involves how we talk and think, which currently hides behind an abstract metaphor of 'cognition', but we can also rethink these to explore even further.

One of the problems is that most people in psychology and psychiatry currently can think about people and their behaviour *only* in one specific way, most commonly as a cognitive information-processing organism, and they *cannot* think in other ways. They cannot realistically view what people do and think about it in innovative ways—they are stuck in the paradigm of the last 50 years and cannot yet see beyond this. This is at its worst when dealing with how people talk and think.

So the purpose of this book is not to present arguments that psychiatry, the DSM (American Psychiatric Association, 2013), clinical psychology, counselling, mental health nursing or mental health social work, are all wrong. I will summarize many critiques as presented by myself and others in the first three chapters, but will also defend some of the many useful things we have learned through these disciplines, although this will be more rescuing some of the effective practices rather than rescuing the theories or conceptualizations (Guerin, 2016a, 2016b).

My real aim for this book, though, is to go beyond any critiques of the past and help readers *explore* more concrete new ways to observe and deal specifically with mental health issues from many angles. How mental health is conceptualized is an extremely important question. Different conceptions of mental health have led to changes in how interventions are conducted, how people are treated, whether or not drugs are given, how research is conducted, how results are interpreted, what is excluded as belonging to another domain ('That is not a mental health issue; that is only a social work/ housing issue'), how criticisms are formulated, and, just as importantly, what services get funded. It also means that some people can be considered as having 'problems' while others are considered 'normal' even though they or the people around them might all be suffering greatly.

My goal is to centre '*suffering*' as our main focus, since I will show that 'mental health' suffering is part of any other suffering and is not essentially or metaphysically different. The ways it has been incorrectly treated as being something different will be examined in this chapter and Chapter 4 more specifically. This means that we need to analyse all the types of suffering together and not divide the universe into the mental and the physical. They are both intertwined in the real world and they each influence the others. The focus will therefore be on suffering, distress, stress, misery, but here focused on those forms of suffering *usually said* to be caused by 'mental health issues'. We will find more naturalistic or ecological ways of talking about this as we go (Chapters 2 and 3). The reader is urged to begin thinking about what they actually mean by 'mental', and in what situations they even use that word.

In Chapters 1 and 4, I try and identify some of the properties that have made practitioners treat 'mental health' as something very different from other suffering, and the metaphors they have mistakenly used to bolster this. None of this will change the fact that people suffer and that people labelled as having 'mental health issues' suffer in a different and severe way. I am not here to say that psychiatry and psychology have mistakenly said that 'mental health' issues are painful when they are not. They are.

In all, even if you do not like the ways I am rethinking mental health, I want this book to show you that it can be done—we *can* think in totally new ways about mental health—and that the way is open for you to rethink in your own way. The real aim is to explore and move beyond the current. I like my way because it makes everything more observable and concrete, and not just hidden in theories and abstract metaphors—even 'thinking' itself will be shown to be observable and concrete.

How do people attribute 'mental health' issues to behaviour?

There are many current ways to 'identify' someone as having poor mental health or a mental illness. Here are some of the most common ways of identifying mental health and illness that apply to almost all methods of identification:

- A person acts in a way that is not considered usual or normal.
- A person talks in a way that is not considered usual or normal.
- A person acts or talks in a way that indicates they are *likely* to behave or talk unusually.
- A person acts in a way that is considered dangerous, irrational, unsafe or not functional, to themselves or to others.

These points, of course, paint a huge canvas of human actions. The problems with this are that:

- The methods of determination differ and are sometimes in conflict.
- Some imply a cause or a treatment that others do not.
- Most are based on different and very selective observations to either arrive at the identification or to confirm the identification.
- There are some 'official' versions of identifying mental health and illness that gain priority in many settings.

In particular, the DSM-5 Diagnostic Manual (APA, 2013) has credence in almost all government and hospital settings in the Western world. It requires 'accredited' persons to make those judgements. So you only can 'really' get a diagnosis if a qualified (that is, trained in a particular way of thinking) medical person says so according to diagnostic criteria. I will pull apart the behaviours utilized in doing this in Chapter 4.

But let us look first at some examples to show how you might try to differentiate what is a mental health issue or not. These are fictitious but based upon plausible, real events or disguised events from my experience. They are not presented to show you the true answers; they are here to get you thinking and then rethinking about how we even begin to judge 'normal' from 'problematic' mental health. Then we can begin looking at how we judge 'mental' health from any other health.

Box 1.1

- Just because I always wear a hat to work but one day do not, this does not mean that I have a mental illness. Likewise, just because I kill someone (which is not normal) who has stolen all my money and run off with my partner does not mean I will be diagnosed as having mental illness (although I will be put in prison). However, if someone takes my hat away and I shoot them, mental health questions will be asked.

- If I say that Jesus or God talks to me at night and I am a devout Christian, then mental health questions might not be asked (some denominations might). If I say that the large boulders on my Country were left after an Ancestor from my Dreaming moved through the area, then mental health questions might not be asked. If I say that I have just started hearing voices telling me that my mother-in-law is the Devil, then mental health questions might be asked.

- If I lose my job and report that I am extremely sad, but I continue to look for a new job and do day-to-day chores, then mental health questions will not be asked (although a social worker might organize some support for me). If I lose my job and begin spending all day in bed, not eating, and not talking to anyone at all, then mental health questions might be asked.

Now consider a few more examples, and judge not just whether *you* consider these might be mental health problems but also what other people might say. Remember that the point is not to get a correct answer but to *observe what you are doing when you think through the examples.* Think carefully about what you are doing when you do this and what you are basing that judgement on. Even if you refuse to make a judgment, consider instead why are you refusing, and what would you need to know or do to resolve that?

Box 1.2

- A woman is walking down a street when a man runs out of a store with a knife and stabs her as he runs away; when she has recovered she begins to stay inside her home and avoids going out.
- A woman feels dissatisfied with her life and arranges to go and spend six months in a Buddhist monastery meditating.
- A war Veteran does a good job at work and is a good family man but every once in a while he starts ranting in a strange way and ends up leaving work or home for the day and gets very drunk; the next day he acts as if nothing happened and is quite functional again.
- A young woman spends all her holidays and money parachute-diving off very high mountains, and gliding down; she also gets flown by helicopter to the tops of snow-covered mountains and then skis down very dangerous slopes.
- A young woman maintains a job but spends all her weekends going out to pubs with friends and getting drunk; she also takes some drugs each night by herself at home but no serious drugs.
- An Australian Indigenous man is feeling poorly and arranges for a Ngangkari (traditional healer) to visit him; the Ngangkari goes through a process of catching the man's 'spirit' which has become loose and putting it back into the man.
- A middle-aged man has an executive job in a bank and a happy family life but he suddenly declares that he feels his life is superficial, so he gives up his work completely and he now lives on welfare and works as a volunteer for a charity part-time, while spending more time with his family.

The point here is not whether you are right or wrong in how you judge these, although it is very instructive to have friends read them independently and then discuss what you come up with.

The main point is to think about what exactly we are doing to even make the attributions that some behaviours are 'symptoms' of mental illness and others are not. In some cases there is an obvious *context* that sways you or persuades you to think that there are no mental health issues, and even that this might be very healthy behaviour, but without that context, you might be swayed to think that the person does have a 'mental health' issue. Hearing God or your Ancestors talk to you is okay, but hearing your cupboard talk to you is not. But what about if your God talks to you and tells you to go and kill people, is that okay still? What if you are not Christian at all but suddenly report hearing a Christian God talking to you (I have seen this)?

What I would like you to learn from these exercises is that *your attribution of whether actions are even 'mental health' issues or not closely depends upon what you know about the context, and the metaphors or theories with which you think about such things*. And, moreover, in most cases we are judging the actions that we see against what are considered 'normal', 'understandable', or 'speakable' contexts. I will use *'speakable'* to mean that you can give a good story alongside your judgement that will convince people of your version (regardless of the truth).

None of this means that non-normal looking behaviours are actually okay; the point so far is getting you to see the many ways that people judge behaviours as being of concern or not. In fact, 1) lots of non-normal looking behaviours are of real concern, but we still need to put what is happening into a fuller context and not rely solely on that judgment against the 'norm'; 2) there are also lots of 'normal' behaviours that are seriously problematic; and 3) there are also lots of non-normal behaviours that are not only okay but also creative and useful.

Problems with identifying mental health and an alternative way of thinking

> Just what the soldiers classified as mental cases were suffering from baffled most people at the time. Though shell bursts apparently triggered off most of the patients, only 3 per cent of those classified officially as 'shellshock' cases had actual brain lesions. In February 1915 the Lancet could only suggest molecular commotion in the brain as a result of high-frequency vibration. John Bull, Bottomley's sensational magazine widely read by the troops, advertised Dr. Muller's Nerve

Nutrient (guaranteed not German), 'The primary trouble in all phases of nerve exhaustion', ran the advertisement, 'is the semi-starvation of the nerve cells, the reason being that the sufferer fails to extract from his daily food the precious, concentrated nutrient that nerve cells live and thrive on.' As an opinion, it was no further from the truth that official medical pronouncements of the time. . .

(Winter, 1978; Death's men: Soldiers of the Great War, p. 130)

It has been pointed out by many people that a real problem with attributions of mental health and illness is that the attributions frequently depend upon what is considered 'normal'. I am going to argue that it is worse than just this, and depends on whether the 'context' for the behaviour is *salient*, and this sometimes means whether it is 'normal'. Risk-taking by gliding off mountain cliffs is certainly not 'normal' for most people but we can understand something about the contexts for what that person is doing and why they might find it attractive. So there is a 'speakable' story we can tell about why it is ok, and which will refer to some reassuring contexts: 'It is perfectly safe, Mum, there are safety ropes, and everyone else is doing it now.' We certainly would not call up the local mental health service and attempt to have such a person admitted.

On the other hand, a young woman spending all her time and money partying is not necessarily unusual in many groups, but we might imagine circumstances in which we would begin to think (identify) that she has a mental health problem—perhaps if her work starts suffering or she continues in that way over a period of years. For another of the examples given earlier, people know (a salient 'speakable' story for context) that many war Veterans have trauma problems, so would the person presented above have a mental disorder if he continues at work except once in a while going on a bender? How can we be certain since we can barely understand what he must have been through and how he must have been affected? The problem, then, is that any 'speakable' story we give for our reasoning will be sadly lacking in real experience and instead based on what we have seen on television.

So, I am not arguing that judgments of 'normality' are always problematic, but I believe there are problems which are slightly different, as my form of questioning suggests. There are several facets to this that you must consider, which I have tried to show in Table 1.1. And note that these are not only about mental health judgments but are common in many domains of knowledge.

TABLE 1.1 Typical observations and conclusions about people

How we typically 'observe' or know about a person

From a short timeframe of visual observations
Visual observations in an unusual context for that person
Verbal reports from the person
Verbal reports from others
General knowledge we have picked up about that 'type' of person

---

What we conclude about that person

The behaviour is due to cause X if:
  If that cause is salient
  If we observe it during the short timefame
  If that cause is socially acceptable as a cause
  If that cause is able to be articulated and justified
  If that cause is 'speakable' and makes a good story
  If it fits with our prior knowledge of that 'type' of person
If none of the above then that behaviour will be attributed to various verbal abstractions,
  generalizations, and essentialisms:
  Mental disorders: 'They have a mental disorder or illness that is affecting them'
  Race: 'It is something about this race of people that predisposes them . . .'
  Culture: 'It is a cultural thing'
  Indigeneity: 'It is part of their Indigenous histories'
  Brain dysfunction: 'There is an unidentified brain problem'
  Evolution: 'It is a hard-wired problem'
  Dysfunctional cognition and decision-making: 'They processed information
  wrongly'

Here are some notes now to help clarify where we have got to so far in our rethinkings:

1. *Just because some action can be considered 'normal' does not mean that no help is required—there can still be suffering.* A young woman getting drunk and taking drugs most nights of the week might be normal in some groups but she probably needs some help to change.

   One of the most common 'normalities' used in mental health identi-fication is that of 'normal life functioning'—a person is okay unless they can no longer function in a normal way. This implies that a person of refugee background is basically okay even if they cry a lot about family members who were killed in the war, but if they can no longer make lunches for their children or wash their clothes then this is a mental health issue. Similarly, this is difficult to judge in the case above of the bank executive who gives up his job to go on welfare and do charity work—is there something seriously wrong with him because he is no longer functioning properly, or is he actually functioning properly for the first time ever now because he is not focused on getting profits for the bank but instead focused on his family and charity work? And what about the woman who goes to live in a Buddhist monastery? Is she also perhaps functioning perfectly for the first time in her life? The question of 'functioning' and 'dysfunctional' will be given some serious rethinking in Chapter 4, and in Chapter 6 I will show it is actually the new neo-liberal version of the old 'irrational = insane'.

2. *If there is an obvious, salient or 'speakable' cause then the behaviour is explained that way; if there is no obvious cause then the behaviour is explained as 'internal', 'psychological', or 'mental'.* This works in many ways. I have seen professionals suggest that a person of refugee background is acting in a peculiar way *because* of previous trauma, purely because that seems a salient cause, and *even though they know almost nothing else about the person and could be wrong.* I have seen professionals suggest that a person does not have mental health issues *because* they are of a particular cultural group who often do that sort of thing, *even though they know little else about the person and could be very wrong.* They usually preface these judgements with 'this is based on my wide experience', but if they have been relying on salient 'causes' during all their wide experiences then this is circular.

(I do not mean to pick on professionals here; I use them just to emphasize that this is widespread and serious. Lay-people usually make worse judgements because professionals at least get exposed to a lot more variety and experiences with people in their work life than lay-people do, although professionals can be blinkered by their professional training about what causes what. Professionals are also usually under external time constraints and resource limitations that make their jobs less than what they themselves would like, and psychiatrists are forced to arrive at DSM decisions by professional and governmental rules.)

3. *Assigning causes to any behaviour in reality is extremely complex.* I am not discussing the philosophy of 'true' causation here, but discussing the study of how people in everyday life find and assign causes to people's behaviour—their own as well as others. This is extremely complex and involves how we have learned the very language that we use to talk about behaviour (Edwards & Potter, 1993; Guerin, 2016b; Lee, 1986, 1988). The upshot is that such discursive considerations should at the very least make us wary about simply attributing any non-normal action or talk to a cause, or to label such actions as a symptom of 'mental illness'.

This means we need to look more carefully at what we are doing when assigning something to the category of 'mental illness', and we need to spend far more time observing and documenting the person's contexts. This is one theme I will pursue in this book, and it raises a question about whether psychiatrists and clinical psychologists are even the best people to make these judgements.

So it would be worthwhile reading through the examples given earlier, and really try to work out what you actually know and what you do not know. What causes were jumping out at you and what assumptions got your silent acquiescence? What would you need to really understand the context of these persons' behaviour? What do you think when there is no 'obvious' or 'salient' cause jumping out at you? Is it suddenly an 'internal' cause? Do you get a 'speakable' story or mere waft of information that justifies what you will decide?

4.   *We should look for the contexts in which the behaviours emerge rather than a cause of those behaviours.* This is a more difficult point to get across since it goes against a lot of Western thinking (Guerin, 2016a, 2016b). Sometimes it comes with words and phrases such as 'holistic', 'systems approach' or 'ecological approach'. One ecological way I like to think of this it to consider that the sun does not *cause* a plant to grow, nor do the nutrients in the ground *cause* a plant to grow. Rather, we think in terms of there being many contexts needed in order for a plant to grow, and also many contexts in which plants die or grow slowly. These contexts include not just sun, water, nutrients, etc., but also a *lack* of large objects falling on the plant, a *lack* of dogs digging up the plants, weak competition from the plants growing next to it, etc. Note that many of these contexts are negative ones (an absence of something) and therefore difficult to think of, observe, and factor into a judgment of cause.

> Social scientists have badly misunderstood Indian customs. . . When they look at Indian customs, particularly in relationship to plants and animals, and say, 'Indians have this great taboo that something is going to happen unless they do certain things with plant and animal remains,' I think that this is taking the Western quadrant and projecting onto the Indian psyche a cause-and-effect relationship with the world. . . In this cooperative enterprise between humans and other life-forms, you cannot leave a cycle of relationships undone or hanging loose.
>
> *(Deloria, 1999, p. 226)*

In the same way as Deloria's quote, I find it more useful to *think of 'mental health' and illness as occurring outside the person*—as the external contexts in which a person is embedded rather than as an 'internal' state caused by one or two simple (meaning easily identified, salient or 'speakable') causes. This obviously makes it more difficult to draw a line and declare that everything on this side is mental illness and everything on the other side is mental health. But that is how things are, and only some conceptualizations force us to try and find a clear borderline (see *Anti-Kraepelin* below).

5. *There are many ways that context and causes are hidden from superficial observations, especially in a one-hour professional interview.* Another less obvious point is that there are many ways in which contexts (and also causes if you still wish to think that way) are hidden from us and therefore get passed over when attributing mental illness to someone's suffering. As already alluded to, I believe that if no obvious causes can be found then most people in the world attribute the cause or context to either something supernatural or else to an inner or internal determination. If you always wear a hat and one day you do not, and if there is no obvious cause to this change, then I will conclude that you have internally *chosen* to do this. If I know instead that a work colleague made fun of your hat the day before, then this becomes a salient and very speakable external context for 'explaining' the absence of the hat, regardless of the truth. But without knowing that context, or even knowing how to look for it in most cases, I would get the attribution askew.

This point is huge, because our Western ways of thinking assume that there can be internal causes unconnected from external contexts that lead us or cause us to do certain actions—we choose, decide, believe, opine, etc.—and they supposedly take place somewhere within us, or in undefined minds, psyches, or cognitive processes. But what if I was to tell you that we only ever make attributions of cause to an internal cause (or homunculus) when: (1) there is a commonly held belief to that effect; or (2) if there are no obvious, observable external conditions causing it? This is what I am suggesting, and attributing mental health and illness to a 'mental state or cause' is just one prominent example of this misguided causal thinking (Guerin, 2016a). The answer will be to focus on (2) and look better.

Putting some of these pieces together, what this means is that *assigning contexts (or even causes) becomes a direct function of how much we know about and can observe a person's external context and history of contexts.* This means that 'He decided to buy the blue car' really translates as 'I have no idea why he picked the blue car, so I have relegated the cause to a vague, internal "deciding" process.' This is reflected in Figure 1.1.

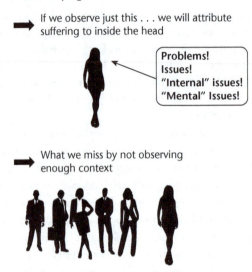

FIGURE 1.1 Observations with and without context

6. *A lot of mental health issues arise from, or are entwined with, how we talk and use language, and this has been poorly analysed in the past.* This argument will be spelt out more in Chapter 3, but how we frame and talk to others and to ourselves—obsessive thinking, for example—is extremely important. But we can look at this in a new way when we consider thoughts and thinking as also arising from the external or ecological contexts in which we live, as social discourses rather than as something mysterious originating 'inside' us that we possess or own (and hence must take responsibility for).

7. *The above points apply to all peoples but the issues arise more often when dealing with people who are very different from you.* This point tries to spell out that the issues to be raised apply to everyone—when we make a judgement about any-one's mental health—psychiatrist and lay-person alike. However, because we understand the context less for those who are different to ourselves, who-ever you might be, these questions have arisen most noticeably for *different* others. This especially applies to Indigenous mental health around the world, and transcultural mental health, which will be examined in Chapters 7 and 8. However, the same questions apply to judgements of mental health even within a Western system and applied to Westerners (e.g. Bentall, 2003). I am arguing that some groups have historically criticized these judgements first (Indigenous and transcultural mental health) because practitioners have been less familiar with the people and the contexts for their lives.

It gets worse, though: in addition, we are usually in a worse position *to find out about* the context of someone's behaviour when that person is different to us than if they are similar. So even if we realized that we needed more contextual observations it might be harder for us to get those observations for people who are different from us.

8.   *This in turn means that the understanding used to judge mental illness depends upon your general and specific social relationship with that person.* It is not that you can 'empathize' with someone similar to you, but as (7) above points out, you are likely to be able to make observations of someone's context who is similar to you more easily. The social relationship certainly also applies to how well you can help that person, but here I am saying is something stronger—that how you make a judgement about mental health depends on your social relationship with that person, because the extent of that relationship determines how well you will know their contexts. (And there are other discursive dangers in just assuming that empathy gains you anything; Shuman, 2005.)

Non-Western ways of identifying mental health

While more will be discussed in later chapters (7 and 8), I would like to say something here about non-Western ways of identifying 'mental health issues' so I do not give the impression that Western ways are the only, or exclusively best, ways. Remember that I am not deciding yet if any judgements are true; I am just summarizing how judgements are made.

The main features we have seen so far appear to be similar in non-Western judgements. While the terms, metaphors and concepts of an 'internal mental illness' are often not used, except more recently or in translations by missionaries or other Westerners, the observation of 'non-normality' and 'lack of normal functioning' are commonly viewed as problematic—even though they might be very, very different. The main differences to Western attributions of problems include these:

- much more emphasis in the judgements around *social and community functioning* rather than exclusively *individual functioning* like Western diagnoses (see Chapter 8);
- attributions to external, spiritual and non-material 'causes' rather than a mind, the brain or another 'physical' or bodily substrate metaphor, but there are many exceptions, such as 'spirits' residing in bodily organs causing the problems;
- the dynamics of change and intervention for such problems are played out in social and community relationships rather than inside an individual's head;
- these social relationship contexts for problems are very complex in most cases and very sophisticated.

As will be written about in Chapter 2 and more fully spelled out later in Chapter 5, these differences are very much connected to the massive changes in social relationships which have occurred over the past few centuries in Western countries (stemming from capitalist forms of resource distribution). Whereas Western people were once also based in large family and community groups for most of the resources they needed in life, we now spend the majority of our Western lives as individuals dealing with strangers for whom we have no familial, strong or life-long attachments; no obligations or responsibility beyond a contractual arrangement for exchanging money and services. I will argue later that it is the changes in these social properties that have changed the nature of identifying and treating life stresses, crises and problems (Chapter 5).

So what we call 'mental health' problems get recognized or identified in kin-based communities and extended families when the social functioning of the *community* is out of kilter, whether or not any individual is behaving differently. If no salient social causes are noticeable (like someone is lazy or cheating the group, or some salient or unexpected community event has occurred), then the causes are attributed to a range of possibilities: witchcraft, bad spirits, jinn, bad intent, etc. These words just listed are our Western words, however, and the actual practices are much more subtle and social than our words imply (e.g. Evans-Pritchard, 1937). What is of importance to note is that the people determining the existence of such problems, often translated as shaman, healers, wise people, elders, etc., are known to be carrying out extremely subtle social observations and negotiations even if they appear to use something like a strict divination method. They are sizing up the whole social context of the communities for their 'diagnosis', not just following a rigid method with an individual.

So, the important points for now are that:

- similar behavioural events are observed in judging 'mental health issues' as for Western methods (like those behaviours listed in Chapter 4);
- the attributions of cause do not usually get placed into bodily causes or the brain (some interesting exceptions occur in social anthropology but they are nothing like our medical brain metaphors);
- these methods are subtle and based heavily in social and community events rather than individual events;
- all this has changed, because the forms of social relationships have been changed hugely in Western societies.

Problems with current ways of identifying mental health

Traditionally in the West, psychiatric and psychological models of mental health have been predominant, especially in terms of the power to make judgements about people and their health for legal purposes. The models used have been various but all worked around an essentialism such that the 'processes' and issues occurred *inside* a person and the intervention involves changing the person's thinking, feeling, behaving, etc. (Guerin, 2016a). The outside context around a person was really only considered insofar as it was conceptualized as how a person 'perceived' the casualty of that problem, or their 'representations' of outside problems, insofar as they could articulate those representations. Interventions were mostly aimed at changing those 'inner' perceptions or representations, usually by talking-therapies. *Most commonly, anything having a strong or obvious external cause would not even be classed as a mental health issue at all.*

Many people have given arguments, however, that psychology and psychiatry have taken an overly essentialistic approach in talking about mental health, and problems are artificially put 'into' the person rather than enough attention being given to the social, cultural and physical (resource) environments which give rise to the behaviours. I have tried to address some of this above by getting you to think through some examples and your explanations, while not trying to be anti-psychiatric and throw the very substantial baby out with the bathwater. Professionals often say that *they have not seen any external contexts* that might have caused the issues, but my question will be: how well have you really looked? Is the 'cause' of the problem 'inside' the person or have you just not looked hard enough, spent enough time looking, or do not know even what to look for in the person's external contexts? (Chapters 2 and 3 will briefly give some methods for doing this.)

The extreme working of such essentialistic discourses leads to some of the paradoxes commonly found in mental health thinking. For example, the position implies that if only the person could 'think' the problem in a different way, or reframe the problem which is inside themselves, then the problem will be solved. This puts the responsibility for change solely on the person, it should be noted, and can be a hidden form of *blaming the victim.* It also leads to attempts to change the 'thinking' by pharmacological means, since 'internal' invariably leads psychiatrists and psychologists to *biological metaphors of the problems*, and their thinking then automatically assumes that a chemical change can solve the problem if reframing does not.

What is ignored in these extreme versions is that changing thinking about having no food, conflicts, no employment, discrimination, etc., does not immediately solve anything. If someone is starving, has family fights ongoing, and has no work or money, then attempting to get them to reframe this more positively is not going to help. One discursive move when professionals face this paradox is to define those outside sources of influence as beyond the realm of mental health issues. Cognitive behaviour therapy is an example of this since only a reframing or change in thinking is intended, not what is done with that afterwards, and other changes in the person's life are relegated to social work. The 'mental' specialist is only there to deal with the perception or thinking about problems, not to solve the external conflict that led to that thinking. That is handed over to a social worker or other professionals (Heller & Gitterman, 2011). Thus begins my arguments to also get rid of a division between health and mental health problems.

There are two questions, then, although I wish to focus more on the second one here. First, the question arises of whether 'mental' health issues are really something uniquely 'psychological' or whether they are just one aspect of external conflicts and problems in life, or the misguided ways that people have tried to cope with those external situations.

This first question of different viewpoints therefore becomes a question of *how far you believe the etiology of behaviours that are seen in 'mental illness' pertains to the context in which a person is immersed rather than something purely about an individual* separate from their context. Most people working in indigenous mental health areas opt more for the former, and I will later argue in Chapter 5 that external context only 'appears' to be less important for those living in Western societies because of the predominance of 'stranger' relationships (Guerin, 2004, 2016a). This is the hub, I believe, of a major divide in the mental health literature, and it is no accident that both the Indigenous and multicultural mental health areas have been the prime discursive domains to raise these discussions since the determinants of mental health seem so different. Women's mental health *should* also have been seen differently but has been accommodated in the Western framework as something being wrong inside women, because of the commonly patriarchal views of professionals (more in Chapter 6).

The second question is about how much of the external context should be recorded, observed and taken into account when dealing with mental health issues—regardless of whether you follow myself and others in believing that everything is externally controlled. On this second question, it has been strongly argued for several reasons that researchers and practitioners in this area should be more inclusive of recording and taking into account contextual material rather than excluding such details. First, as will be seen later in this book, many Indigenous Australians differ in significant and diverse ways in how they run their lives and relationships than the majority of people involved in mental health services. Social anthropologists have long suggested that such issues are complex and depend on complexities that are just not obvious to others immersed in Western society. Second, it has been argued that the ways in which many Indigenous Australians behave is a function of social, historical and political impacts on their ways of life over many decades (Hunter, 2007). Hunter (2007) wisely wrote: 'Summarizing mental health status, then, is fraught with the twin dangers of generalisation and decontextualization—context is critical' (p. 88).

Questioning current psychiatric and psychological treatment justifications

Having seen some of the pitfalls in how we all judge whether a behaviour is about 'mental health' or not, I will now look at the professional guide. As already mentioned and is well-known, the DSM (APA, 2013) is the standard 'diagnostic tool' for psychiatric and psychological practice. Less well known is the foundation for the underlying thinking or theory of this 'tool'. The approach was first lobbied strongly by Emil Kraepelin, a psychiatrist from the early twentieth century. He followed a medical model that 'mental illness' behaviours are symptomatic of 'underlying' physical diseases. One must look closely, he thought, mostly within the brain, for the lesions and tumours and other diseases that lead to the aberrant behaviours.

To make this plausible, Kraepelin attempted to arrange the symptoms into groups or categories which would supposedly predict the physical basis of the disease in the brain. This was meant to mimic doctors and physical health: the way groups of physical symptoms (fever, cough, chest pain, nausea, vomiting or diarrhoea) could predict an underlying physical condition and illness (pneumonia).

I will go through some criticisms of this approach below, but will give two comments here to orient readers who have never known this basis and who need to see the problems with this way of thinking itself. First, this system was *invented* and not *discovered*. Kraepelin went looking for groups of 'behavioural symptoms' to make categories, even though establishing categories is fraught with dangers, as is well known in discourse analysis. Second, *the underlying diseases of the brain or chemical imbalances were never found* and only vague links were found amidst lots of theorizing.

The important point for now is that this way of thinking still underlies the DSM even though it has been changed and expanded in many ways. There are assumed to be *discrete and separable clusters of mental health physical diseases which can be predicted by discrete groupings of behavioural symptoms*. These clusters are said to be separate and there is little or nothing in between, except for what are assumed to be rare 'co-morbid' symptoms. Perhaps the most scary and most damaging point is that these clusters are wrongly talked about as having been *discovered* rather than *invented* or *constructed*, and they are supposed to have a physical basis in reality even though none have been found.

So, it is assumed now that the DSM structure is a 'real' thing and not a theory or metaphor. But it is not. Medical science has found inflammations of the throat and lungs which produce pneumonia and account for all its symptoms; but this is not true for the proposed clusters of 'mental illnesses'. They are metaphorical only (Guerin, 2016a).

The final point for now is that many or most of the 'anti-DSM' proponents have not really proposed any other way of dealing with the area, and new proposals are usually vague. While I am using many of their criticisms in a different way, we do not yet have an alternative. People do suffer from the behaviours mentioned in the DSM and if we want the focus off the DSM/Kraepelin clustering approach we must be able to show plausible alternatives. That is why this book and work from others (e.g. Bentall, 2006) are trying to give some sort of basis for thinking of an alternative and using that to reduce suffering.

Having said this, I will argue and demonstrate (Chapter 4) that we can dispense with the underlying theory and assumption-making of the Kraepelin approach and yet still utilize the descriptions of behaviour which have been amassed in the DSM. If they are based on observations rather than suppositions (as is the DSM structuring and grouping), then we can yet find this a very useful resource. I will make extensive use of this in Chapter 4. Unfortunately, the DSM and Kraepelin approaches do not take much context into account with their individual-centred approaches, so the DSM has very little in the way of *contextual observations* of the behaviours involved; they are just listed behaviours. Researching case studies on the *contexts* which give rise to and change the behaviours that lead to 'mental health' suffering is our next step I believe. More later.

Discursive analysis of the DSM basis

To find the basis for the categorical groupings in the DSM we must therefore look to a discursive analysis of the *words* which have been used rather than the reality of underlying diseases in the brain (which elude us).

(This is similar to what is called the 'sociology of diagnosis', but that research rests more on the use of more physical health criteria than on the DSM psychiatric criteria; Brown, Lyson, & Jenkins, 2011; Jutel & Nettleton, 2011.) I will follow one theme here to deconstruct the language used in psychiatric talk, and Chapter 4 has others.

The Kraepelin approach really goes back to Carl Linnaeus (1707–1778) and the beginnings of animal taxonomy. Linnaeus' method was that you should make a lot of observations about animal bodies, or behaviours in our case, categorize what you see into clusters of genera, families, and species, and then attempt to *discover* (by observation rather than theory) the underlying physical '*substrate*' (this is the word they use) which can differentiate the clusters.

Table 1.2 illustrates some of the uses that have been made of this *category/list methodology*, and you can see the animal taxonomy and general medicine examples, such that the clusters are grouped with respect to the underlying *substrate*. So, for example, with medical observations of fever, chest pain, nausea, vomiting, or diarrhoea, plus test results, we can suggest either pneumonia or food poisoning (simply put). Animal taxonomy uses mostly bodily features, especially the reproductive organs, to place animals into taxonomic clusters.

TABLE 1.2 Examples of the use (and misuse) of taxonomic clustering

Observations	Examples of observations	Clusters with an example	Underlying 'physical substrate'
Animals and their physical features	Reproduction physiology, body features and shape, genetics (rarely behaviour which is frowned upon)	Species, family, genus, subspecies → spiders, scorpions and pseudo-scorpions are related in Class Arachnida	Genetics, physiology and morphology
Medical symptoms	Fever, cough, chest pain, nausea, vomiting, or diarrhoea	Range of diseases → pneumonia	Bodily disease → inflammatory condition of the lung primarily in alveoli

(continued)

TABLE 1.2 *(continued)*

Observations	*Examples of observations*	*Clusters with an example*	*Underlying 'physical substrate'*
Current 'mental' and behavioural symptoms	Depressed mood and/ or loss of interest or pleasure in life activities for at least 2 weeks and at least five of the following symptoms: 1. Depressed mood most of the day. 2. Diminished interest or pleasure in all or most activities. 3. Significant unintentional weight loss or gain. 4. Insomnia or sleeping too much. 5. Agitation or psychomotor retardation noticed by others. 6. Fatigue or loss of energy. 7. Feelings of worthlessness or excessive guilt. 8. Diminished ability to think or concentrate, or indecisiveness. 9. Recurrent thoughts of death.	DSM category system → major depressive episode or major depressive disorder	Bodily disease, usually hypothesized brain lesions; or dysfunctional cognitive/ brain processing structures; or chemical imbalance (but all theoretical and none has ever been found)
Behavioural symptoms or complaints, and strong contextual observations, such as in this book	As above (description plus 1–9)	Any clusters are just patterns in the situations or strategies of the person's external context or environment, but this is likely to be highly idiosyncratic	The physical 'substrates' are the external contexts and environmental conditions and strategies (e.g. social, cultural, historical, opportunity, and economics)

Kraepelin in the early twentieth century sought to do the same with 'mental disorders' and tried to categorize behavioural symptoms into clusters of an underlying mental illness, and this is the approach still used today by the DSM. If we know the behavioural symptoms we can work our way through a taxonomy to place the mental illness into a disease group, and then assume that some underlying physical (brain) lesion is causing these. It gives the surface appearance of a 'real science', like biology and medicine, but no underlying substrate is actually provided.

Jumping now to the bottom, Table 1.2 shows that for a contextual approach like the one in this book, the clusters can actually be real but are made of observable but idiosyncratic *environments* or *contexts* of a person with behavioural 'symptoms'. There is no assumption of generalizable diagnoses, and *any patterns or clusters that are discovered reside in the environment not the person.* So, there is indeed a physical substrate to the behavioural clusterings—the *so-called physical substrate of 'mental health issues'* is *the environment, the person's world!* The environmental contexts *are* the physical basis (social, cultural, historical, opportunity, and economic), not the brain. The equivalent of the DSM clustering into axes, etc., is the contingency structure of each person's external world. *But they are therefore generalizable only insofar as the environment is stable and generalizable.* Figure 1.2 shows this in more detail.

Anti-Kraepelin arguments

I next want to outline some of the arguments people have made against the approach used in the DSM and other 'diagnostic tools' for judging mental health. This is not about trashing the DSM or psychiatry, but showing some weak assumptions in the metaphors used (and showing that they *are* just metaphors). There has been a lot of criticisms of psychiatry and the DSM use but I only want to examine the main assumptions. I will utilize the behavioural observations contained in the DSM in Chapter 4 for some discursive re-analysis.

The approach was first promulgated by Emil Kraepelin (see Bentall, 2003, 2006), and the assumptions of the general and more recent approaches have been put clearly by Klerman (1978, pp. 104–105), even if he did not endorse them all. There were nine main assumptions of Kraepelin (the headings below) and I will work through some notes about each of these. My notes might not convince you but I want to get you rethinking rather than convinced.

1. *Psychiatry is a branch of medicine.* Psychiatry might be defined as a branch of medicine but that does not mean that the study and treatment of all 'mental health' must be within the domain of medicine or psychiatry. Mental health must include understanding social, cultural and economic

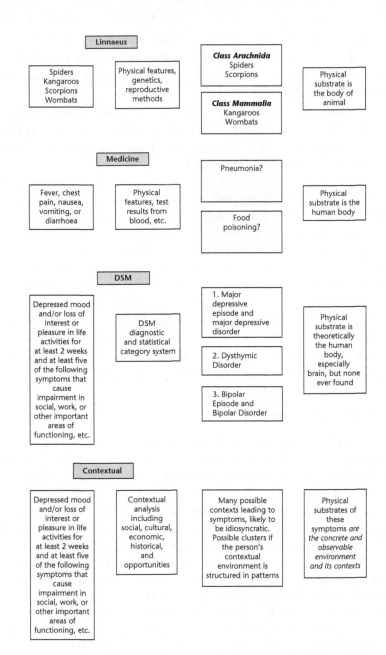

FIGURE 1.2 Traditional classification systems with more details and how to replace the current psychiatric classifications with an external contextual system.

aspects of people's lives, and studying medicine is not sufficient for this. The skills and method for understanding these contexts are not given in medical training except superficially (see Rose, 1962, quoted below).

2. *Psychiatry should utilize modern scientific methodologies and base its practice on scientific knowledge.* While this sounds good, there are contentious issues about what counts as 'scientific' in the realm of 'mental health'. For instance, I will argue in later chapters (Guerin, 2016a, 2016b) that even positing a 'mental' domain is unscientific since what is implied by the concept is intrinsically unobservable. Others have argued that the Kraepelin approach itself is not scientific (Bentall, 2003, 2006). I will also argue that the 'scientific methods' currently used to study mental health behaviours are not the best ones to use.

3. *Psychiatry treats people who are sick and who require treatment for mental illnesses.* This simply begs the question of what is meant by 'sick' and how we judge that.

4. *There is a boundary between the normal and the sick.* Again this begs the question or what is normal and what is sick. This and point (3) are really *conceptual or metaphorical definitions of how psychiatric words are to be used.* They do not add anything beyond defining words. Almost all people with 'mental health' diagnoses are suffering, but the boundary is very blurred, as mental health experts from social work and nursing know.

5. *There are discrete mental illnesses. Mental illnesses are not myths. There is not one but many mental illnesses. It is the task of scientific psychiatry, as a medical specialty, to investigate the causes, diagnosis, and treatment of these mental illnesses.* There is little good evidence that what are defined as mental illness are actually discrete (Bentall, 2006). Indeed, the best evidence for 'discrete' illnesses has been comorbidity which is treated as a minor occurrence, but evidence suggests that it is way bigger than realized. The point about 'myths' depends on your metaphors. If this phrase is meant to imply that people suffer when they are in conditions identified here as 'mental illnesses' then, yes, they are certainly not myths; people suffer badly from all the events being talked about. However, if the current *metaphors* or *conceptualizations* of 'mental illnesses' are meant to be a non-myth then this again simply begs the question entirely, and is again merely a statement of definition. Suffering is not a myth, but that there are 'mental' realms at all, that the illnesses are discrete, and that there are many, are all just verbal statements of unexamined beliefs.

6. *The focus of psychiatric physicians should be particularly on the biological aspects of mental illness.* Like (1) above, if psychiatry wishes to focus only on

the biological then that is fine, but this does not even begin to cover what we need to know to identify or treat 'mental illness'—all the contexts which give rise to behaviours. My view from later chapters is that focusing on the biological is actually not very useful for identifying and alleviating the suffering of people who are currently classified as 'having mental illnesses' since it inhibits observations elsewhere in the person's life. If point (6) is taken seriously, then psychiatrists should not actually be treating 'mental illness' since the biological aspects are not the most important for identification and change. Professionals with better systematic experience and knowledge of social, cultural, economic, and opportunity inequalities should be treating such behaviours:

> By some historical accident, the study of the unhappy or disturbed personality has been assigned to physicians, perhaps the least equipped of all investigators of man to deal with the problems. Unlike others in the biological sciences, physicians have next to no training in scientific methodology, and—more important—they are trained to look for causation in the organism rather than the organisation.
>
> *(Rose, 1962, p. 537)*

7. *There should be an explicit and intentional concern with diagnosis and classification.* Again, this assumes from above (5) that there are, in fact, discrete groupings or clusters of events which make up 'mental illnesses'. If you disagree with that, then the major focus on classification is unwarranted, and likewise if diagnosis means placing 'symptoms' into classifications. But diagnosis *is* extremely important if that means, instead, a focus on observing and documenting the entire contexts for problematic behaviours—social, cultural, bodily, historical, environmental, and economic contexts—and analysing how they strategically fit together and how they might be patterned by the external contexts. That is certainly important diagnosis.

8. *Diagnostic criteria should be codified, and a legitimate and valued area of research should be to validate such criteria by various techniques. Further, departments of psychiatry in medical schools should teach these criteria and not deprecate them, as has been the case for many years.* Again, it all depends on (5) and (7). If discrete clusters do not occur or do occur but due to social and cultural events rather than biological events (Table 1.2), then such classifications certainly are important to teach.

9. *In research efforts directed at improving the reliability and validity of diagnosis and classification, statistical techniques should be utilized.* Depends on (5), (7) and (8).

So what is being proposed through this book, and by others I am feeding off, is not a disregard for science and evidence, and using some woolly, utopian New Age ideas about mental health. It is a re-focus to in fact be *more scientifically stringent* by carefully *documenting and analysing all* the events surrounding a person's suffering, rather than making huge jumps in thinking based on abstract psychiatric and psychological theories (metaphors) and their assumptions about vague 'mental' events and vague references to an unknown biological 'substrate' which underlies all their suffering, and then assuming that if you could only change the biological substrate you will relieve the person's suffering. That does not even sound very scientific when put this bluntly.

This new(ish) approach here is actually more difficult and requires much more time and effort on the part of the practitioner than the DSM/Kraepelin approach has needed. And you can no longer do it just from the confines of your professional office, nor rely upon whatever titbits of information you might have picked up about various people and their social, cultural, and economic settings. I argue, therefore, it is more 'scientific' (if that is even important) because it is about observing more before you judge and intervene.

Imagine seeing someone suffering from (mild) electric shocks because they have touched some live wires. With the current approach, it is as if you must assume that their suffering arises from a mental issue with a biological substrate in the brain, and your only method is to try to find a way to shut off that mental disorder through changing their biological substrate of pain. However, why not just turn off the electricity? Change the external context?

The argument usually given to counter this is that psychiatrists and psychologists *cannot see* anything like an external electric shock happening with 'mental disorders' so they cannot fix that and *must* assume a hidden biological basis. But going back to the beginning of this book, however, I am arguing instead that *they have failed to see the external contexts* which bring about the suffering, and only because of their assumptions, limited observation skills, belief in a category system, and lack of knowledge about subtle and hidden contexts for human behaviour (Guerin, 2016b; Rose, 1962). It is not their fault, as the Rose quote above implies; they have narrow training in understanding people and their contexts and they have legal pressures currently to diagnose à la the DSM. If they were able to spend more time training with contextual observations they *would* see the external events leading to the suffering.

And those who were seen dancing were thought to be insane by those who could not hear the music.

(Variously attributed to Nietzsche, Anne Louise Germaine de Staël, anonymous, and many others)

A final concern with diagnostics, which again will surface throughout this book, is that when we name something, frequently we then stop careful observation. Our life training is to look at something long enough to verbally name it, so it is socially useful, and then observation stops or reduces (Guerin, 2016b). This again is a major problem with the Kraepelin approaches, because *the goal becomes highly focused on naming* the 'underlying' disorder and classification rather than observing as much as possible in the contexts of the person(s) suffering. This focus was explicit in (7), (8), and (9) above. I personally have seen both psychiatrists and clinical psychologists do this; they observe a person with me and soon state a probable classification, and meanwhile I can see so many other social and cultural events still occurring which are relevant to the person's suffering that they have missed. And usually, any post-naming observations they make are directed at confirming their named classification rather than seeing more of what is occurring in front of us.

Many of the same arguments I have given have been made by others, sometimes in a different form. In particular, the work of Bentall (2003, 2006) is very useful and is much more detailed with evidence than I have given here. He proposed a re-focus onto people's 'complaints' or 'symptoms' (I usually call these 'events or behaviours related to the suffering') rather than the extremely narrowing focus on diagnostic categories and forcing there to be discrete categories of separable 'mental disorders'. For example, he stresses (with evidence) that environmental factors can, and already have, accounted for many of the issues in mental health, what I will call in this book the contextual factors, and which are observable, unlike 'mental' or 'private' events. Writing of events labelled 'psychosis':

> When all of the psychotic complaints have been explained [with environmental or contextual observations], there will be no 'schizophrenia' or 'manic depression' left behind awaiting explanation. The approach that I advocate is not only more scientific than the Kraepelinian approach, but also more humane.
>
> *(Bentall, 2006, pp. 220–221)*

Brain and drugs in explanations

Something needs to be said here about the role of the brain in all this. It is commonly assumed that the brain must figure importantly in mental health, but if you have understood the points in this book so far, you will begin to see why this might not be so crucial. However, the brain is clearly involved in human behaviour, so what is its role?

First, what is loosely designated as 'mental' cannot be seen so it has been automatically taken to reside inside the head of people, and hence automatically equated with the brain. But if you reject the 'mental' as being useful (Chapter 3), then the brain and any other 'biological substrates' are not so important even if they are involved. We will see later how to rethink your ideas so that thinking is done outside of people, not in their heads somewhere.

Second, it has been argued (and I will spell this out more below) that the attribution of mental illness to a mental or brain 'cause' only arises because we have not yet learned to properly use contextual observation to see all the external contexts within which people's behaviours or symptoms arise (Guerin, 2016b). The social, language, historical, and cultural contexts in particular are typically hidden and difficult to observe or to report (especially in just a one-hour interview). When this is done more systematically and thoroughly, the attributions to 'mental' or biological causes vanish. Practical ideas of how to do this better are given in Guerin (2016b).

Finally, the brain and our biology are clearly involved in *everything* we do as humans but they are not crucial nor are they the source or cause of our problems. They are equally involved when eating an orange, reading Camus, or laughing at a joke as they are in a psychotic episode; no more, no less. They do not hold the clues, or the answers.

This is the same argument as I gave earlier about the suffering from electric shocks having a biological basis and then from this inferring that the cause and removal of the suffering *must therefore be biologically based*. Once we start observing more of the contexts or 'environmental factors' (Bentall, 2006) in mental health issues, however, the need to refer to any of brain, biological substrate or mental as *special* ingredients will disappear. Or when someone washes their hands many hundreds of times a day we can measure an increase in blood flow to their hands but this does not mean that their hands 'cause' their compulsive behaviour; more blood flow, electrical activity, or heat in a part of the brain does not mean that part of the brain 'caused' any behaviour.

Finally, the evidence for actual brain changes in mental health also needs to be critically examined. First, given we do not know what 'mental health' even means how can one correlate that with brain changes? The research only uses abstract 'diagnoses' of mental health to set up control groups in brain experimental work, but this use of diagnoses is very contentious. It is no basis for claiming differences between groups. Second, the research is almost entirely correlational, meaning that measured brain changes are correlated with diagnoses as the measure of 'mental health'. Correlations never prove cause, as we are taught in our first year of university.

And third, where there is evidence of brain changes (correlated with diagnostic criteria for mental health), the correlation can always means something else is causing it all which is unrelated. Two examples, the second one with the brain. Hearing voices has been correlated with symptoms of distress, leading some to claim that hearing voices causes stress and is a mental illness. However, other evidence suggests that it is other people's reactions to hearing voices—the stigma and discrimination against the hearer—which causes the distress, not the voices (Thain & Guerin, 2016). And second, Zipursky, Reilly, and Murray (2013) reviewed the evidence carefully that schizophrenia is a degenerative brain disease and found little evidence for this. Of importance for here, they noted:

> MRI studies demonstrate subtle developmental abnormalities at first onset of psychosis and then further decreases in brain tissue volumes; however, *these latter decreases are explicable by the effects of antipsychotic medication, substance abuse, and other secondary factors.*
>
> *(Zipursky et al., 2013, p. 1, italics added)*

This is a good illustration of 'correlation is not cause' since the evidence suggests it is the associated drugs, including the anti-psychotic medications, which cause any brain changes, not the behaviours labelled as 'schizophrenia'.

Once again, my purpose is not to trash brain studies but to get you rethinking that there are other possibilities. As mentioned, the brain is certainly involved in most of what we do but so is moving the body, the eyes, and the head (Gibson, 1979). Once brain technicians start looking more at the relation between brain functioning and the contextual functioning of people, I think we will learn a lot more than from correlations to verbal 'mental health' measures.

Cognitive psychology and clinical psychology

Psychology sits in a curious position in these debates. In some ways it is a handmaiden to psychiatry, and in principle gives importance to 'mental' processes, the brain, and biological substrates. In another way, it has a long reliance on (somewhat simplistic) theories of learning within which people are said to behave purely from what they have learned and this means external factors not reliant directly on any biology (at least no more than does eating oranges or reading Camus). But despite a long history of studying behaviour as behaviour, most psychologists believe that 'cognitive processes' are somehow different to other behaviour and that these 'processes' coincide with or are identical to the ideas of 'mental processes'. There is no evidence for this—it is theory.

My conclusion (Guerin, 2016a, 2016b), of which I will say more during the book, is that psychology has been an historic 'dumping ground' for 150 years to try and explain any human events which cannot easily be seen to have a direct biological basis (in the way that coughing without any inflammation can be called 'psychosomatic') or any 'obvious' or salient external causes which can be easily seen (a client reports hallucinations and cannot tell the therapist an external cause for this or a make a good, 'speakable' story).

So, this really goes back to the beginning of this book and how we judge causes (Table 1.1). My point is that *when we can see no obvious causes in the body or the external world, we call the events either psychological or mental, and it has been the 'right' or domain of psychology and psychiatry to explore these.* More recently the metaphor of 'cognitive' has been used with this same discursive functioning (Guerin, 2016a).

Much more will be said about cognition in Chapter 3 since I will argue more substantively there that what are currently called 'cognitive' and 'mental' events are really language events which have been learned externally and arise from external contexts (and yes, that their contexts are ones that are very difficult to observe). But it is of interest to note here *a certain tension between the cognitive metaphors of psychology and the biological substrate metaphors of psychiatry.* This has not caused much direct friction between the groups because the assumption is made that cognitive processing will *one day* be shown to be wholly the same as brain processing and the 'mental', and the circle will be closed. But it does imply a view that what we call 'thinking' occurs wholly within a person (in their brain presumably, not in their big toes) independently of any external influence in the present. I will argue against this in Chapter 3 also.

For now, though, I will outline a few ways in which cognitive psychology has been melded with ideas based on behavioural theories to 'explain' mental health problems. These metaphors are currently the strongest in psychological intervention (*cognitive behaviour therapy*, CBT). But to reiterate, these cognitive theories or metaphors do not cite the brain directly but make hidden assumptions that the brain carries out the cognitive processing, it happens inside humans, and that this will be shown one day in the future. If cognitive processing turns out to be language functioning (Chapter 3), however, then we can retain the ideas of 'cognitive' disorders in mental health but without needing the brain directly involved (just mechanically as argued in the previous section). This will point us to what we should be observing to actually find the external contextual controls over 'cognition'.

The move to CBT began with people like Aaron Beck (1976), who argued that mental illness is not strongly different to other behaviours. He argued using a cognitive metaphor (Guerin, 2001, 2016a) that people process information around them to arrive at decisions and choices. Like other research going on at that time with cognitive biases in information processing (see Kahneman, 2011; Thaler & Sunstein, 2008), Beck argued that when people (or their information processing systems actually) make mistakes in processing, or are biased in their decision-making because of the structure of information processing, then we get cognitive disorders occurring which are the basis (he wrote) of many mental illness. The main 'cognitive metaphor' assumptions are below:

Box 1.3

- People 'take in' information and then process and compute to make decisions which then control their behaviour.
- People 'take in' information, process it and then decide how to attribute causality to events and people.
- People 'take in' information, process it and then decide what beliefs they will 'possess'.
- People 'take in' information, process it and then make *mistakes and have biases* in what they decide.

Some of these 'cognitive disorders' and cognitive biases are set out later in Table 3.4, including some from Beck and some from other cognitive biases research. For example, people in therapy might report that they are depressed because they never do anything correctly and always make mistakes. Beck would describe this by saying that they are making a cognitive mistake of 'selective overgeneralization'—that they are taking a few examples of times when they did something in error and then overgeneralizing this to their whole life. In essence, it is a cognitive mistake in processing the information and in theory this occurs because of a cognitive (and implied brain) structure.

I will come back to this and the cognitive models in Chapter 3, and I will totally rethink each of the proposed biases in a new way from discourse analysis. To give you a heads up, we will see that the patterns are based on very common *language strategies* which are learned and maintained by our (external) social audiences, not because of any cognitive structuring of our brains. The events which are described are better analysed in terms of discursive strategies which we use all the time in life and which are concrete and can be observed. In Table 3.4, in fact, I will give equivalents from discourse analysis to account for these 'mistakes' and 'biases' listed above.

Other Western versions of 'mental illness'

I have gone through the psychiatric and clinical psychology models mostly, but there are many other ways Western researchers have approached 'mental health' to make sense of what is happening when people are suffering in these 'mental health' ways. Most of these will be detailed later, especially in Chapters 2 and 3, but I will note one of importance now.

I have already highlighted the key work of Richard Bentall (2006) in arguing against the Kraepelinian approaches of diagnostics and mental and brain assumptions. Not coincidentally I think, he is also one of a number who have actually tried to give evidence and observations of how ordinary external factors are involved in mental health issues (Fryers, Melzer, & Jenkins, 2003; Gottlieb, Waitzkin, & Miranda, 2010; Guerin & Guerin, 2012; Pilgrim, Rogers, & Bentall, 2009; Tew, 2005; Tew, Ramon, Slade, Bird, Melton, & Le Boutillier, 2012; Varese et al., 2012; Walker, Johnson, & Cunningham, 2012).

For example, Varese et al. (2012) present evidence that the occurrence of serious childhood problems including poverty and forms of abuse can be found in most of those who develop major psychoses later in life. And Fryers et al. (2003) reviewed evidence showing that eight out of the nine clear studies they identified linked common 'mental disorders' to social inequalities, especially socio-economic inequalities.

I will not say much more about these here only because they will be incorporated into the full discussion of contexts in life and their relevance to 'mental health' in Chapters 2 and 3. Chapter 4 will then surgically extract the observed behaviours out of the DSM and elsewhere, remove the idea that these behaviours cluster into diagnostic or brain disease categories, and then look at analyses of how these 'mental illness' behaviours might arise from the external strategic contexts of people who are labelled as having 'mental health' issues.

Summary

- We have been thinking about the 'psychology' of people in wrong ways for a few centuries.
- We can rethink 'psychology' in terms of external contexts—a 'post-internal' discipline which will include all the social sciences.
- We can apply new ways of rethinking 'psychology' to explore new ways to rethink 'mental health'.
- Mental health is a form of suffering not in principle different from other forms of suffering.
- Assigning causes to any behaviour in reality is extremely complex.
- We should look for the contexts in which the behaviours emerge rather than a cause of those behaviours.
- There are many ways that contexts and causes are hidden from superficial observations, especially in a one-hour professional interview.
- Attributions of whether actions are even 'mental health' issues or not closely depends upon what you know about their context, and the metaphors or theories with which you think about such things.
- Assigning contexts (or even causes) becomes a direct function of how much we know about and can observe a person's external context and history of contexts.
- If there is an obvious, salient or 'speakable' cause then the behaviour is explained that way; if there is no obvious cause then the behaviour is explained discursively in abstract terms: as 'internal', 'psychological', 'supernatural', or 'mental'.
- The above points apply to all peoples but the issues arise more often when dealing with people who are very different from you.
- This in turn means that the understanding used to judge mental illness also depends upon your general and specific social relationship with that person.
- The so-called physical substrate of 'mental health' issues is the environment, the person's world, as it is for any form of suffering.
- Psychology has been an historic 'dumping ground' for 150 years to try and explain those human events which cannot easily be seen to have a direct biological basis or any 'obvious' or salient external causes which can be easily seen.
- When we can see no obvious causes in the body or the external world, we call the events either psychological or mental, and it has been the historical 'right' or domain of psychology and psychiatry to explore these but that is not immutable.
- Cognition is language functioning in social context which is controlled externally and socially.

References

American Psychiatric Association (APA). (2013). *The diagnostic and statistical manual of mental disorders* (5th Ed.). Washington: APA.

Beck, A. T. (1976). *Cognitive therapy and the emotional disorders*. Madison, CT: International Universities Press.

Bentall, R. P. (2003). *Madness explained: Psychosis and human nature*. London: Penguin.

Bentall, R. P. (2006). Madness explained: Why we must reject the Kraepelinian paradigm and replace it with a 'complaint-orientated' approach to understanding mental illness. *Medical Hypotheses, 66*, 220–233.

Brown, P., Lyson, M., & Jenkins, T. (2011). From diagnosis to social diagnosis. *Social Science & Medicine, 73*(6), 939–943.

Deloria, V. (1999). *Spirit and reason: The Vine Deloria Jr reader*. Golden, CO: Fulcrum Publishing.

Edwards, D., & Potter, J. (1993). Language and causation: A discursive action model of description and attribution. *Psychological Review, 100*, 23–41.

Evans-Pritchard, E. E. (1937). *Witchcraft, oracles, and magic among the Azande*. Oxford: Clarendon Press.

Fryers, T., Melzer, D., & Jenkins, R. (2003). Social inequalities and the common mental disorders. *Social Psychiatry and Psychiatric Epidemiology, 38*, 229–237.

Gibson, J. J. (1979). *The ecological approach to visual perception*. Boston, MA: Houghton Mifflin.

Gottlieb, L., Waitzkin, H., & Miranda, J. (2010). Depressive symptoms and their social contexts: A qualitative systematic literature review of contextual interventions. *International Journal of Social Psychiatry, 57*, 402–417.

Guerin, B. (2001). Replacing catharsis and uncertainty reduction theories with descriptions of the historical and social context. *Review of General Psychology, 5*, 44–61.

Guerin, B. (2004). *Handbook for analyzing the social strategies of everyday life*. Reno, NV: Context Press.

Guerin, B. (2016a). *How to rethink psychology: New metaphors for understanding people and their behavior*. London: Routledge.

Guerin, B. (2016b). *How to rethink human behavior: A practical guide to social contextual analysis*. London: Routledge.

Guerin, B., & Guerin, P. (2012). Re-thinking mental health for indigenous Australian communities: Communities as context for mental health. *Community Development Journal, 47*(4), 555–570.

Heller, N. R., & Gitterman, A. (2011). Introduction to social problems and mental health/illness. In N. R. Heller & A. Gitterman (Eds.), *Mental health and social problems: A social work perspective* (pp. 1–17). London: Routledge.

Hunter, E. (2007). Disadvantage and discontent: A review of issues relevant to the mental health of rural and remote Indigenous Australians. *Australian Journal of Rural Health, 15*, 88–93.

Jutel, A., & Nettleton, S. (2011). Towards a sociology of diagnosis: Reflections and opportunities. *Social Science & Medicine, 73*(6), 793–800.

Kahneman, D. (2011). *Thinking, fast and slow*. London: Penguin.

Klerman, G. L. (1978). The evolution of a scientific nosology. In J. C. Shershow (Ed.), *Schizophrenia: Science and practice* (pp. 99–121). Cambridge, MA: Harvard University Press.

Lee, V. L. (1986). Act psychologies and the psychological nouns. *The Psychological Record, 36,* 167–179.

Lee, V. L. (1988). *Beyond behaviorism.* Hillsdale, NJ: Erlbaum.

Pilgrim, D., Rogers, A, & Bentall, R. P. (2009). The centrality of personal relationships in the creation and amelioration of mental health problems: The current interdisciplinary case. *Health: An Interdisciplinary Journal for the Social Study of Health, Illness and Medicine, 13,* 235–254.

Rose, A. M. (1962). A social-psychological theory of neurosis. In A. M. Rose (Ed.), *Human behavior and social processes: An interactionist approach* (pp. 537–549). Boston, MA: Houghton Mifflin.

Shuman, A. (2005). *Other people's stories: Entitlement claims and the critique of empathy.* Chicago, IL: University of Illinois Press.

Tew, J. (2005). *Social perspectives in mental health: Developing social models to understand and work with mental distress.* London: Jessica Kingsley.

Tew, J., Ramon, S., Slade, M., Bird, V., Melton, J., & Le Boutillier, C. (2012). Social factors and recovery from mental health difficulties: A review of the evidence. *British Journal of Social Work, 42,* 443–460.

Thain, A., & Guerin, B. (2016). The contexts for everyday experiences of hearing voices: A textual analysis of Romme et al.'s *Living with Voices.* Unpublished paper, University of South Australia.

Thaler, R. H., & Sunstein, C. R. (2008). *Nudge: Improving decisions about health, wealth, and happiness.* London: Yale University Press.

Varese, F., Smeets, F., Drukker, M., Lieverse, R., Lataster, T., Viechtbauer, W., Read, J., van Os, J., & Bentall, R. P. (2012). Childhood adversities increase the risk of psychosis: A meta-analysis of patient-control, prospective- and cross-sectional cohort studies. *Schizophrenia Bulletin, 38,* 661–671.

Walker, C., Johnson, K., & Cunningham, L. (Eds.). (2012). *Community psychology and the socio-economics of mental distress.* New York: Palgrave Macmillan.

Winter, D. (1978). *Death's men: Soldiers of the Great War.* London: Penguin.

Zipursky, R. B., Reilly, T. J., & Murray, R. M. (2013). The myth of schizophrenia as a progressive brain disease. *Schizophrenia Bulletin, 39,* 1363–1372.

2

CONTEXTUAL ANALYSIS FOR MENTAL HEALTH

We have seen in the last chapter that rather than try and fit all the behaviours, symptoms, or complaints of a person suffering into a 'mental illness'—by which I now mean behaviours for which the external contexts leading to suffering cannot be easily observed—we need instead to observe, analyse, and intervene (where appropriate) the external contexts for those separate behaviours or symptoms in more detail. This is viable but it is perhaps becoming clear that psychology and psychiatry do not have the best methods for doing this, neither the conceptual nor observational methods. This is especially so with symptoms involving talking and thinking for which most psychologists cannot even contemplate a 'post-internal' version of these.

The next two chapters, therefore, aim to show briefly one way to begin this task although I by no means have all the answers (Guerin, 2016b). Any approach will have to draw on all the social sciences since we need to learn how to observe and analyse people's life strategies across all contexts (see the Rose quote in the previous chapter). It must attempt to draw together the interdisciplinary studies and methods to observe and think about human behaviours in their social contexts, so we can put mental health 'symptoms' into a bigger, or at least broader, contextual frame. It needs to focus on observations of the real contexts from which the behaviours and complaints arise, and not theories and hypotheses which signal to me only that detailed observations were not made.

There have been a lot of researchers working to find new ways to rethink psychology, psychiatry, and mental health. I have learned from them all, even if I disagree over some points and do not always quote them

(Bentall, 2003, 2009; Bentley, 1935; Beresford, 2002; Bhugra, 2013; Billig, 1999; Bracken, 2002; Bracken et al., 2012; Bracken & Thomas, 2005; Cochrane, 1983; Cromby, Harper, & Reavey, 2013; Crowe, 2000; Edwards, 1997; Giddens, 1991; Han, 2004; McGruder, 2001; Potter, 1996; Powers, 1998; Rose, 1962; Rose, 1998; Smail, 2005, 2012; Tew, 2005).

So, what is different in the account to be given here, if it stems from all these other researchers and thinkers? I believe there are a few key points I have developed *through these others* but which stand out here as a new package (Guerin, 2016a, 2016b):

- a strong commitment to seeking out and *observing* the details of people's contexts before naming abstract notions as 'explanations';
- a strong commitment that all human behaviour arises through other people because all our resources come through other people in some way or another—everything we do is social (has a social context and social consequences);
- language use is complex and hidden, but is always a social exchange— we never affect the non-people environment through words without other people;
- what we do, our total behaviours comprising doing, saying and think- ing, are just actions which arise from our unique contexts;
- our behaviour arises from our contexts and is not driven by our thinking, which is itself a behaviour arising from our social contexts;
- applying this consistently to all of the behaviours which we currently call the 'inner' life of people; so there is no 'inner' life, experience, phe- nomenology or personal theatre, but instead there are the language and other responses which we have learned through our life but do not say out loud (Chapter 3);
- and above all, when you fixate on a factor, mechanism, process, dis- ease, issue, experience, cause, symptom, diagnosis, or cognitive state, which you want to say leads to, correlates with, seems associated with, or causes mental illness, always but always ask this question instead: *what contexts brought about this factor, mechanism, process, disease, issue, experience, cause, symptom, diagnosis, or cognitive state? What contexts gave rise to them?*

This last point underlies everything in this book. For example, we will see in Chapter 7 that some mental health symptoms for many women arise from focusing their 'self' on their looks, attractiveness or body image. But that is not the real problem. The real question is: *what contexts*—social, cultural, historical, economic, and opportunity—*give rise* to this excessive focus on appearance? We will see that all those contexts are involved: the present par- ticular issues are from a historical focus developed over a period in Western society (cultural) based in outcomes for capitalism (economics) and shaped by both the society in general (unequal opportunities for women; often via media) and the people in social relationships who give consequences based on appearance (the patriarchy). The same focus and problems for women have occurred in other societies through different contexts, but currently it is a big problem partly because of the widespread media shaping, which reaches more people than in the past, and partly because the current capitalist system relies heavily upon female appearance to sell products.

I cannot outline everything in full detail since that requires a lot of experience and reading of social sciences beyond what I could say, but I will give enough here I hope to understand how we can use this version of questioning for analysing the suffering from 'mental health' issues. The material will be spread over two chapters since to rethink how talking and thinking fit into people's life strategies and external contexts is difficult to get across (especially if you have been brought up on easy cognitive theorizing), and will take up the entire Chapter 3. This is important material, though, because of all those events in life for which we cannot easily see the external contexts from which they arise, the so-called 'mental' events, the events involving talking and thinking are most important. As mentioned in Chapter 1, this includes what is currently called 'cognition', and currently includes much of therapy because CBT is (perhaps unknowingly) about observing, analysing, and changing the contexts for talking and thinking.

My plan is that in the chapters following Chapter 3 I will try and make all these contextual analyses clearer by providing very specific examples based around 'mental health' suffering. This will include Chapter 4 looking at the DSM lists of behaviours currently thought to have an underlying biological substrate (we will then begin to see the underlying 'environmental substrates'; remember that the DSM clusters might not be wildly wrong, they are just not clustered by biology!), and looking at particular groups who might present with the same 'symptoms' but who have completely different contexts producing those symptoms. The latter will include the important groups of Indigenous peoples, women, and people in refugee and other oppressive contexts. I will also make some suggestive comments in Chapter 5 about how the social structuring of modern life—society, capitalism, ecology—shape some of the specific contemporary mental health complaints of Western people living in Western societies.

The basics of contextual analysis

The general pattern for analysing the contexts of people's lives is that there will be social strategies (possibly involving historical and cultural features) primarily arising from *access to resources* via *audiences or populations/groups.*

This means that some economic analysis is usually needed (but in the broad sense of how the resources for life are distributed through social networks), as is more context around the social relationships involved with those audiences and populations, and some of the tricky resource analyses. This in turn will usually involve digging into the more particular strategies for the particular contexts that have developed over time, typically including some strategies for secrecy and finding out, and for trust in the resource exchanges in some of the social relationships.

The above paragraph was put tersely, but what it meant was that our behaviour comes from the environment around us and we have been shaped by past environments to behave in certain ways, all of us very differently. In order to understand why people do what they do, we have to observe and explore that person's total environment, social ecology, or context. This especially includes all their social relationships and cultural and community relationships which shape so much of importance, and also their broad economic context which just means how they get the things they need and want (resources) and who they get these through. This needs good contextual observation skills, and a good knowledge of all the social sciences.

The above is what a typical social analysis might look like. Some is new and some not new, but most is new in the sort of interdisciplinary package I have presented (Guerin, 2016b). To give an example, for someone seeing a clinician with 'psychological' problems (ones for which we cannot see an immediate 'cause'), we might do the following:

- find out the resources (in a broad sense) they are getting and how they access these, through what social channels or networks (are there conflicts or problems here?);
- find out all their main relationships, including those with strangers, acquaintances, immediate family, kin and friends networks (are there conflicts or problems here?);
- find out what is exchanged in each relationship, taking special note of the subtle resources (reciprocity; what is the person getting from and giving to each relationship?);
- find out what, in the person's life, they keep hidden from each of those persons (what dynamics are going on here?);
- find out about each of those persons they try and monitor or keep up with (who are they tracking closely in life and what resource conflicts might be behind this?);
- find out how much and in what ways the person would trust all those others (which relationships does the person rely on or get support from?);

- find out something about the person's overall ecology, opportunities, and economics (in their life what opportunities have they had and what did they miss out on; what resources are not available to them?);
- find out how the person believes each of those persons-in-relationships would most like them to act and behave (what do they think each of those persons would like from the person in therapy?);
- find out the stories and verbal strategies they use to negotiate the above with the people in their worlds (which stories and reason-giving work and which do not work; what have they had to invent in stories to negotiate their worlds and their resources and to maintain their relationships; what stories about themselves—called identity work sometimes—have they had to construct for their different relationships or audiences?)

This is the sort of thing a social analysis involves, and within this analysis there are all sorts of strategies we would look for. As we will see below, if the person's main social relationships are not those common in Western societies (that is, are not stranger relationships) then the analysis will look very different because the contexts for their behaviours will be very different. The reason why the mental health of non-Western groups (such as in Chapters 7 and 8) seems different is because their life contexts are different and give rise to different behaviours (and different forms of suffering) not because they are 'racially' or essentially different in some way.

Hidden or difficult-to-observe contexts

I have mentioned several times that many contexts which give rise to our behaviours are difficult to see (especially if you sit in an office all day). I have also made the point that in these cases the 'cause' is then typically referred to an 'explanatory' metaphor of 'psychological', 'mental' or 'mind', or some metaphor of a biological substrate. So attempting to observe contexts in a person's life that are inherently difficult to observe will feature in a large way in this book because it is an important facet of mental health analysis.

To help us get oriented to this point, Table 2.1 shows several ways that the contexts for behaviour can be hidden, and therefore (I am arguing) the 'odd' behaviours become attributed to a 'mental' or 'inner' cause and illness. They are discussed in more detail in Guerin (2016a, 2016b), but are important to recognize in this book because they form the main contexts under which the attributions to mental events, as we explored with examples in Chapter 1, are made.

TABLE 2.1 Ways that contexts or causes for behaviour can be hidden, leading to a false attribution of a 'mental' cause

---

- You have not spent enough time observing all that person's behaviours and actions; even if you have good reasons for this—it takes too long, your boss will not allow extra time, your research needs to finish quickly—you will still miss out and have to resort to averages or abstract theorizing.
- You have not spent enough time observing in context.
- There are historical events and contexts that you have not observed or have not found out about.
- There is something that the person has successfully avoided or escaped from in the past by doing what they are doing and you cannot observe that outcome because it does not actually occur anymore since it is successfully escaped or avoided.
- There are key elements of the context for behaviour that are not present in the current situation so you cannot see them.
- There are key elements of the context for behaviour that the person has kept secret or is hiding for other contextual reasons.
- There are key elements of the context for behaviour which simply do not fit into (your) ordinary experience and so are not observed even though they potentially could be.
- The behaviours work well because the contexts are not obvious; even for 'normal' behaviours it is often best to not know the contexts in which someone's behaviour towards you arises.
- Where language use (including thinking) is prevalent in a context, as the social control of language is frequently difficult to observe without a lot of effort.

Some contexts are by nature difficult to observe, such as historical contexts and contexts in which a person successfully avoids or escapes another context thereby leaving nothing for you to observe. Similarly, a lot of the important contexts for any event arise from people and other events that are not present at the time (or no longer present in the case of historical contexts), so it requires extra observation or questioning to find out about these.

In other cases, a person keeps part of the context secret or hidden because of the social relationships or other contexts, and in many cases our sequences of social behaviour and our relationships work better if we do not know the external contexts that give rise to them. For example, if I thought that you said you liked me or liked being with me only because that gives you access to my rich family, then that would sour our relationship for me—so in this way we are also often shaped to ignore or keep secret some contexts that might be having an influence. We do not go around telling our friends what might be in the relationship for us; so while we do get all our resources through our relationships, we are shaped not to highlight this.

The other main way we fail to observe contexts is when we do not observe long enough or in the best ways. This often comes about in psychology because academics have professionally acquiesced that short-term research and interviews are satisfactory for understanding people. Psychologists must extend this and learn from social anthropologists and some sociologists that more time and intensity of observation are needed before we can really understand why people do what they do. We can also fail to observe context because our experiences in life have not given us the skills to observe what is going on. This is why experts often see things in a situation that we laypersons miss.

The final case of the missing contexts, very prevalent when dealing with suffering from 'psychological' problems, arises because of the use of language and the fact that language use arises only from social contexts but again, it works well only because the social contexts are hidden. Language just seems to occur without consequences but this is because their true source of impact is social and hidden (Guerin, 2016a). And people often just do what we ask them to do, seemingly without reciprocation, although this is misleading because we rarely ask people to do things they will not do anyway. When we start to see how discursive analyses can dredge up the social contexts for language use, in Chapter 3, this will become clearer.

The point is that these sorts of difficulties will be ever-present when dealing with the materials in this book on mental health. This is also why it is understandable that academics and practitioners have resorted to imaginary metaphors to describe and try to understand (at least abstractly) the social strategies of developing suffering labelled as 'mental illness' in context—it is not easy to observe most of the contexts that give rise to the behaviours and complaints surrounding 'mental health'.

The dangers, however, of these hidden contexts are that we invent abstract or theoretical metaphors to cover up our lack of observations, and these theories then *begin to seem observable*, especially disguised as self-reports. Figure 2.1 shows some of these dangers that have been mentioned, and some of the ways academics and laypeople alike have filled in the lack of contextual observation with metaphors. Like the many thinkers I have learned from (Bentley, 1941a, 1941b), *my goal is to get rid of the 'interior design' approach to psychology, as it were, and replace it with a plausible form of 'landscape gardening or ecology'*.

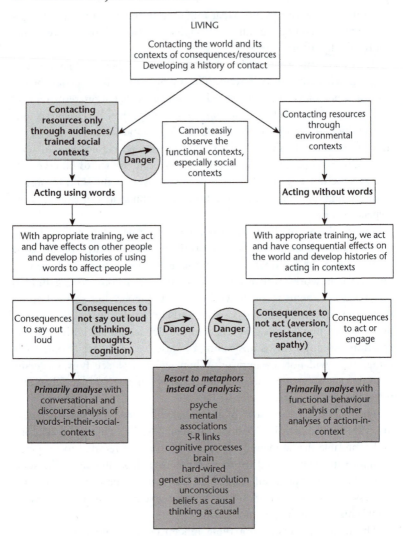

FIGURE 2.1 Ways in which analysing contexts can present dangers from hidden contexts or contexts that are not easily observed, highlighting three common dangers

Five contexts for people's behaviour

What I wish to do next is to outline briefly and sketchily five important contexts to guide your initial observations and analyses of human behaviour. These contexts will be fleshed out more in following chapters using mental health behaviours as the material to be analysed. They are not exhaustive or final but just useful ways I conceptualize context which seem to help me observe and think through tricky examples. I have not made them up but learned them from across all the social sciences, each of which emphasizes them in different ways, and more importantly I have learned from my experiences working closely with people and communities very different from me. In the end, all contexts form a whole for each person's life without division, and all attempts to categorize are artificial and fail, but the divisions can be useful to start. In the end, in fact, you should be observing all these with any human behaviour—none is ever excluded from real human life.

Social contexts

Everything we do is done in a variety of social contexts, whether we can see these easily or not (Guerin, 2001a, 2016b; Pilgrim, Rogers, & Bentall, 2009). This might be from a close family which controls, advises, shapes, or otherwise influences what you do, or it might come from strangers who determine what you can do and the ways in which you do those things (especially abstract bureaucracies). It is important that you find ways to analyse these often hidden social contexts and how they influence you if you wish to understand yourself and others (Guerin, 2016b).

I find it useful to look for several categories of social relationships to begin with. But more importantly, rather than just getting a list of these people, it is vital to observe how these people fit into the social life patterns, the resources the person accesses and requires, the dependencies, the networking, what is exchanged in these relationships to keep them going, the conflicts arising from resource problems and the conflicts arising from multiple relationships impacting on each other. That is your social analysis; not merely listing people or just the type of relationships, but their social properties.

Table 2.2 presents some of the more simple social properties and dynamics of three broad categories which I will use to outline the material here. The only way to really learn them is to participate with people and observe and question carefully. This is particularly important for those forms of relationships with which you are not familiar. The most common problem, of course, occurs with people brought up in Western societies, where they have a diet of 90 per cent strangers per day and 10 per cent close family and some friends, who then go to work with people from kin-based communities who might not understand how these relationships work. I have also seen many issues and problems for people living in strong kin-based communities who cannot work out how you are supposed to relate to strangers.

TABLE 2.2 Social properties of three broad categories of relationships

---

Stranger relationships

Form of reciprocity: exchange within a society of strangers is primarily done via money.

What you can get done is typically by paying someone and can be done at a distance, and in principle there are: no other social relationship involved; no other social obligations; does not usually impact on other areas of life.

Personal influence will depend upon having economic (resource) status, often contextualized as a show of commodities.

Monitoring: will often not see them again, and others will not see each other (e.g. your family probably sees and knows very few of the strangers you deal with in life).

Accountability mainly through public rule-following and policing, institutionalized.

Avoidance and escape of consequences is easy especially if wealthy, and people can easily withdraw from social relationships. Secrecy and lying are also easy since you do not usually have to see the persons again.

Conformity & norms: will usually be towards what is publicly available and especially on media and through government and high-status (rich) citizens.

Kin-based relationships

Form of reciprocity: tend to be taken-for-granted obligations that are not questioned often; not onerous because the same is reciprocated.

What you can get done depends heavily upon the family social relationships. The same people will be relevant in most arenas of life.

Personal influence will be important and depend upon the status of the family in the community networks and the person's status within the family. Time spent talking therefore rather than rule-following.

Monitoring: will see most of the people regularly, and the others will see each other regularly so there is much mixing of events and information.

Accountability is through complex family systems with historical context frequently utilized.

Avoidance and escape of consequences is difficult and is limited mostly to secrecy and language strategies, or forming coalitions among kin; on the other hand, the family and community will protect from many negative consequences.

Conformity and norms: Usually will be directed towards what community sees as important and often reflected in historical precedence or ritual practices.

Friend and immediate family relationships

Form of reciprocity: usually there are specific supports that are returned in some way but these vary.

What you can get done depends upon your networks and the reciprocity you provide. The people are usually not relevant in all other arenas of life; so if you go to a gym you might go with a friend but perhaps not, and your family will not be involved in this.

Personal influence will depend upon your status within networks, but because people in your network do not know each and everyone else, you will need more verbal persuasion for influence; your family might have little influence in the networks of your friends.

Monitoring: will see some of the people regularly, but not others. The others will not all see each other regularly, except if family perhaps.

Accountability through public rules and policing, and through network members' contacts.

Avoidance and escape of consequences is only easy if constantly changing networks or if high status within networks, or there are coalitions within networks (cliques); you can keep things with the smaller groups fairly easily, such as secrets with friends can be kept secret easily from your family.

Conformity and norms: usually directed towards what best friends or closest family perceive is important.

Stranger relationships. In the modern Western world, probably the largest number of relationships is now with strangers. We get so much of the resources we need in life from strangers and we have to learn to deal with strangers in ways that will not get us exploited yet gain the resources we need. Relationships with strangers have some interesting properties which vary hugely from those involved when dealing with communities, family, and friends. I will also suggest in Chapter 5 that much of the modern increase in anxiety and depressive disorders arises from having to deal with strangers on a daily basis to achieve any outcomes in life. For example, this includes all the people we work with usually (unless you work in a family business) and all the people from whom we buy our life requirements at shops and malls.

To give just a few ideas of the social properties of strangers which shape our behaviour (Guerin, 2016b), strangers have no history with us, no other consequences or obligations to us, and they usually cannot monitor what we do in other parts of our life. They themselves are devoid of other consequences to us, so if they exploit us nothing else will happen to them (unless you take action through even more strangers such as the police). They are not monitored or checked usually by our family and friends, and in fact our family and friends might know little about the people we deal with every day of the week. On the other hand, if something goes wrong with the relationship either party can usually just walk away and not have to deal with the other ever again, which can occasionally be useful. Whereas many disputes in former days were resolved within families, albeit not always peacefully (Johnson & Earle, 2000; Waller, 1988), the modern world has a range of societal-imposed systems to deal with problematic stranger interactions, such as police, armies, law courts, ombudsmen, community groups, and many types of tribunals. But these involve working through even more strangers.

The point here is that to survive in life now we all need a large range of skills to either interact successfully with people we have never met before and might never again meet and who have no real responsibility towards us, or to find ways to avoid such interactions by using money or other people to buffer those stranger interactions, or by just avoiding people. The reader can hopefully begin to see how coping with this modern form of relationship can lead to the 'mental health' issues in modern life, and this will be fleshed out later in this book.

Finally for here, it is worthwhile remembering that for those living in Western societies, having a large percentage of our relationship time spent with strangers is something *new* in human history, or at least only 300–400 years old. In the past, most social encounters every day of the week were with people related to you, who knew most of the other people you knew (your family), and who could be made accountable to most of the other people you knew (family, that is). There has not been a very long period yet (in terms of human existence) of working out strategies to handle the conflicts and issues which arise from dealing with unaccountable strangers. This is true both on a large scale of obtaining and distributing resources (Western economics), and, as we are pursuing here, on the small scale of people's everyday lives. Yes people, we are all still making this up as we go along—and this even includes foreign policy (Alkon & Agyeman, 2011; Cryan, Shatil, & Piero, 2013; de Soto, 2000; Fleming, 2015; Guérin, 1970; Klare, 2012; Kolbert, 2014; Leonard & Sunkara, 2016; Löwy, 2015; Pinchbeck & Jordan, 2011; Polanyi, 1944; Sandal, 2012; Sennett, 1998; Stiglitz, 2013).

Kin-based community relationships. A second broad category of relationship I use, although there are as many types of relationships as there are life situations, is the extended or kin-based family. These are family groups in which the members mostly interact on a daily basis with each other, often intermarry into the community of those families, they monitor and know what is going on with most of the members, are obliged to, accountable to, and are responsible for, other members of the family, and they share their resources within the family in many ways. There are certainly conflicts, and kin-based families and communities are not conflict free and happily peaceful the whole time (Johnson & Earle, 2000). But the point is that they usually have their own ways of dealing with conflicts, for better or for worse.

Once again, the properties of maintaining relationships in extended families (and even establishing them requires a special set of skills for outsiders such as researchers), are very different from other forms of relationships, although the human race has had almost its entire history developing these. Of importance for this book, *they produce different issues for the members which means the 'mental health' complaints and symptoms might look the same but will arise from very different contexts and need different ways to change them.* For example, most conflict issues (for individuals) arise from things going on in the family or community, so there are not really any 'individual' or 'mental' issues. The solutions with (intact) kin-based families also arise from within the family; usually some relation in that large group monitoring each other extremely closely will know what is going on and support any individual caught in a messy situation. In Māori whanau, for example, children often go to live somewhere else in the family if there are issues happening; in a very natural way traditionally, which is not seen as problematic.

Understanding the dynamics and properties of kin-based relationships is a necessity for anyone trying to work with 'mental health' issues for both non-Western people and also with many people living within Western societies but in kin-based communities. What has been learned about people helping people in Western societies might be fine, and the interventions work, but it is a whole new ballpark when you step outside of working with people whose main relationships are with strangers. In Chapters 7 and 8 we will see that this is actually very common and almost always true for those working with people from Indigenous, refugee, or oppressed communities. And to make it worse, many of these kin-based families and groups are struggling because they are forced to live within Western societies where their kin-based relationships cannot help them; and they and their children are having to learn to deal with and trust strangers in order to get any resources.

Friends and close family relationships. A third broad category of relationship, although one which can be limited for those living in kin-based communities, is a set of friends who are close but not related to you or your family in any way. While different in some ways (especially legal ways), the close members of current Western nuclear families are now very similar to being friends, and behave towards each other in some similar ways to being friends rather than being related like extended families. Again, the common social contexts in these relationships give rise to properties which are very different from those of both kin-based family and strangers (Guerin, 2016b; Table 2.2). For example, secrets can be kept better with friends since there is less cross-monitoring between a person's relationships than happens with family (where everyone finds out about everything!); friends often stay separate from family; friends can therefore give more independent advice if this is something important; and you can do things with friends that others might never hear about (hence no consequences). On the other hand, when it comes to the crunch (such as having a serious illness), friends have no other ties and can easily avoid any long-term responsibility for each other if that arises.

There are many twists and turns and strategies to all this, and once again, remember that every case or context is idiosyncratic to a large degree; here I can only give a brief smattering. When I begin to relate the symptoms of mental health to their contexts we will see more of how the forms and properties of relationships affect and give rise to various behaviours (Gottlieb, Waitzkin, & Miranda, 2010; Pilgrim et al., 2009; Tew, Ramon, Slade, Bird, Melton, & Le Boutillier, 2012). The main point here is that social contexts envelop all our behaviours and so dealing with relationships, and how we do this, is vital to living in a way that we want, and not in living an unwanted way.

Cultural contexts

Cultural contexts in a broad sense are the shaping and support given by a community or group of people for behaviours that would not occur otherwise, and frequently these become behaviours unique to that group. This often occurs where a community or group live in isolation from other people, or live in opposition to or conflict with other communities nearby, but not always. If you and a group of friends go away for a few weeks together isolated from other people or surrounded by strangers, you develop behaviours (jokes, reminiscences, ways of doing things) that others do not share and will not understand when you get back home (some things you do might appear weird to the people back home). But communities living in mountainous regions or other forms of isolation for centuries with few visitors (or at least strangers) will develop a large number of such behaviours and ones that maintain longer than the transient ones with friends (e.g. Campbell, 1964; Hammel, 1968; Oliver, 1981).

What this means for analysis is that many behaviours are supported by social contexts which are unique to one group of people only, and this can make it difficult to observe why those people act that way, because you are not privy to all the social strategies or the history of that group. This is another form of hidden contexts which make it difficult to understand the behaviours—and I have already (over)stressed that these commonly get referred to as mental health issues because they are not understood.

With kin-based families and communities and other groups, such as those based around religions (which are often kin-based as well), the cultural behaviours supported only by that group become very important and very meaningful in life. This comes about because all the resources you gain from such communities are dependent upon behaving in those 'cultural' ways. Cultural changes do occur but they can be slow. Cultural ways of behaving within 'nuclear' families, workplace friends, and outside-work friends are also important, but often the person's main sources of resources in life are not contingent upon those behaviours in the way they usually are for kin-based relationships. So, for example, I can go along with the 'cultural' ways things are done at the workplace where I work but I can disregard them totally once I finish work every day. And being relationships based with strangers and acquaintances, my work colleagues are less likely to monitor my behaviour outside of work hours (it would be stalking!) so no one will check up whether I continue the same practices out of the office. But the resources gained through participating within kin-based groups also become contingent on the cultural practices so they are very important to life strategies.

So, in analysing behaviour we must look to how some behaviours are supported or occasioned by special groups that have developed their own ways of doing things—the cultural context. There are two opposite problems with this. First, because they are difficult to observe and the people are usually unfamiliar to you, these cultural influences can be missed and some other analysis given to the behaviour—you might not know what to even look for. Second, even though these are difficult to observe commonly, and therefore missed, it has also been too easy in mental health to blame behaviours on 'cultural practices' as if that explains anything.

In fact, naming something as 'cultural' actually requires you observing and describing the social groups involved in that behaviour, what the person does to be part of that group, and what resources they get access to through being part of that group. *Calling some behaviours 'cultural' without these further observations and documentation does not explain anything.* The real understanding is from the contextual descriptions.

Economic contexts

The ultimate bases for behaviour are the resources we need, and our families and communities need to survive. Getting and distributing these resources is our economic context, and can range from how people hunt and gather resources and share among a kin-based family group, to how people earn money and spend it in shopping malls. The point here, well-known in all the social sciences except psychology, is that different economic contexts produce very different behaviours (Guerin, 2016a). Most behaviours require a good knowledge of a person's economics to understand why they arise, and they can seem peculiar otherwise.

The forms of economics can have very subtle and strategic effects on people and their behaviour (e.g. Fryers, Melzer, & Jenkins, 2003; Walker, Johnson, & Cunningham, 2012). Just finding that poorer people (in terms of monetary wealth in Western capitalism) have more reported 'mental illness' tells us little about how this arises (if it was indeed measured properly). We need good descriptions of how the whole context of economics functions for those people, and in my experience this usually also involves the person's family history of economics, and strongly involves the contexts of opportunity and lack of opportunities that they have had because of the situations into which they were born. There are multiple life pathways that are different for different people but which might end up with a behaviour treated as a 'symptom' that looks the same for all of them. Stressing out about many modern economic problems can produce similar looking 'mental health' behaviours but they arise from different contexts.

I will only make a couple of extra points here (see Guerin, 2016a). First, the economic context of a person's life is often ignored in clinical psychology because the model is that it is the brain or cognitive functioning that is disturbed, and this should be independent of economic networking. Second, economics will re-occur in a major way in three other sections of this book. Not far below we will see that a major 'opportunity context' is economic status. With different economic contexts, life provides very different opportunities for other behaviours—otherwise unrelated to the economics itself—to arise. We will also see in Chapter 5 that much of the contemporary 'mental health' must be understood in the context of people living in modern societies with a strong capitalist or neo-liberal economy. The current economic system has changed human behaviour hugely and mental health issues follow from that. Finally, in Chapter 8 we will see that there are major hidden contexts needed to understand anything about Indigenous mental health, and one is the imposition of capitalism during colonization.

Opportunity contexts

One context in life which determines a lot of what we do, and what we do not do, concerns the opportunities available to us. Briefly, a lot of resources, or the opportunities to access resources, depend upon the structuring of relationships and economics historically and culturally. This is usually called *stratification* in sociology. This is different in every group and every society, but typically there are different life opportunities to someone born into different: classes of society, races, colour, gender, and some more specific opportunity differences. Of course, these often compound each other (*intersectorial*).

It is unfortunately common that behaviours in these different loosely named groups are 'explained' in terms of the group membership itself, rather than what the differences in opportunity contexts have allowed people to do or not. For example, most Indigenous groups around the world have had 'odd' behaviours explained as due to something essentialistic to those people ('because of their indigeneity'; 'that is an Indigenous thing'), whereas it is most often brought about by lack of good opportunities provided by colonialists or something caused more directly through social relationships with colonialists—such as violence, abuse, and stealing land (Guerin & Guerin, 2012, 2014; Waldram, 2004). Much of the 'Indigenous mental health' area arises from these problems, as we will see in Chapter 8.

But the problems with opportunities and mental health are even worse. We have seen already that behaviours which are labelled as 'mental health issues' are often ones which interfere with the person's 'normal' functioning. This disruption leads to further contexts of reduced opportunity—such as a reduction in money and other resources. This means that they get a double whammy of issues, to put it scientifically. But they actually get a triple whammy because being in these conditions, especially when some unnameable behaviours have led you to lose income or friends is very stressful, and this stress can further exacerbate the issues (Bourdieu, 1999; Cochrane, 1983).

So, in modern Western society in particular, as we will see in Chapter 5, having unequal opportunities leads to stress which will in itself often be a context for mental health behaviours, as well as this all changing the contexts of opportunities available to the person to further exacerbate the issues:

> Society can thus be seen as responsible for promoting mental illness in two respects. First, by putting some of its members in more stress-inducing situations than others and, secondly, by depriving them of the material and psychological resources required for dealing with such stress. It is perhaps little to be wondered at that many people who apparently benefit greatly from a particular course of psychiatric treatment relapse very quickly when they are returned to their original social environment with their coping resources unimproved.
>
> *(Cochrane, 1983, p. 183)*

So, it is imperative that people working with 'mental health' understand the stratifications in society and how they play out in the particular groups they are working with, and appreciate the complex interplays of contexts here. The idiosyncratic mixtures produce many variations of context in which the same-looking behaviour arises but in very different ways and needing different interventions.

Examples of this will be a constant feature of Chapters 7 and 8. In particular, we will also look at the opportunities not available to women compared to men, and the limited opportunities available to refugee and other oppressed groups in Chapter 7. As we will see, differences in 'mental health' behaviours in these groups, such as between men and women, has usually been attributed to their gender somehow, whereas it is the opportunities and lack of opportunities in patriarchal societies that leads to the behaviour.

Historical contexts

Analysing how behaviour arises from a person's past contexts and the role of that historical context in current behaviour seems easy but is very difficult. It represents a tricky case of everything we saw in the last chapter about focusing wrongly on salient, 'speakable' or 'persuadable' explanations. Pointing to an event in the person's past seems a reasonable 'explanation' for what they are doing now, but this leap is hazardous (Fischer, 1970; Guerin, 2001b; Kirmayer, Gone, & Moses, 2014; Maxwell, 2014; Mohatt, Thompson, Thai, & Tebes, 2014; Paradies, 2016).

Clearly, the past is related to what is happening in the present, but the urge to call this a 'causal relation', while strong, is mistaken: *the past gives rise to the present but does not cause it.*

It is because, as I have probably over-stressed by now, the arena of mental health has been built upon behaviours which arise from contexts which are very difficult to see, that 'history' has frequently been pulled in or opportunistically used as a 'cause' of those behaviours: Freud's childhood stages, PTSD, early attachment, childhood trauma, etc. More recently, the terms 'historical trauma' or 'collective trauma' have functioned in this way also and have rightly been criticized for pretending to be causes (Kirmayer et al., 2014; Maxwell, 2014; Mohatt et al., 2014; Paradies, 2016). These histories are certainly all involved in the current behaviours and the suffering arising from the person's mix of contexts, but they cannot be used as a 'cause'. That is why I ask they be treated as contexts for current behaviours.

I will present four suggestions to help your skills with historical context. First, if historical events do not cause current events but gives rise to them, this means that you need to analyse exactly which of the early *contexts* was changed so as to lead to the current contexts. This means we must examine much more closely than we normally do the history of all the other contexts at that earlier time: economic, social, cultural, and opportunity. You need to trace from the 'big' or salient events in question *how other things were changed for that person, not how the person was changed 'in him or herself'.*

So, as an example, knowing someone experienced a childhood trauma is not enough of an analysis; you need to examine:

- what events brought about that situation which allowed that traumatic event to occur;
- how those events changed the social relationships, the cultural patterns of the groups, the opportunities for the people involved, and the economic or resources networking of the people involved at that time.

Any of those contexts (or all of them) could have changed from that traumatic event and given rise to the contemporary situation. Figure 2.2 tries to give the idea of this in the second row.

The second suggestion is to trace what brought about those salient life events. What early contexts in the person's life gave rise to the salient ones which we focus on? There will be clues there for your analysis, since even big or salient events do not occur spontaneously out of nothing. The historical analysis, therefore, could be that the conditions which allowed or brought about the big life event will be important and might have actually

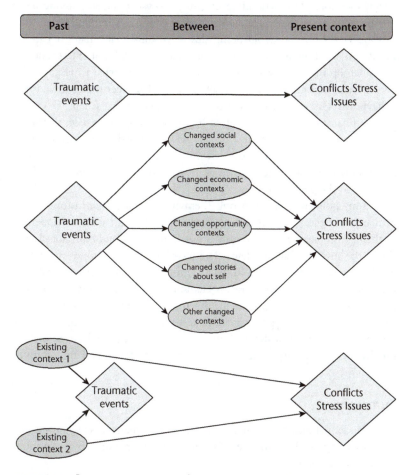

FIGURE 2.2 Common way to consider traumatic events in history, with two alternatives

given rise to the contemporary crises irrespective of the traumatic event itself (this is at the bottom of Figure 2.2).

The third suggestion to help you with historical context goes back to my earlier point in Chapter 1 that when we name things then we typically stop looking. This equally applies to history. A very real problem with big or salient life events is that we can easily name them (and make a good story around them) so we stop looking at the other contexts in the contemporary situation and, as my first two suggestions suggest, in the past as well. *Naming salient life events as causes makes us complacent about digging for more.* I have seen this, for example, with professionals talking to refugees who, as soon as the clients mention a traumatic life event, stop analysing and stop asking more questions—clearly, there is a traumatic event causing everything here.

One way I try and avoid doing this is to think that whatever bad life event you are dealing with, other people have had the same life event and *not* ended up the same way. So the question to ask is: what is *specific* to this person's past and present contexts (all of them) that gives rise to the current behaviours? This may or may not turn out to include that salient life event.

The final suggestion to help with history is *strategic usurpation*: that some regular pattern of behaviour can be used—usurped—for another strategy (Guerin, 2016a). In this case we have already seen one example: that professionals can 'use' the historic event to make it appear like they have understood the person's issues.

But my point here is that people themselves can use their historic events in many strategic ways which have nothing to do with what is happening to them. And please note: this only occurs sometimes, and I am not placing this as the answer to all problems. The most simplistic version is that a person blames the historic event in their life for all their problems so that they escape having to deal with those problems, or they use it as a way to assuage people so they stop bugging them. But there are countless more ways this can occur in very complex strategies and this simplistic strategy probably does not occur often. Talking about an early life event could even make a good story for *initiating* friendships, for example, and be useful and positive.

Summary

- Contextual analysis requires a strong commitment to seeking out and observing the details of people's contexts before naming abstract notions as 'explanations'.
- Plus, a strong commitment that all human behaviour arises through other people because all our resources come through other people in some way or another—everything is social (has a social context and social consequences).

- Language use is complex and hidden, but is always a social exchange—we never affect the non-people environment through words without other people; *words do not refer to things, words refer other people to things.*

- Our behaviours arise from our contexts and are not driven by our thinking, which is itself a behaviour arising from our social contexts and needs its own exploration.

- We must apply this consistently to all of the behaviours which we currently call the 'inner' life of people; so, there is no 'inner' life, experience, phenomenology or personal theatre, but instead there are the language and other responses which we have learned through our life but are not said out loud.

- Contextual analysis of someone's behaviours must therefore consistently:

  o find out the resources they are getting and how they access these, through what channels or networks (are there conflicts or problems here?);

  o find out all their main relationships, including those with strangers, acquaintances, immediate family, kin and friends networks (are there conflicts or problems here?);

  o find out what is exchanged in each relationship, taking special note of the subtle resources;

  o find out what, in the person's life, they keep hidden from each of those persons;

  o find out about each of those persons they try and monitor or keep up;

  o find out how much and in what ways the person would trust all those others;

  o find out something about the person's overall ecology, opportunities and economics (in their life what opportunities have they had and what did they miss out on; what resources are not available to them?);

  o find out how the person believes each of those persons-in-relationships would most like them to act and behave;

  o find out the stories and verbal strategies they use to negotiate the above with the people in their worlds (which stories and reason-giving work and which do not work; what have they had to invent in stories to negotiate their worlds and their resources and to maintain their relationships; what stories about themselves—called identity work sometimes—have they had to construct for their different relationships or audiences?);

  o in analysing a person's history, the past is related to what is happening in the present, but the urge to call this a 'causal relation', while strong, is mistaken: the past gives rise to the present but does not cause it.

References

Alkon, A. H., & Agyeman, J. (Eds.). (2011). *Cultivating food justice: Race, class, and sustainability*. London: MIT Press.

Bentall, R. P. (2003). *Madness explained: Psychosis and human nature*. London: Penguin.

Bentall, R. P. (2009). *Doctoring the mind: Why psychiatric treatments fail*. London: Penguin.

Bentley, A. F. (1935). *Behavior knowledge fact*. Bloomington, IN: Principia Press.

Bentley, A. F. (1941a). The human skin: Philosophy's last line of defense. *Philosophy of Science, 8*, 1–19.

Bentley, A. F. (1941b). The behavioral superfice. *Psychological Review, 48*, 39–59.

Beresford, P. (2002). Thinking about 'mental health': Towards a social model. *Journal of Mental Health, 11*, 581–584.

Bhugra, D. (2013). Psychiatry needs a broader focus. Interview in *The Guardian*.

Billig, M (1999). *Freudian repression: Conversation creating the unconscious*. London: Cambridge University Press.

Bourdieu, P. (1999). *The weight of the world: Social suffering in contemporary society*. London: Polity Press.

Bracken, P. (2002). *Trauma: Culture, meaning and philosophy*. London: Whurr.

Bracken, P., & Thomas, P. (2005). *Postpsychiatry: Mental health in a postmodern world*. Oxford: Oxford University Press.

Bracken, P., et al. (2012). Psychiatry beyond the current paradigm. *British Journal of Psychiatry, 201*, 430–434.

Campbell, J. K. (1964). *Honour, family, and patronage: A study of institutions and moral values in a Greek mountain community*. New York: Oxford University Press.

Cochrane, R. (1983). *The social creation of mental illness*. London: Longman.

Cromby, J., Harper, D., & Reavey, P. (2013). *Psychology, mental health and distress*. London: Palgrave.

Crowe, M. (2000). Constructing normality: A discourse analysis of the DSM-IV. *Journal of Psychiatric and Mental Health Nursing, 7*, 69–77.

Cryan, D., Shatil, S., & Piero. (2013). *Introducing capitalism: A graphic guide*. London: Icon.

de Soto, H. (2000). *The mystery of capital: Why capitalism triumphs in the West and fails everywhere else*. London: Black Swan.

Edwards, D. (1997). *Discourse and cognition*. London: SAGE.

Fischer, D. H. (1970). *Historians' fallacies: Towards a logic of historical thought*. New York: Dover.

Fleming, P. (2015). *The mythology of work: How capitalism persists despite itself*. London: Pluto Press.

Fryers, T., Melzer, D., & Jenkins, R. (2003). Social inequalities and the common mental disorders. *Social Psychiatry and Psychiatric Epidemiology, 38*, 229–237.

Giddens, A. (1991). *Modernity and self-identity: Self and society in late modern age*. Oxford: Polity Press.

Gottlieb, L., Waitzkin, H., & Miranda, J. (2010). Depressive symptoms and their social contexts: A qualitative systematic literature review of contextual interventions. *International Journal of Social Psychiatry, 57*, 402–417.

Guerin, B. (2001a). Individuals as social relationships: 18 ways that acting alone can be thought of as social behavior. *Review of General Psychology, 5*, 406–428.

Guerin, B. (2001b). Explanations of bereavement, grief, and trauma: The misuse of both mental and foundational terms. *European Journal of Behaviour Analysis, 2,* 154–161.

Guerin, B. (2016a). *How to rethink psychology: New metaphors for understanding people and their behavior.* London: Routledge.

Guerin, B. (2016b). *How to rethink human behavior: A practical guide to social contextual analysis.* London: Routledge.

Guerin, B., & Guerin, P. (2012). Re-thinking mental health for indigenous Australian communities: Communities as context for mental health. *Community Development Journal, 47*(4), 555–570.

Guerin, B., & Guerin, P. (2014). "Mental illness" symptoms as extensions of strategic social behaviour: The case of multicultural mental health. *Rivista di Psicologia Clinica, 1,* 67–81.

Guérin, D. (1970). *Anarchism: From theory to practice.* New York: Monthly Review Press.

Hammel, E. A. (1968). *Alternative social structures and ritual relations in the Balkans.* Englewood Cliffs, NJ: Prentice Hall.

Han, C. (2004). The work of indebtedness: The traumatic present of late capitalist Chile. *Culture, Medicine and Psychiatry, 28,* 169–187.

Johnson, A. W., & Earle, T. (2000). *The evolution of human society.* Stanford, CA: Stanford University Press.

Kirmayer, L. J., Gone, J. P., & Moses, J. (2014). Rethinking historical trauma. *Transcultural Psychiatry, 51,* 299–319.

Klare, M. T. (2012). *The race for what's left: The global scramble for the world's last resources.* New York: Picador.

Kolbert, E. (2014). *Field notes from a catastrophe: A frontline report on climate change.* London: Bloomsbury.

Leonard, S., & Sunkara, B. (2016). *The future we want: Radical ideas for the new century.* New York: Metropolitan Books.

Löwy, M. (2015). *Ecosocialism: A radical alternative to capitalist catastrophe.* Chicago, IL: Haymarket Books.

Maxwell, K. (2014). Historicizing historical trauma theory: Troubling the transgenerational transmission paradigm. *Transcultural Psychiatry, 51,* 407–435.

McGruder, J. (2001). Life experience is not a disease or why medicalizing madness is counterproductive to recovery. *Occupational Therapy in Mental Health, 17,* 59–80.

Mohatt, N. V., Thompson, A. B., Thai, N. D., & Tebes, J. K. (2014). Historical trauma as public narrative: A conceptual review of how history impacts present-day health. *Social Science & Medicine, 106,* 128–136.

Oliver, D. (1981). *Two Tahitian villages: A study in comparison.* Provo, UT: Brigham Young University Press.

Paradies, Y. (2016). Colonisation, racism and indigenous health. *Journal of Population Research, 33,* 83–96.

Pilgrim, D., Rogers, A., & Bentall, R. P. (2009). The centrality of personal relationships in the creation and amelioration of mental health problems: The current interdisciplinary case. *Health: An Interdisciplinary Journal for the Social Study of Health, Illness and Medicine, 13,* 235–254.

Pinchbeck, D., & Jordan, K. (Eds.). (2011). *What comes after money? Essays from 'Reality Sandwich' on transforming currency and community.* Berkeley, CA: Evolver Editions.

Polanyi, K. (1944). *The great transformation.* New York: Rinehart.

Potter, J. (1996). *Representing reality: Discourse, rhetoric and social construction.* London: SAGE.

Powers, W. T. (1998). *Making sense of behavior: The meaning of control.* New Canaan, CT: Benchmark Publications.

Rose, A. M. (1962). A social-psychological theory of neurosis. In A. M. Rose (Ed.), *Human behavior and social processes: An interactionist approach* (pp. 537–549). Boston, MA: Houghton Mifflin.

Rose, N. (1998). *Inventing our selves: Psychology, power, and personhood.* Cambridge: Cambridge University Press.

Sandal, M. J. (2012). *What money can't buy: The moral limits of markets.* London: Penguin.

Sennett, R. (1998). *The corrosion of character: The personal consequences of work in the new capitalism.* London: W. W. Norton.

Smail, D. (2005). *Power, interest and psychology: Elements of a Social Materialist understanding of distress.* London: PCCS Books.

Smail, D. (2012). Draft manifesto for a social materialist psychology of distress. *Journal of Critical Psychology, Counselling and Psychotherapy, 12,* 93–107.

Stiglitz, J. E. (2013). *The price of inequality.* London: Penguin.

Tew, J. (2005). *Social perspectives in mental health: Developing social models to understand and work with mental distress.* London: Jessica Kingsley.

Tew, J., Ramon, S., Slade, M., Bird, V., Melton, J., & Le Boutillier, C. (2012). Social factors and recovery from mental health difficulties: A review of the evidence. *British Journal of Social Work, 42,* 443–460.

Waldram, J. B. (2004). *Revenge of the Windigo: The construction of the mind and mental health of North American Aboriginal peoples.* Toronto: University of Toronto Press.

Walker, C., Johnson, K., & Cunningham, L. (Eds.). (2012). *Community psychology and the socio-economics of mental distress.* New York: Palgrave Macmillan.

Waller, A. L. (1988). *Feud: Hatfields, McCoys, and social change in Appalachia, 1860–1900.* London: University of North Carolina Press.

3

CONTEXTUALIZING LANGUAGE AND THINKING (COGNITION) FOR MENTAL HEALTH

In all the fields of mental health both talking and thinking are very important behaviours —indeed pivotal—to consider and rethink. Sigmund Freud even wrote: 'If we ask ourselves what is it that gives the character of strangeness to the substitutive formation and the symptom in schizophrenia, we eventually come to realize that it is the pre-dominance of what has to do with words over what has to do with things' (Freud, 1915/1984, p. 206).

In addition, the biggest movement in clinical psychology over the last decades has been cognitive behaviour therapy. This has used a 'cognitive processing' metaphor to pretend that people have something like an inner agent, computer, or a control centre inside them making decisions, coming up with their thoughts, making (mis)attributions about people and events, and having inner beliefs and attitudes which directly determine some of their behaviour. Below and elsewhere (Guerin, 2016a, 2016b), I have suggested that 'cognitive' events are real, but they simply mean behaviours involving language, which means that analysing the external contexts for language and thinking are once again of vital importance to understanding mental health. They have special *social* properties which certainly make them look different to the rest of our behaviours, but they are no different in principle to any other behaviour.

The historic move of looking more closely at thinking and talking by imagining them as metaphorical 'mental' cognitive processes has been helpful within some therapies, to spur on some new ways to do therapy, but these approaches do not contextualize the behaviours properly as we saw in the last chapter—describing their social, historical, cultural, and other contexts. Indeed, it seems that the cognitive models have dissuaded this form of observation. And for some behaviours, however, such as hearing voices and 'distorted thinking patterns', the cognitive conceptualizations are not working well and a new approach is required that involves more of the context. Further, as we will see below, using a cognitive metaphor escapes having to deal directly with real-world social contexts because the 'social' just becomes representations in someone's head; whereas a more careful analysis of language use and thinking shows that they are essentially involved with *concrete and observable* social contexts and doing various things to people.

If we are going to replace the cognitive metaphors with 'post-internal' descriptions of context, what do we need to account for to make this plausible and useful for therapeutic actions? Below are the sorts of real events I think we need to be able to account for if we want to change the cognitive metaphor:

- what the 'single-channel' of cognition really means;
- 'metacognition' and thinking or talking about your cognitive processes;
- why there seem to be two systems of cognition and decision-making;
- how reframing verbally for people in therapy works to affect their other behaviour;
- attributions and misattributions in many forms and how they work;
- how people 'possess' beliefs;
- how (or if) people's beliefs affect their other behaviour;
- what leads a person to state a belief and follow it in a consistent way if beliefs do not control our behaviour;
- why people do not do what they say they are going to do;
- what is people's cognitive sense of self-identity or ego;
- how people 'make' decisions (as statements or actions);
- how people make replicable 'biases' in their decisions (statements);
- how voices can be heard and reported as real voices;
- how all the above can be different in different contexts (social relationships, cultural, economic, etc.).

To do this, I wish to first give a brief overview of one way to (re)conceptualize talking and thinking (aka cognition) as arising from our external social and other contexts—not an easy task to do quickly and especially so for rethinking thinking as events outside us and not inside our heads (Guerin, 2016a, 2016b). After this I will go through some of the points listed above to show how we can think beyond the cognitive metaphors in which psychologists are currently stuck (see also Edwards, 1997). My main use of translating the cognitive metaphors into contextual analysis, however, will come from using all this to examine mental health behaviours and complaints in later chapters, and *getting the problems and solutions for what are currently called 'mental' issues out of the head.*

Rethinking talking and thinking

The general idea for rethinking talking and thinking is that both are behaviours like any other (Guerin, 2016a, 2016b). The do have special properties, but in general, all our behaviours arise out of the strategies and arrangements of our social, cultural, historical, economic, opportunity, and other contexts. Talking and thinking are no different except that they are always part of social contexts (the only way they can be trained). In certain contexts, certain thoughts will 'occur' to us or we will talk in certain ways. Change those contexts, and the thinking and talk will change. Simple to say this, much more difficult to show the nuanced contextual details and to convince people.

Luckily, the research from areas of study variously called discourse analysis, conversation analysis, the analysis of verbal behaviour and sociolinguistics have been pursuing something like this approach with language use for many years. Indeed, we will see below that discourse analysis already has the most plausible alternatives to (cognitive) attribution and other theories within cognitive social psychology (Edwards & Potter, 1993). Like the approach here, discourse analysis, conversation analysis, and sociolinguistics treat our talking as a behaviour which occurs in social contexts, and they therefore study language as an embedded social activity, not something we devise in our heads. In theory, at least, one cannot study language without also studying concurrently how those uses of language function within the social, cultural, historical, and other contexts of the people talking (or thinking). As I have written elsewhere—you cannot study language by studying the words alone (Guerin, 2004)—even studying the structure of language, its syntax, is about how syntax functions within social and cultural contexts.

Of most importance to understand, then, is that language use is meaningless outside of its social context. Language use is a behaviour such that the only thing it can do in this world (and hence be shaped by having effects) is to change the behaviour of someone who has also spent time learning that language (Guerin, 2004, 2016b). No matter how long or hard we say 'Please stand up and clap your hands above your head' to a cat or to a non-speaker of English, they will not do anything (unless we prompt in another way of course).

The upshot of this for the current approach and for discourse analysis, conversation analysis and sociolinguistics is that *we must always find out what any language usage is doing to people and what it has done in the past to people*—how it fits in with their social strategies of life, how it is embedded in what they are doing and its consequences. This is not always easy, and requires some special methodologies which are unfamiliar to most psychologists, but it is the only way to understand the use of a language segment in a social setting (Guerin, 2004, 2016b). So for any types of language, we must not ask 'What does that mean?' or 'Is that true?', but ask '*What is saying or thinking that doing to people and what has it done to people in the past?*'

One advantage of this approach is that it forces us to observe more closely the contexts surrounding any talking or thinking that a person does. We do not pretend to 'explain' language behaviour by positing some unknown inner existence or space where all these 'cognitive processes' can take place independently of the rest of the concrete universe and our lives. But this does mean that hard work needs to be done with observations and contextual descriptions rather than theorizing happily with made up models and metaphors.

This was nicely put by Arthur Bentley (1935) many years ago in discussing the absurdity of using metaphors such as 'mental' or 'psychic' when trying to theoretically position a '*locus*' for an individual to control their own behaviour (a misguided task, we will see later). He wrote that language and thought, for example, are not found in the head or in a mental domain:

> [the] locus is not some 'point' in the brain—itself linguistically as incoherent as the 'pointless' psychic—nor the brain as a whole, nor even the human organism as a whole. As for 'language' so also for 'thought.' *The locus lies in many human beings interacting with all of their interconnecting materials and processes,* not in some arbitrary space and time adopted from the procedures of other branches of investigation, but in such space and time as may be developed in the full range of the study.
>
> *(1935, p. 149, italics added)*

The basic idea is that through our long history of experience and learning ever since we were born, we have learned to behave in certain ways with our bodies in certain contexts, and this includes what we attend to or look at. If given a piano there is a range of actions we can do although we can only do one action at a time usually. We cannot play the keys 'properly' and also clap our hands at the same time. There is nothing mystical about this.

But, we have also spent a huge part of our life learning to *say* many things, and we do this when we see or do almost anything; we have a huge variety of ways to talk and comment, and to influence our audiences in this way if said out loud. But only one out loud at a time, also. Simply put, *one of the most frequent things humans have learned to do in absolutely any situation is to talk or comment, even if no one is listening or the many responses are not said out loud.* Our important, common, or relevant audiences do not even need to be present once it is learned.

We must remember, then, that talking (including thinking) is one of the most common things we do in life; we see or experience something and begin talking whether or not people are present, whether out loud or not out loud; we can even say contradictory things concurrently since we have many different and contradictory audiences shaping us. And so when something happens or we see something, usually we are chattering out loud (or not out loud) long before we begin to do anything with our body, arms, or legs.

So, we have a lot of concurrent talking going on as things happen around us in life because we have many audiences who are important (and all our most important consequences come through people), but most of this does not get said out loud. The many unsaid conversational snippets (both listening and saying) are usually called thoughts, but I like to call them '*thinklings*', to include both 'conscious' (rehearsed) and 'unconscious' thoughts (Guerin, 2016a). And often the language response is our one and only response and we stop 'focusing' on those things once we have 'said' (named, usually) them.

The point here is that for any of the life contexts we are in, we do not get to say out loud most (only one at a time) of the language responses we have learned for different social contexts (audiences) but these still occur simultaneously with any 'out loud' talk, and so *there are concurrent multiple thoughts if we have multiple relevant audiences*. This constitutes thinking and other events called consciousness, hearing voices, ideas, concepts, etc.

These events are very real and have the same reality as the language that we use out loud but without them actually being said out loud (although the consequences are likely to be different which is an important difference). So they are like any other behaviours, but for humans we most especially learn to talk with respect to objects and events, more than anything else we do.

Special features or properties of talking

The two most difficult ideas to comprehend when contextualizing talking are first, that it only occurs through people, and second, that *because of this* we can say things which have no basis in the world whatsoever (except for the trained and changeable effects such talk has on people). To understand the first point, we can adapt the methods and ideas from discourse analysis to help us to find the ways language use is embedded in, or arises from, our social contexts and social strategies in life. I do not just randomly say out loud 'I believe that cats are closely related to foxes'; I say it within a history of social conversations, perhaps competitive strategies with the people listening (maybe competing over time as to who knows the most).

My particular version of discursive analysis integrates other versions but is open-ended, and for convenience works with analysing two common functions of talking (and hence thinking): (1) *getting people to do things* and (2) *developing and maintaining social relationships* with people (Guerin, 2003, 2004, 2016b). I will not go through these since the details are not important here (see Table 3.1), and there are other good systems. But within these two main functions there are a wealth of strategies that are typically found *in both talking and thinking*: rehearsal of stories, excuses, attributions of responsibility, 'facts', attitudes and opinions, hedging or mitigation, rumour and gossip, reasons and explanations, secrets and hiding, lies, arguing and counter-arguing, pleading, identity management and face-work, and questioning or 'fishing' for details (see Billig, 2008; Burman & Parker, 1993; Edwards, 1997; Edwards & Potter, 1993; Eggins & Slade, 1997; Jaworski & Coupland, 2006; Kitzinger, 2000; Potter, 1996).

These discursive strategies are entangled in people's idiosyncratic social and cultural contexts, and this will apply to thinking just as to other conversational and discursive actions. But we must keep in mind that talking is all about

TABLE 3.1 One way to rethink language use (talking, writing, or thinking) as an embedded social activity

Main functions of using language:

- getting people to do things
- developing, maintaining, and repairing social relationships with people

Some strategies typically found in talking (and thinking) to achieve the functions:

- rehearsal of stories which can include all those strategies below
- portraying the world as 'facts'
- making excuses
- attributions of responsibility
- stating 'facts' and 'beliefs'
- saying humorous things such as jokes
- stating attitudes and opinions
- hedging or mitigation
- preventing challenges to what is said
- use of extremes
- use of abstract language to prevent challenges
- threatening or bribing (verbal bullying)
- telling rumour and gossip
- giving reasons and explanations
- keeping secrets and hiding things
- telling lies
- arguing and counter-arguing
- pleading
- identity management and face-work
- questioning or 'fishing' for details

our concrete social contexts, whether this is something said by a client with mental health issues or by the therapist trying to help that person by talking in exchange for money. All language use is a behaviour which only does things to people and is only shaped by social contexts therefore. It is part of our whole social context and its strategies and is not a separate domain somewhere in a mental or processing environment, independent of the world. (Remember the words of Bentley quoted earlier: 'The locus lies in many human beings inter-acting with all of their interconnecting materials and processes.')

The second difficult point above was that we can do anything with language precisely because it does not directly relate to the non-social world (only through the training of listeners; Guerin, 2016a). If I were to say, 'Hey! I just saw Elvis leaving the building and I told him to give us a concert next week', we should not worry about the truth or falsity of this statement. What our contextual analysis needs to focus on most is *what does saying this sentence do to its audiences*. What are the social effects when someone says this, especially when someone says obviously false facts? It certainly is false but it can still have a powerful effect on that person's life (keeps people away from them, makes people laugh and like them, etc.).

The more philosophical point is that if language use did not arise solely from our social contexts and our social/cultural language training activities, then this would mean that saying the word 'cat' would be constrained in some way by real live cats and we might be restricted when we use it. It would be like this: just as my fingers cannot make piano music without a piano, in this new strange world I might not be able to say 'cat' at all if there was no real cat present, if saying 'cat' was determined by the real world. However—and luckily!—because language use is about affecting people (and not cats) we can say anything we like and the only constraints on truth and reality are what people do when they hear us—the consequences from listeners. Thus is born all the creativity and great literature from talking, writing and thinking, as well as all the falsities, lying, delusional talk, and word salads.

The final point about language use strategies will be important when we look more at cognitive models of 'thinking disorders' and how to contex-tualize these models. This is about what looks like people reporting their 'beliefs'. People portray the world and state what they believe, but our ques-tion is: what social contexts give rise to this? But because this is important in mental health models I will make one point here, and discuss 'beliefs' more when discussing specific mental health complaints (Chapter 6).

Most discourse analysis treats examples of such talk as the speaker trying to convince the listener to believe what they believe, and therapies typically do the same. I might tell everyone in conversation that research has shown that coffee causes you to go blind, that cats evolved from foxes, that I am the worst person in the world, that if I go outside people will laugh at me, or that I am the king of England. I seem to be attempting to portray my version of my world and convince you it is true.

But we need to expand our contextual analyses. Saying 'beliefs' is also a large part of initiating and maintaining social relationships (our second function in Table 3.1) and, in such cases, the idea of actually convincing the listener might not be functional. So talking about research that coffee makes you go blind is probably not commonly done to actually persuade your listeners but done simply to engage them and facilitate friendships with a laugh.

As another example, stating beliefs can also get the listener to do something (our first function), but something *which might have nothing to do with stating your 'belief'*. Telling you I am the king of England is a good way to escape or avoid social contact, for example, as I mentioned earlier, but has nothing to do with the belief I use for this. Telling you that I am the worst person in the world, or that if I go outside people will laugh at me, will be similar but probably more complicated (more layers of past audiences). And remember in this that we are not analysing what *really* happens when I go outside—*we are analysing my making of the statement to you* that if I go outside people will laugh at me. The two events will likely have very different contexts that give rise to them and different consequences.

So, in summary, telling 'beliefs' (in fact any use of language) can be unrelated to convincing the audience, but instead relate to contexts of:

- entertaining the listener
- getting the listener to like you
- getting the listener just to listen to you
- getting the listener just to pay attention to you
- getting the listener to do something unrelated to what is being said.

So, when someone is portraying the world, establishing facts, warranting their accounts and explanations, or otherwise giving 'beliefs' about the world, there might be several outcomes:

- getting the listener to fully believe them forever after (e.g. the listener makes the same claim to others in the future)
- getting the listener to believe them for some specific event or period
- getting the listener to learn what they say and be able to repeat
- getting the listener to just listen
- getting the listener to just go along with them or even pretend to agree
- getting the listener merely to not challenge what they say (or maybe not in front of people).

These two analyses will be discussed in more detail later but it is important here since so much of cognitive behavioural therapy and observations of mental health behaviours and complaints is about stating 'beliefs' or accounts of the world (establishing facts). I would like you to remember that contextual analysis opens up hugely the canvas of human behaviours we can now *observe* that relate contexts to stating beliefs. Stated beliefs are not a simple belief-memory dump as occurs usually in cognitive models of mental health issues. And if you think about this quote by Janet, memory is also actually storytelling and needs to be analysed as discourse in its social contexts:

> Memory, like belief, like all psychological phenomena, is an action; essentially, it is the action of telling a story. Almost always we are concerned here with a linguistic operation, quite independent of our attitude towards the happening.
>
> *(Janet, 1925/1919, p. 661)*

Special features or properties of thinking

We have so far looked mostly at talking, but rethinking 'thinking' is especially difficult, because there have been centuries of thinking being assumed to be events occurring inside us somewhere—a psyche, a mind, a mental domain, the brain, or in a cognitive processing structure—and to be events which originate there and control our other behaviours. But we can truly rethink 'thinking' when we appreciate that it arises and occurs outside of us in the way that happens for any behaviour, by treating it as *language use we have been socially trained or shaped to use with our audiences in context but which is not said out loud*. So, just as everyday conversation and discourse can be analysed within its social and strategic contexts and there are typical forms of conversational strategies found (see Table 3.1; Guerin, 2003), similarly *these will also occur for thoughts and thinking*.

The events we call thinking or 'having thoughts' have had a long history of being talked about as private or unobservable events that go on inside an individual, usually as a form of 'psyche', mind or brain activity, but many have questioned this (including Wittgenstein, Vygotsky, Bentley, Bakhtin, Cooley, Ryle, Kantor, Skinner, Rorty; see Fernyhough, 2016; Guerin, 2016a; Hodgkiss, 2011; Leiman, 2012; Rapaport, 1955; Robbins & Rumsey, 2008; Soyland, 1994).

Contextually, therefore, *thinking only arises from and exists in the contexts outside of us*. What we call thinking is a variety of ways we have learned over many years to talk *as if to others*, even though only one of the many responses can get said out loud at any time—we only have one mouth. This is also the origin of the 'single channel hypothesis' in cognition.

When faced with this rethinking, a metaphor is sometimes given that thinking is simply the 'inner' version of talking, like an inner speech, by which we can influence *ourselves* to do things when we think them. 'Talking to yourself', however, despite being an everyday expression for thinking, is not an accurate one, it is a misunderstanding. You are not actually the audience for your own thoughts. Thinking is more like '*talking with your audiences about events but not out loud*' than it is like 'talking-to-yourself about events'. See if that helps you readjust to thoughts existing outside of you.

So I am suggesting that we can approach this all in a new way by analysing thoughts as part of 'everyday social conversational responses with our normal audiences but which are not said out loud'. This uniquely combines contextual analyses of the thinking-in-its-social-contexts with discourse or conversational analyses of the thoughts themselves. *Most importantly, I think, this means we can observe and describe the (external) contexts in which thoughts arise in the same way that discourse analysis currently does for talk which is spoken out loud*. We do not have to limit our analyses of thinking by treating thoughts as private and unobservable events.

We can at last 'see' thinking! But not in the place it has been presumed to reside for centuries. Its 'physical substrate' is not the brain but the external contexts in which we are all embedded which give rise to using language— social contexts.

What this is also saying is that if we know all the contexts for a person (in principle, that is), and all the language they have been shaped to say in different situations, we could (in principle, remember) predict accurately what they are thinking. We should be able to 'read their mind' (Guerin, 2016a, 2016b)! But this is not a form of magic. If I know from everything about your context that you are having major economic and financial problems, and that you cannot do a lot of things you would like to because of money problems, I can predict that you are likely to be thinking about both money and the people in your life and the networks related to money.

The above was written 'in principle', but the more practical upshot is that *the more I know your life contexts in detail, the more I can know what you are thinking*. This is no different to saying that the more I know your life contexts in detail, the more I can know what you have in your office at work: if I know you are an architect, I can predict many things that will be in your office; if I know you have a close family I can know you are likely to have a photo of them in your office; if I know that you have a fascination for trains, I can predict you are likely to have a picture on the wall of trains or a model of a train on your desk.

So the language responses we have been shaped to say in different circumstances are not hidden in some metaphysical domain inside our head;

they are contextual arrangements no more hidden than the things in your work office. And the more I know about you the more I can guess those things you are thinking without hearing you actually say them out loud. I hope you can begin to see why this rethinking is so very important for dealing with 'mental health' issues and suffering from thinking events.

'Rethinking thinking' therefore opens up exciting possibilities that current mental health treatments could be talked about in new ways and lead to even more efficacious treatments or to treatments that suit a wider diversity of people and circumstances. There have been some initial attempts to apply linguistic analyses to various forms of 'thought disorders' (Barch & Berenbaum, 1996; Bentall, Corcoran, Howard, Blackwood, & Kinderman, 2001; Gladstone & Parker, 2003; Leudar & Thomas, 2000; Leudar, Thomas, McNally, & Glinski, 1997; McCarthy-Jones & Fernyhough, 2011). But with a thorough discourse analysis applied to thinking we can do a lot more. Three particular forms of language strategies—attributions, intrusive thoughts, and the strategic use of beliefs—will be of specific importance in discussions below of mental health in life.

In summary, research on thoughts and thinking has been stifled I believe by limiting 'observations' of thought to the *verbal reports of thoughts* in almost all clinical and non-clinical applications, and this is only because thoughts have been assumed to be private and not directly observable. But the reporting of thoughts is itself another behaviour shaped usually by different audiences. Clinically relevant thoughts have therefore been assumed to be 'dysfunctional' internal cognitive processes rather than normal conversational behaviours shaped by external (but perhaps still 'dysfunctional') social contexts or audiences but which are not said. With social and discursive analyses to explore the contexts for thinking in detailed ways, new ways forward will be found.

When are there words and when are there not?

Before going on, I want to say a little about judging whether we are dealing with words or not, whether talking, writing, or thinking. I mentioned above that we can say anything with words because their consequences are only in social context rather than the rest of the environment, but this also means that in many places in life it is difficult to judge if we are dealing with words and our social realities or the other realities of the world.

Whereas Western philosophy has been directed (since Plato) at finding complete certainty of knowledge *in words*, much of 'Eastern' philosophy has been directed at showing how words were being disguised as, or pretending to be, the real world, and finding ways (such as in Zen) to unmask this 'veil of Maya'. I have compiled a brief list in Table 3.2 of tests to give you a clue whether words are being used (shaped by audiences) or actual engagement in the real (non-word) reality. While these are not always correct, hopefully they can help you sort the word events from the non-word events.

The items in Table 3.2 will help you decide whether someone talking to you is partially or totally using words, and if they are supposed to be describing some event whether they are exaggerating or embellishing. You can see these in action from Zen Masters if you read the Zen koan (e.g. Reps, 1957; Shigematsu, 1988). To give an example, if someone says to you 'Wow, we all went to the burger place last night and took over the whole joint for the night' then the talk is probably more about words and a story, even if some real events took place. (This was probably said, however, to entertain and maintain social relationships not to tell the stark truth about the previous night, so this does not matter; in fact, doing this is better than a boring story meticulously reporting what took place.)

TABLE 3.2 Tests to give you a clue that words are being used (behaviour which is shaped by audiences) rather than the real (non-word) reality (behaviour shaped by the consequences of what the world does to you)

- If it is abstract it is probably a word event
- If it is generalized it is probably a word event
- If it is active it is probably a non-word event
- If it is concrete it is probably a non-word event but there are social strategies in which concrete verbal descriptions are used as a ploy to make it seem more real (Potter & Edwards, 1990)
- If it is singular or specific it is probably a non-word event
- If you repeat the behaviour over and over, are the effects like repeatedly hitting a wall with a brick or does the repetition produce other effects, more like the effects you get from people when they are bored or exasperated?
- There are good language methods for determining whether someone is lying (a word event) although not full-proof (Houtson, Flloyd, & Carnicero, 2012)
- If it can be easily said or can be said clearly then it is probably a word event
- If it makes a good story then it is probably a word event
- If it needs a lot of arguments rather than observations then it is probably a word event
- If you need to be convinced of it then it is probably a word event
- If the person is looking towards other people during the behaviour, then it is probably a word event; if they are looking towards the relevant environment during the behaviour then it might be a non-word event.
- Imagine the person reporting this in front of a judge and jury; would it hold up?

Box 3.1   We live in the Matrix now!

You will recall in the movie that people in the future world are being kept alive in a post-apocalyptic wasteland so AI machines can live off their energy. But the people are plugged *visually* into a huge virtual reality program that gives them the illusion of living in a 'normal' world (that is, the Matrix). So at the start of the movie you (and the hero, Neo) think there is just our normal world because everyone is seeing the world through the program, but it is all an illusion. They try to break through the illusion by hacking into the software running the Matrix and inserting themselves as characters in 'there' to destroy the virtual reality program/Matrix. It is all really being controlled externally in a wasteland world run by machines.

I have previously suggested that *language use is the original virtual reality* (Guerin, 2016a). We learn and act as if our words are the real things. We regularly give words precedence over the actual experiences we can have, and we trust what is said over and above what we see and experience. We no longer trust observation but do trust things we *hear* people saying. Stories we hear or read are more convincing than what we see, and a good story can even persuade us that we did see or experience something when we did not. I also noted that when we name something that we see, we stop looking and exploring our world—the naming was the goal, and we now have something to talk about and a story to tell people.

Further, our worlds and lives are now filled with words, everywhere. Even this book. We spend more time reading and talking than looking and experiencing. When something happens in life we can respond based on previous experiences or we can prepare to talk about whatever happened. The latter now gets priority. It is as if our first instinct now is to have something ready to say about everything around us, rather than respond in other experiential or engaging ways. Now I want to go fully to the dark side and suggest that this is just like The Matrix in the movie by that name, and we are already living in it, Mr Anderson . . .

Basically then, all the above suggests that words are acting like our Matrix: we live now in a world of words where the reality is what is said, and what is said gets first priority. This Matrix is here and now and we are living it. We actually live an experience-deprived existence: have you ever seen or interacted with most of the animals you can talk about

(continued)

(continued)

(zoos do not count—they are mostly about words and telling stories later)? We can tell stories about all sorts of animals and post about them on Facebook but never actually interact or behave with them.

In exchange, we are given a huge comforting world (Matrix) of words that we all agree implicitly to treat as if we know them for real, and we can tell stories about them (all second- or third-hand of course), and name 'facts' about them, and have opinions and beliefs about them although we have never seen or interacted with any of it, get sympathy and a range of emotions from the words we use about them, and be able to place most of it on Facebook for moral outrage effects. This includes fictitious characters called 'pop stars' or worse, 'TV personalities', who we all talk about as if we knew them almost. They are really real to us. (One person shot John Lennon even though Lennon was only pure words for that person up to the final point.) And all this is supported (the 'software' and the AIs) by our social worlds of learning to respond the same to words and everyone implicitly agreeing to go along with this as if the words were then the real thing.

There are some benefits, obviously, in using words, but there are long-term downsides as well. Of most importance for mental health: (1) our worlds become abstract (like words are) and the concreteness of life disappears; (2) we also start treating *people* as if they ARE the words we use about them, and no longer experience them and our relationships in more engaging and experiential ways, and we do not see their diversity because it is not captured by words very well; (3) we start treating imaginary things that only arise from talking as if they were reality, and so anxieties, gloom, and slogans become real to us far too easily and we cannot easily shake them off as merely linguistic illusions.

Luckily, and it is no accident, methods for re-prioritizing experience over words are becoming more prevalent, with Zen, mindfulness, Gestalt therapy, Third Wave therapies like ACT, etc. When you believe that your neighbour is listening to you through the walls secretly at night, this means that words have taken over your Matrix and this all appears to be the absolute reality for you. When you say to yourself (from somewhere) that you are worthless and depressed; again, words are taking precedence over experience—the Matrix is feeding you glum words of gloom that you cannot seem to shake.

But also remember the important point from all this: that your words are shaped from the people around you, not from inside you, since the Matrix is actually created out there in the external social world and is not an inner reality (also like the post-apocalyptic wasteland in the movie which is hidden). But in everyday life it sure appears to be real, just as it did for Neo at the start of the movie before he saw there were cracks in this illusory world (or cracks in our stories and words in our case). He was like a proper Zen Master, then, stopping you from responding to everything around you with words and getting you to respond to the objects, events, and experiences themselves. So we begin to see the cracks in this word-created world we live in.

Rethinking general cognitive processes

Now I will look at some more detailed features of the cognitive approaches to see how we might deal with these in a contextual approach; what is added to a new rethinking, and how we can still capture what is important. In all the following chapters, then, we will look at examples of how our thinking about mental health behaviours specifically can change when we rethink 'cognitive processes'. I would not spend the time doing this excepting that the 'cognitive' approach is the most frequent one used in mental health talk currently, and thinking is a behaviour with extremely difficult to observe contexts.

The history of metaphors in psychology is a constant fight to place 'thinking' and some of 'language' into a private or inaccessible space—the mind, the brain, private events, etc. The idea is to allow (theoretically) that *new events can then occur within these private spaces which are not dependent anymore on external contexts.* This the panacea or alchemist's gold being sought *to explain everything for which we cannot see obvious external events or contexts.* And that is what I am, in general, disagreeing with, and think we have to just dig deeper in describing external contexts and take longer to do it, not invent theoretical private spaces that can generate non-external events, not take the easy way out with quick research methods and then theorizing to fill in the gaps from inadequate observations.

So, as one example, we might be said to learn stimulus response associations externally at first but *we can then do things with those networks of associations in the private spaces* (usually the brain) *without further external contexts.* This becomes 'thinking', whereas I am arguing that thinking is external not private. For cognitive psychology, as another example, we might commence cognitions by seeing something external (perception) but this is turned into information representations which are then passed to an information processor within an unobservable space (the brain or a mental processing area). Once there, the cognitive representations are said to be changed and augmented in many ways *independent of the external environment*, so says cognitive theory. Both of these become like a 'run-about inference ticket' (Prior, 1960) in which anything goes, we can invent any model, and we then also get a sort of *ipso facto* argument as the 'explanation'.

So, what is the cognitive metaphor? A rough idea culled from many sources goes like this. We wander around the world and take in information through our senses. This information is passed to a processing 'centre' and processed in some ways, using decision-making processes, action processes, using memories which are recalled from a storage area, and using 'executive' processes to oversee all this.

There is a processing environment, therefore, something like the following, although versions differ, and this one is simplistic in any case:

sensations → perception → memory → retrieval → cognitive decisions → action

There are many problems myself and others have dealt with elsewhere and I will not repeat the details here (mostly in Guerin, 2016a):

- that this is supposed to have an unchanging environment along which new information is passed but the structure remains unchanged;
- that this is supposed to occur moment-by-moment (very quickly) in real time so we get actions done;
- none of the details of structure or pathways are provided, observations are actually only ever of 'externally' observed behaviours or verbal reports;
- the models are all underdetermined, they are hypothetical, and new models and processing 'modules' can be invented at any time;
- there are major confusions in all these literatures between word events and non-word events.

To look ahead, the major cognitive mental health models then state that in the middle of all this processing, we make natural or unnatural mistakes or errors in the processing and hence are born our mental illnesses. This mostly occurs in the memory and decision-making sections of the processing, but some theorists have utilized the 'sensations into perception' modules to 'explain' other mental health issues.

It is important to say a bit more about three points, now that we have seen the models in general. First, all the evidence for these models comes from external observations, but weak ones—we cannot measure directly any of these hypothesized processes. Attempts have been made to locate some of the hypothetic processes in some brain 'substrates' but these require a whole new slew of assumptions, and interpretations of correlations.

Second, and my major practical concern, once people work with hypothetical models they tend to stop observing the contextual details and just look for small, indirect observations which might support or refute their models. It restricts what we see in the person's real world because the models then channel us to look for only certain events, and whole other contexts go floating past without any attention given to them. Economic contexts and economic opportunities are two major examples of this that rarely get observed because there is nothing of this in the cognitive models since the social basis to all this has been excluded in order for the model to occur within the head.

Third, all the work on memory and executive control does not differentiate word and non-word events very well, and, more importantly, does not differentiate the two different types of consequential contexts from which they arise. Verbal reports are typically taken to be the same as the non-word events they appear to report, especially when reporting what are called thoughts, feelings, or beliefs. But most of the time reading about the models of central controls and executive controls we are at a loss as to whether these are referring to word or non-word events despite the different contexts for their appearances as behaviour. In these cases, remember the Janet quote earlier.

Having got very critical of cognitive modelling, there is certainly much that is useful in what they have done, and the therapies based on the ideas have certainly made some inroads into dealing with language use in mental health issues, even if from incorrect metaphors. Below I will first suggest how the main tenets of cognitive theory can be viewed as behaviour in context (external context, not inside the gooey grey matter), with much of the focus being on the contexts for talking and thinking of course. Following that I will go through some areas of cognitive theory and give more details of what we can use and how we can translate these, and begin to translate the useful therapeutic applications.

Translating 'cognitive' to 'contextual'

Table 3.3 provides some examples of the tenets of cognitive theory and how we can rethink them in terms of external contexts giving rise to the behaviours, including talking and thinking.

TABLE 3.3 Translating some main tenets of cognitive theory into a contextual observation approach

Cognitive approach	Contextual approach
People 'take in' information and then process	What we do, say, and think (all are variously called 'decisions') arise from the contexts in which we are embedded and that have shaped us in the past
The cognitive system computes to make decisions	The 'decisions' are 'made' (shaped by) in the contexts in which we live; we act within those contexts based on our past and the 'locus' for the decision-making is therefore external
The information 'taken in' is limited sometimes or is 'single channel' only	We can learn multiple verbal responses to situations but if 'rehearsing' as thoughts or saying out loud, then we can only speak one thing at a time
People 'take in' information, process it and then decide, for example, how to *attribute causality* to events and people	Instead we ask: 'What effect does making that *causality attribution* have on people, or has it had on people in the past?' (Edwards & Potter, 1993)
People 'take in' information, process it and that processing decides what *beliefs* they 'possess'	'What effect does telling people that *belief* have on people, or has it had on people in the past?'
People 'take in' information, process it and then make *mistakes and have biases* in what they decide	'What effect does telling people those "biased" statements have on people, or has it had on people in the past?'
People do not do what they say they are going to do	Saying and doing both arise from social and other contexts but not necessarily the same ones; why would you expect them to always coincide?
'Metacognition': thinking or talking about your cognitive processes	What you do or say will be a part of your context, so it can give rise to other responding
How reframing verbally for people in therapy works to affect their other behaviour	Whatever a therapist says is part of a social context with a history of consequences, so the 'reframed thinking' does not control the future behaviour but behaviour can change from the social contexts of a therapist talking (indeed that is the idea)

We process information from local events around us through sensations and perceptions	Probably the strongest and most frequent thoughts which 'pop into our heads' resonate with our immediate contexts—the rest are 'quieter' conversations as it were, unless of great consequence. So if you suddenly see someone steal another person's purse and run, most of your thinking will be conversations to tell now or later about this event as it unfolds. This thinking does not control your running and helping that person, but if you have had those behaviours shaped already, you will likely do this.
Dreaming shows the internal thoughts and cognitive processes because there is no external input	Things do not have to be present even when we are awake for the contexts to give rise to thoughts. I can be at work and suddenly a thought about my mother 'pops into my head'. Dreaming is no different except that many of the editing and critical thoughts (from different audiences) might not be present. This version also suggests two interesting properties to me: (1) *dreams appear weird* when we wake up because they are not connected to any of our immediate contexts upon waking (it's cold, need coffee, blankets askew, work today), and (2) since there is no context for them when you wake up, *you are unlikely to be able to say them,* so people report that they cannot remember (say) their dreams upon waking. This is because none of the people or surroundings that were in your dreams are present when you wake up. Luckily . . .
'People only use 10% of their brain's cognitive capacity when they think.'	Forget what the brain does, what this means is that of all the external contexts with consequences so that we are ready to talk (thinking), we attend to or speak only 10% of those that are occurring.

In general, all the bits of the models are actually outside the body in our contexts; that is our substrate, shaping us to behave in certain ways. Our *remembering* to behave in those contexts is also, therefore, outside of us, and we do not need an internal memory storage area from which we retrieve everything; that would be too slow for the proposed moment-by-moment processing into action required (Guerin, 2016a). The reason it is said that we need an internal memory storage is that people can 'remember' things (mostly the research is to do with word-remembering, however) and this can take place without an immediate or present 'stimulus'. Hence it has been concluded that we must store everything in the brain and therefore we must have 'represented' it in some internal form beforehand.

But all this reasoning about memory can be side-stepped once it is understood (at a gut, practical level) that contexts affect us even when they are not present, and we will usually have multiple word-events going on anyway (Guerin, 2016a). Contexts are nothing like a 'stimulus'. The earlier cognitive reasoning for a memory storage given above is actually a throwback to the older idea that we *must* have a stimulus present if we are responding to it. The cognitive models pointed out in the 1960s how this does not occur usually, but they then concluded wrongly that this must mean we *must* always have built an internal representation (like an internal stimulus) instead (of everything actually, which is another worry) for when we respond in the absence of the stimulus. This is why I emphasize that we behave even if the context is not actually present (Guerin, 2004, 2016b). (I even argue that saying that we 'see' a stimulus is very misleading anyway and is a word event in terms of Table 3.2; Gibson, 1960, 1979; Guerin, 1990.) Ironically, in this way the cognitive models are actually still based on the very old stimulus–response behaviourisms.

So with cognitive theory, for example, people are said to 'take in' information, process it and then decide how *to attribute causality* to events and people around them. With the present approach, on the other hand, it is more useful to ask 'What effect does making that *attribution* have on people, or has it had on people in the past?' Or again, for the cognitive models people 'take in' information, process it and this processing decides what beliefs they will 'possess'; here we must ask 'What effect does telling people that *belief* have on people, or has it had on people in the past?' Or again, people 'take in' information, process it and then make *mistakes and have biases* in what they decide; here we must ask 'What effect does telling people those "biased" statements have on people, or has it had on people in the past?' Our question is useful to observe and disentangle how those beliefs, attributions, and biases have functioned when embedded in all our other social behaviour, by observing the social strategies as well as the words that are said. How do they fit in with our other strategies and behaviours of life?

I will now go through a number of areas which are important when thinking about mental health and show some of the ways to translate the cognitive into the contextual. More importantly, this will also show you which new types of observations you can now make to enhance your understanding of these events.

Two 'systems' of cognitive processing

One common feature found in these areas is that two 'systems' of cognitive processing are frequently suggested. The most popular current forms of these are the *System 1* and *System 2* of Kahneman (2011) and the *automatic* and *reflective* systems of Thaler and Sunstein (2008). There are many variations of these, however, and some are given in the below, which expands a table of Thaler and Sunstein (2008), drawing on Guerin (1992, 1994), Freud (1915/1984), Ryle (1949) and many others.

Box 3.2

Without language use	Language use
Knowing how	Knowing that
System 1	System 2
Unconscious cognition	Conscious cognition
Mindlessness	Mindfulness
Wu wei/Nothingness	Yu wei
Tamed monkey mind	Untamed monkey mind
Automatic	Reflective
Implicit cognition	Explicit cognition
Direct contingency controlled	Verbal contingency controlled
Non-verbal behaviour	Verbal behaviour (including gestures)
Unconscious	Conscious
Ucs.	Cs./Pcs.
Uncontrolled	Controlled
Associative	Deductive
Effortless	Effortful
Fast	Slow
Skilled	Rule-following

What can we make of this, instead of just claiming that two systems exist? What I suggest is that we behave in relation to the contexts of our worlds but *our talking and thinking are specialized in relation to their social contexts* so they frequently look different.

Most often, this use of language is about negotiating social relationships with people and might not even be relevant to what is happening immediately around you. So, for example (see Figure 2.1 here), if I need to do a little body-balancing while walking over a rough part of the footpath or sidewalk, this does not need to involve language use *per se*. However, there are always strong contexts around activities which are very much social, in terms of: what you might say if you fall or stumble; comments someone might make about your balancing fiasco; a story to tell after about your moral outrage at the state of the footpaths in this city (or post the comments on Facebook); or a funny story to tell about what happened (maybe exaggerated for more laughter). This part of the walking event is very much about behaving in a *social* context, even if the actual walking is not. But this chattering can also actually interfere with the basic task of walking without tripping over cracks in the sidewalk, with these collateral, but important in your social context, other language and thinking behaviours occurring at the same time.

With this example already we can also imagine a case of someone telling people stories about their skilful balancing act even though their balancing skills were actually bad (they might have to lie if there are punishing social outcomes). We can also imagine another case of a person very skilled at walking and balancing on rough terrain but who is not very literate when talking about what they are doing, or making an interesting story out of this episode. These extremes help you get the idea that the 'walking and balancing' and the 'talking about your walking and balancing' are two independent actions to the extent that they arise from independent contexts and have different sources of consequences: one to do with rocks and footpath cracks, the other to do with anticipating social comments and stories shaped from your social contexts. This I suggest is the basis for the two systems.

So doing things with words is different to doing things without words, not metaphysically but only because there are: different contexts giving rise to the talking; different properties; and different outcomes. This is the gist of the observed System 1 and System 2 differences. Some of the distinctions are not clear-cut, though, and need some spelling out which will also help us focus. But the two things to remember are that any thinking and talking will be occasioned by social contexts not the acting-in-the-world itself (Guerin, 2016a), and that talking and thinking are not different in any metaphysical or essential sense to other behaviours, they are just behaviours which have been trained within specialized social contexts.

Biases in decision-making

Many clinical and mental health phenomena have been interpreted in terms of 'cognitive information processing' models. There has been a lot of work from this gone into looking at how people 'make' decisions (statements) and how people make replicable 'biases' or errors in their decisions (statements). These are called 'cognitive' biases but we will see that they are a result of normal strategic uses of language (perhaps gone wrong) and the conflicting multiple social contexts in which language arises.

The main change in rethinking this comes from describing and analysing the contexts for all behaviours, which includes thinking and hence the contexts for biases. This will then shift our observations *onto* mainly social events external to the person rather than *into* a metaphorical 'psychological space', the head, or a metaphor of the brain (the current fad). Any 'biases' in thinking or 'distorted' thinking just mean that there are other contexts giving rise to another behaviour *which seems to be biased when compared to more 'normal' behaviour*. But nothing is faulty, it is all working perfectly well, in fact, 100 per cent (Guerin, 2016a). It is just that there are other, and perhaps conflicting, audiences or social contexts which give rise to the so-called 'biased' behaviour (see the discussion of 'rationality' in Chapter 6 for more).

For example, Aaron Beck (1976) was an initiator of cognitive behaviour therapy, and suggested that we have faulty modes of cognitive information processing or 'distorted thinking' which lead to various 'mental health' problems. For example, he suggested a distorted thinking of 'overgeneralisation' in which faulty information processing leads a person to overstate that if something happened once it will always happen: 'I don't like going to parties. I tried it once and it was awful.' Clearly, whatever gives rise to this, if this is followed by the person (and this will depend on other contexts of course), then it can lead to life problems. But this is 'explained' as a cognitive processing system gone wrong (even though no independent evidence is given for these processes).

The point here is that whether overgeneralizations are made or not, they can be rethought as normal discursive strategies for external social contexts (Guerin, 2016b, Table 9.2). The strategic use of those statements in social contexts has been shaped and we must focus our energies on observing and describing better the external social circumstances for making such overgeneralizations—and that is also where the clinical interventions will lie. In terms of discourse analysis, for example, this strategy of overgeneralization can be seen as a very common discursive use of *extremes* and *abstraction* to make challenging by audiences more difficult (see my earlier discussion, and some parts of Bandler & Grinder, 1975). The same applies to the other 'cognitive biases and heuristics'.

In a similar way that we saw earlier, 'beliefs' for discourse analysis are ways of talking rather than mental states (Guerin, 1992, 1994). This means that metaphors about 'bias', such as the dysfunctional 'core beliefs' of Rational Emotive Therapy (RET: Bernard, 1981; Ellis, 1994), can be approached by observing the social and cultural contexts in which they might be uttered and the consequences they have had on audiences (Guerin, 2016b). I will discuss these biased or dysfunctional beliefs more in Chapter 6.

These are all examples of clinical issues with thinking which are normally couched in private, unobservable, or unassailable metaphorical terms. But if these are rethought as observable events which are centred on the various social conversations of the person but which are not said out loud, new possibilities for research and treatment become available.

Table 3.4 describes and translates some of the commonly labelled biases from cognitive and clinical psychology into contextual terms that are

TABLE 3.4 Proposed 'dysfunctional' cognitive biases with the cognitive model description and a contextual or discursive account

Clinically relevant 'cognitive biases'	Common explanation or cognitive theory	Contextual or discourse analysis account
Anchoring	A cognitive bias wherein one relies too heavily on one trait or piece of information: 'All I know is that she used the word "jerk"'	People rely too heavily on what can be named (the 'information'), at the expense of what can be done but not named shaped by their contexts
Availability heuristic	When people predict the frequency of an event based on how easily an example can be brought to mind: 'I can't see how she might possibly like me!'; 'I can't think of anything or anyone that might help me'	Relying too heavily on what words can be said or thought ('come to mind') rather than their experience or wordless actions shaped by their contexts
Representativeness heuristic	Where people judge the probability or frequency of a hypothesis by considering how much the hypothesis resembles available data: 'She used the word "jerk" so she must hate me'	People follow words and the similarity between different verbal accounts (which arise from discursive experience and training) rather than on experience or non-word training shaped by their contexts

Arbitrary inference	Jumping to a conclusion without good reason: Might be mind-reading: 'I know she is going to reject me', or assuming the outcomes: 'It's not even worth going because I know I am going to fail.'	Reason giving and establishing (wrong) facts that are convincing. Use of extremes common. Making presumptions that are probably incorrect but difficult to notice in conversation. Strategizing statements to make them look 'as if' facts.
Selective abstraction	Focusing on one aspect of a situation and ignoring the rest: 'I will fail because I made one mistake right in the middle.'	Use of partial facts. Making presumptions that are probably incorrect but difficult to notice in conversation. Using categories incorrectly as a strategy.
Overgeneralization	Overstating that if something happened once it will always happen: 'I don't like going to parties. I tried it once and it was awful.'	Use of extremes. Use of abstraction to make challenging more difficult.
Magnification and minimization	Minimizing positive outcomes and maximizing negative outcomes: exaggerating or catastrophizing	Use of extremes or hedges to maximize and minimize.
Personalization	Falsely taking responsibility for something bad: 'My child failed their test. I am such a bad parent.' Blaming: doing the same but putting the responsibility onto someone else entirely.	Discursive placement of responsibility in opposite way to usual strategies (you are responsible for good outcomes, other people for bad outcomes). Question to analyse is what are the other contextual arrangements so this is arrived at?
Dichotomous thinking	Thinking in black and white; you are either a good person or a bad person.	Strategic use of word categories to establish facts.

(continued)

TABLE 3.4 *(continued)*

Clinically relevant 'cognitive biases'	Common explanation or cognitive theory	Contextual or discourse analysis account
Ignoring the positive or filtering	Focus on the negative aspects only: 'The boss said I did well in the interview but he gave me one strange look in the middle that I think said it all!' Disqualifying or discounting the positive is similar: 'She said she liked me but I know she only felt she had to say that.'	Reason giving in reverse of the usual pattern (emphasizing the negative rather than positive because of the particular social context).

amenable to contextual observations (they are no longer hidden in the head) and discursive analyses. Remember that my goal here is not to say that these phenomena or events do not occur, but to see them as just another behaviour that is based on using language and therefore arising in a primarily social context as social strategies. This is the main thing to focus upon—that when we are dealing with any words, thinking, or talking, the main context will be a social one and the words will be being used strategically within that person's world.

For each of these 'biases' in the Table we can see the language use patterns that are occurring in a social context and the ways they are challenged. It turns out that our contexts and particularly our social contexts persuade ourselves to say and think in ways that use extremes and other linguistic devices.

This is only one version and more recent cognitive behaviour therapy has other 'cognitive mechanisms' that lead to faulty thinking and hence poor outcomes for the client. It should be clear what is going on here. I am not disputing that these events occur, just disputing the metaphor which puts responsibility or a driver into a 'faulty' internal mechanism that is not monitorable (this step in CBT's reasoning itself commits several errors of *distorted thinking,* by the way), and treating the thoughts instead as well adapted to the poor contexts the person is immersed within: the thoughts have adaptive outcomes in their current contexts but lead to poor outcomes as well.

As pieces of discourse, these 'biases' need to be analysed in terms of the resources at stake and the audiences giving rise to them, the audiences maintaining them, and the social strategies they employ. Two advantages of the current proposal is that we have more concrete audiences and resources to examine, rather than vague 'cognitive processes somewhere in the head, probably the brain', and that we have a wider array of methodological resources from the social sciences to describe and explore for challenging these conversational strategies.

The 'erroneous cognitive processing' metaphor mainly leaves out the context for these strategies being used in the first place, in the sense of 'You are jumping to conclusions and this is a wrong or erroneous inference' rather than 'You are jumping to conclusions and stating them here, so what exactly in your social contexts is maintaining that erroneous inference? Why is that discursive strategy being used here and for what resources and for what audiences?' Just because the conversational strategies are opposite to what is *normally* found (remember Chapter 1) does not mean they are 'erroneous' or 'distorted'; the context needs to be described to understand what is going on. The therapist should be exploring the person's contexts to see what audience-resource networking is leading to these arrangements of language use, rather than assuming they are faulty.

All that is being said here is that we can forego the cognitive metaphor and think instead that these are typical language strategies which are used for conversation in social contexts, and that also occur in thinking 'conversations', but that they can lead to problematic outcomes.

Symbols and symbolization

Another form of behaviour related to language and which also arises only in social contexts, is the use of symbols (Canestri, 2007). Like all language use, people cannot symbolize by themselves, and using them needs to be taught. Symbols only work, or make sense or have meaning, if trained with at least one person as audience. So to have symbols you need a trained audience, and the trick for analysis again is to track down the audiences.

So, like other language use, we learn specialized (cultural) ways to behave and talk when presented with symbols, and these can be extremely important parts of our lives—involving reputation, image management, attention, honour, coolness, status, and conspicuous consumption. When they are symbolic *events* we sometimes call them rituals, and we have learned to behave, talk, and think in certain ways in those contexts.

The major analysis point, and especially in clinical settings where something like a shirt or a piece of jewellery is said to be symbolic and important to that person, is to analyse these just as for any discursive analysis. What outcomes are there, and what outcomes have there been in the past, for behaving in these ways in the context of this symbol? What is it doing in the world—what effects is it having? What effects would occur if the person did *not* do the specified ritual or symbolic behaviours?

As should be obvious now, relating this to our analyses of language uses, the contexts are social ones and will always be the effects from past and present audiences. Only people do something different if I am wearing my special shirt or not. So the outcome is social regardless of what is happening in the presence of the symbol or during and after the ritual. But once again this forces us to observe the person's contexts more widely and in more detail. *Symbols, rituals and image might be abstract but the access to resources through people they can provide is very real and observable if you are patient and look outside the immediate situation.*

Attributions and misattributions

I have already said a little about attribution theory above. Attribution theory began in cognitive social psychology to explain how people assigned causes and responsibility to what they saw. If I see someone stumble in the street and knock the person next to them so the precious vase they are carrying falls on the road and breaks, I might conclude that the person stumbling is the *cause* of the items breaking but should probably not really be held responsible. If I found out that the person stumbling was drunk, on the other hand, I might conclude that they were fully responsible for the broken vase. If I found out that the person stumbling was running to catch the other person because they had just stolen the vase, I might hold the thief responsible for the whole episode. If I found that the person stumbling had a rare muscle disorder that makes them occasionally stumble for no reason, I would not like to hold them responsible even if they were the cause of the vase breaking.

This is all especially important for how we explain what we do and what other people do. The ideas of attributions and misattributions there-fore appear in many forms in clinical therapy now but in cognitive models. People are said to process the information they have, or even collect more information, and then 'decide' on or compute the reasons or causes for events. This could be attributing positive causes to people in a maladaptive way ('My husband only yells at me because he is stressed from work, so I should not rock the boat and just put up with his yelling') and negative causes about oneself ('I mess everything up in my life because I am no good at making friends').

The way that cognitive modelling proceeds in social psychology is instructive in helping us rethink to a contextual approach. The original cog-nitive model was to treat people as if they were scientists who took in and processed information around them to make decisions and to make attribu-tions of cause (e.g. Kelley & Michela, 1980). Depending on the information they had, they would come up with different attributions. The Kelley model suggested that people make one of two attributions of social cause; that the person did what they did because of internal or personal causes, or because of something in the situation: internal or external. The information people were said to use was called consensus information (did everyone do this?), consistency information (did this person always do this?), and distinctiveness information (did this person always do this in this situation?).

So the cognitive model was that people gather this sort of information and then when an event worth explaining occurs, they compute their attribution. So if I know the person is always stumbling I will attribute the cause to something internal about them. But if everyone stumbles on this footpath, I will attribute the cause of stumbling to something external to the person (most obviously the footpath or a secret Vogon force-field nearby). If this person stumbles in no other situations at all, then I might attribute the cause of stumbling to something external to them. This gives the flavour of how this cognitive processing model derives predictions, and how it follows from taking on a metaphor of cognitive processing:

sensations → perception → memory → retrieval → cognitive decisions → action

Within the discourse analysis and conversational analysis research there have been some excellent rethinkings of such attribution theory, but rethinkings that the mental health area has not caught up with (e.g. Bonaiuto & Fasulo, 1997; Edwards & Potter, 1993; Harper, 1996; Potter & Edwards, 1990). The main idea is that attributions are a part of normal strategic social interaction and need to be analysed in terms of the social relationships and strategies occurring within those relationships and other contexts. *We do not just compute an attribution based on the information we have collected, but rather our attributions are part of the shaping of people as we speak*, based on current and past contexts of interactions.

So like any use of language, *attributions are a way of doing things to people* not the result of a computation (Guerin, 2016b). It is not that we just compute a slightly biased-in-our-favour attribution, but rather, making the attribution at all is a way of influencing people which can be well-intentioned or not. How it is 'pitched' depends on all else that is going on in that conversation and in the relationship, in the same way that giving the other person flowers is influencing the relationship.

We can only analyse attributions, therefore, in the analysis of all contexts happening. Saying to someone 'You only did that because you are out to get me' can occur in multiple contexts as part of multiple social strategies and have multiple and different effects. It could be a relationship-enhancing joke between two friends, it could be an accusation to anger the other, or it could be a testing to see how exactly the listener responds when it is said. We do not know which of these—or other—strategies are happening without an analysis of all the contexts operating. The words and the attribution itself cannot tell us any of this. Remember: you cannot analyse language use by the words alone.

Similarly, if we are puzzled about what caused a work colleague to yell at another colleague very loudly, we are not being an innocent scientist (Kelley's cognitive model) if we remark out loud that we heard that they also yelled last month at a waiter in a restaurant, nor being an innocent scientist if I report that the person they yelled at seems to get everyone yelling at them sooner or later. In each case my attribution statements are part of the strategic background or social dynamics of talking to this person at work about the yelling incident, to influence them to see the incident in a certain way and give responsibility and punishment to different people.

There is a lot of useful research already done by Richard Bentall and others building attribution models of some clinical thought disorders (but currently relying on a cognitive model). So, for example, attributions of responsibility have been predicted to be more common for intrusive thinking in delusions (Beese & Stratton, 2004; Bentall & Kaney, 2005; Merrin, Kinderman, & Bentall, 2007). While not disputing the prediction, discourse analysis locates these attributions in people's social and cultural strategies, not in the head, so we might get new and more fruitful ways to approach these ideas. I will discuss some of these in Chapter 6 and how we might keep the substance of these ideas but rethink the attribution part in terms of contexts rather than cognitive models. This would also mean new avenues to observe what is going on in such cases, and possible new ways to intervene and change if that is appropriate.

Summary

- One of the most frequent things humans have learned to do in absolutely any situation is to talk or comment, and even if no one is listening or if the many learned responses are not said out loud.
- Talking and thinking are both behaviours like any other; they have special properties, but in general all our behaviours arise out of the strategies and arrangements of our social, cultural, historical, economic, opportunity, and other contexts and talking and thinking are no different except that they are always part of our social contexts.
- Careful observation of language use and thinking shows that they are essentially involved with concrete and observable social contexts and doing various things to people.

- 'Thinking' is language use we have been socially trained or shaped to use with our audiences in context but which is not said out loud.
- Thinking is more like 'talking with your audiences about events but not out loud' than it is like 'talking-to-yourself about events'.
- This means we can observe and describe the external contexts in which thoughts arise in the same way that discourse analysis currently does for talk which is spoken out loud; we no longer have to limit our analyses of thinking by treating thoughts as private and unobservable events.
- The 'physical substrate' of thinking is not the brain but the external contexts in which we are all embedded which give rise to using language—our complex social contexts.
- Thoughts are 'language responding in context' so the contexts for thoughts must be social ones—our relationships, audiences, people; we can therefore have multiple, concurrent 'thoughts' happening all the time and conflicting and contradictory thoughts without a problem normally; if we have contradictory thoughts it is because we have audiences that have shaped us in opposite ways.
- A practical upshot is that the more I know your life contexts in detail, the more I can know what you are thinking.
- We can therefore rethink cognition in terms of discourse analysis, as behaviours arising from their (mainly social) contexts.
- We can also therefore rethink the 'cognitive' phenomena in terms of observable external context; such as biases in cognitive decision-making and the proposed two systems of thought.

References

Bandler, R., & Grinder, J. (1975). *The structure of magic I. A book about language and therapy.* Palo Alto, CA: Science and Behavior Books.

Barch, D. M., & Berenbaum, H. (1996). Language production and thought disorder in schizophrenia. *Journal of Abnormal Psychology, 105,* 81–88.

Beck, A.T. (1976). *Cognitive therapy and the emotional disorders.* Madison, CT: International Universities Press.

Beese, A. G., & Stratton, P. (2004). Causal attributions in delusional thinking: An investigation using qualitative methods. *British Journal of Clinical Psychology, 43,* 267–283.

Bentall, R. P., Corcoran, R., Howard, R., Blackwood, N., & Kinderman, P. (2001). Persecutory delusions: A review and theoretical integration. *Clinical Psychology Review, 21,* 1143–1192.

Bentall, R. P., & Kaney, S. (2005). Attributional lability in depression and paranoia. *British Journal of Clinical Psychology, 44,* 475–488.

Bentley, A. F. (1935). *Behavior knowledge fact.* Bloomington, IN: Principia Press.

Bernard, M. E. (1981). Private thought in RET. *Cognitive Therapy and Research, 5,* 125–142.

Billig, M. (2008). The language of critical discourse analysis. *Discourse & Society*, *19*, 783–800.

Bonaiuto, M., & Fasulo, A. (1997). Rhetorical intentionality attribution: Its ontogenesis in ordinary conversation. *British Journal of Social Psychology*, *36*, 511–536.

Burman, E., & Parker, I. (1993). *Discourse analytic research*. London: Routledge.

Canestri, J. (2007). Language, symbolization, and psychosis: An introduction. In G. Ambrosio, S. Argentieri, & J. Canestri (Eds.), *Language, symbolization, and psychosis: Essays in honour of Jacqueline Amati Mehler* (pp. 1–17). London: Karnac.

Edwards, D. (1997). *Discourse and cognition*. London: SAGE.

Edwards, D., & Potter, J. (1993). Language and causation: A discursive action model of description and attribution. *Psychological Review*, *100*, 23–41.

Eggins, S., & Slade, D. (1997). *Analysing casual conversations*. London: Cassell.

Ellis, A. (1994). *Reason and emotion in psychotherapy*. New York: Birch Lane.

Fernyhough, C. (2016). *The voices within: The history and science of how we talk to ourselves*. London: Wellcome Collection.

Freud, S. (1915/1984). *The unconscious*. (In the Penguin Freud Library Volume 11.) London: Penguin Books.

Gibson, J. J. (1960). The concept of the stimulus in psychology. *American Psychologist*, *15*, 694–703.

Gibson, J. J. (1979). *An ecological approach to visual perception*. Boston, MA: Houghton Mifflin.

Gladstone, G., & Parker, G. (2003). What's the use of worrying? Its function and its dysfunction. *Australian and New Zealand Journal of Psychiatry*, *37*, 347–354.

Guerin, B. (1990). Gibson, Skinner and perceptual responses. *Behavior and Philosophy*, *18*, 43–54.

Guerin, B. (1992). Behavior analysis and the social construction of knowledge. *American Psychologist*, *47*, 1423–1432.

Guerin, B. (1994). Attitudes and beliefs as verbal behavior. *The Behavior Analyst*, *17*, 155–163.

Guerin, B. (2003). Language use as social strategy: A review and an analytic framework for the social sciences. *Review of General Psychology*, *7*, 251–298.

Guerin, B. (2004). *Handbook for analyzing the social strategies of everyday life*. Reno, NV: Context Press.

Guerin, B. (2016a). *How to rethink psychology: New metaphors for understanding people and their behavior*. London: Routledge.

Guerin, B. (2016b). *How to rethink human behavior: A practical guide to social contextual analysis*. London: Routledge.

Harper, D. J. (1996). Accounting for poverty: From attribution to discourse. *Journal of Community & Applied Social Psychology*, *6*, 249–265.

Hodgkiss, P. (2011). *The making of the modern mind*. London: Athlone Press.

Houtson, P., Flloyd, M., & Carnicero, S. (2012). *Spy the lie*. New York: Icon.

Janet, P. (1925/1919). *Psychological healing: A historical and clinical study*. London: George Allen & Unwin.

Jaworski, A., & Coupland, N. (Eds.). (2006). *The discourse reader*. London: Routledge.

Kahneman, D. (2011). *Thinking, fast and slow*. London: Penguin.

Kelley, H. H., & Michela, J. L. (1980). Attribution theory and research. *Annual Review of Psychology*, *31*, 457–503.

Kitzinger, C. (2000). Doing feminist conversation analysis. *Feminism & Psychology*, *10*, 163–193.

Leiman, M. (2012). Dialogic sequence analysis in studying psychotherapeutic discourse. *International Journal for Dialogical Science*, *6*, 123–147.

Leudar, I., & Thomas, P. (2000). *Voices of reason, voices of insanity*. London: Psychology Press.

Leudar, I., Thomas, P., McNally, D., & Glinski, A. (1997). What voices can do with words: Pragmatics of verbal hallucination. *Psychological Medicine*, *27*, 885–898.

McCarthy-Jones, S., & Fernyhough, C. (2011). The varieties of inner speech: Links between inner speech and psychopathological variables in a sample of young adults. *Consciousness and Cognition*, *20*, 1586–1593.

Merrin, J., Kinderman, P., & Bentall, R. P. (2007). 'Jumping to conclusions' and attributional style in persecutory delusions. *Cognitive Therapy and Research*, *31*, 741–758.

Potter, J. (1996). *Representing reality: Discourse, rhetoric and social construction*. London: SAGE.

Potter, J., & Edwards, D. (1990). Nigel Lawson's tent: Discourse analysis, attribution theory and the social psychology of fact. *European Journal of Social Psychology*, *20*, 405–424.

Prior, A. (1960). The run-about inference ticket. *Analysis*, *21*, 38–39.

Rapaport, D. (1955). *Organization and pathology of thought*. New York: Columbia University Press.

Reps, P. (1957). *Zen flesh, Zen bones*. Harmondsworth: Penguin.

Robbins, J., & Rumsey, A. (2008). Introduction: Cultural and linguistic anthropology and the opacity of other minds. *Anthropological Quarterly*, *81*(2), 407–420.

Ryle, G. (1949). *The concept of mind*. London: Hutchinson.

Shigematsu, S. (1988). *A Zen harvest: Japanese folk Zen sayings*. New York: North Point Press.

Soyland, A. J. (1994). *Psychology as a metaphor*. London: SAGE.

Thaler, R. H., & Sunstein, C. R. (2008). *Nudge: Improving decisions about health, wealth, and happiness*. London: Yale University Press.

4

DECONSTRUCTING THE DSM

Having gone through some alternative rethinkings of mental health while pursuing a contextual approach in the last two chapters, we are now ready to look more closely at some specific analyses of various behaviours and contexts closely involved in mental health, and get out of the patterns of thinking raised in Chapter 1—stop thinking of behaviours leading to suffering as arising from a hidden physical substrate inside the person and think of them instead as potentially observable physical substrates *outside* the person of social, economic, cultural, and other contexts.

The usual plan of presenting mental health is to outline the normal DSM diagnoses, causes and etiologies, and then consider some special cases such as ethnic or cross-cultural mental health. However, from a contextual approach this begs the question of what is even normal (Crowe, 2000; McGruder, 2001). Contexts are just there and there is no question of which one is 'normal'. We could talk about which arrangements of contexts are the most *frequent*, but that is very different. Even in that case, however, peoples of the Indian subcontinent and China are usually covered in the 'cross-cultural' sections of 'Western' textbooks, even though they make up over half the world's population, and are certainly the most 'frequent' doers of every behaviour.

Strategies of life

The broad picture painted so far is that our behaviours arise from our external contexts, even our talking and thinking although these are specialized within social relationships. To understand and change our behaviours we must describe and analyse the contexts in which we are embedded, and those we have been embedded in previously if important. We need more detailed analyses of the contexts and strategic patterns that emerge and this requires bringing all the social sciences together (see Table 1.2 in Guerin, 2016a). We will gradually work our way through more complex analyses of human contexts and strategies.

Strategies of identifying mental health issues

The idea of 'mental health' we arrive at from a contextual analysis is that they are behaviours like any others that humans do—not original, metaphysically unique, or defined by a special biological substrate or disease. They have been brought together only by the history of theorizing and practice with the hodgepodge of cases that have historically been presented by society to 'mental health' experts to handle. For example, if a person is lacking money and needs a job this is not typically seen as a life problem for which you need to see a psychologist or a psychiatrist—probably you would see a social worker, a financial advisor, a life-coach, or a work-employment agency. If a person started seriously disrupting their life by arguing that the CIA was keeping them out of work, then a psychiatrist or psychologist might be sought.

So, if you remember Chapter 1, then behaviours and the problems with behaviour which are presented to 'mental health' experts are typically done so for a few very loose reasons:

- difficult-to-see contexts from which they arise (hence the free-for-all theorizing that has gone on for over a century)
- behaving in ways that prevent life functioning
- behaving in ways that prevent other people from their normal life functioning
- persistence of unusual symptoms or behaviours over time
- behaving in ways that are not considered 'normal' (Crowe, 2000)
- presence of several problem issues in life with these same properties.

So basically, if there are behaviours causing conflicts or problems and if they have the properties listed above (especially the first point), then they will usually (in Western societies) be called 'mental health' issues and the person or persons will end up consulting a 'mental health' expert (or sometimes a religious leader, imam, or community elder). If there is a conflict or problem without these properties, there are others they will consult (social worker, a financial advisor, a life-coach, or a work-employment agency).

But it is important to remember that *these do not define or reveal the essence of an authentically 'mental health' problem*; if anything, they only show the essence of:

- how we construct categories of 'mental health'
- what sorts of issues in life we even call by that name
- what sorts of issues end up with 'mental health experts' because no one else will deal with them (except some religious leaders and traditional healers).

This is what defines what we call mental health in reality; not the theorizing, categorizing, and metaphors of disease that occurred later. These are the contexts which group or define mental health behaviours, not some essence or disease of our bodies. Mental health is constructed and determined through observing behaviours-in-context during life strategies, not by measuring some brain or other substrate essence. These are all just metaphors and theories we have used up until now, and the promises of breakthroughs in brain research.

You might also remember the quote in Chapter 1 by sociologist Arnold Rose (1962), that it was accidental but unfortunate that in the nineteenth century the medical professions were assigned this task of treating people with the conditions listed just above. They were not suited to what was really happening in such cases and did not have the training to properly find out.

So, in terms of a contextual analysis, we can instead further draw out *normal* strategies for each of these and try to identify more closely those contexts from which 'mental health' issues commonly arise and then get maintained in context. For example, a key property of recognizing mental health problems found here was that the behaviours usually have *difficult to observe contexts*, which in terms of a contextual analysis (Guerin, 2016b) usually further means (from Table 2.1):

- hidden parts of contexts
- parts of the contexts that are made secret by other behaviours or other people
- results of historical parts of the person's context that were idiosyncratic
- the result of escape or avoidance strategies which are successful so that the contexts being escaped or avoided are not easy to observe
- they are behaviours arising from ritual, symbolic or cultural contexts that strengthen social relationships but they appear to be doing other things
- they are based on language behaviours and most language use arises in difficult to observe social contexts
- they are language behaviours arising in contexts in that strengthen social relationships but they appear to be doing other things.

These are all normal strategic ways that the contexts for what we do become difficult to observe and articulate. The point is that we can, and will, identify and observe these with detailed contextual observations. They are not hidden from us in a mental realm or in the brain.

Mental health conflicts: locked in, blocked out, and knocked around

The idea of life is that we engage with the world through working within social relationships to obtain resources and maintain those relationships. We engage all sort of strategies for this which depend on the particular contexts which are available and how they link to resources. A large part of what we do involves doing things to people with language. We get 'locked into' some patterns, often because local opportunities are out of our control or we can only work through local contexts. In all of this engagement in the world of people, resources, and the distribution or networking of resources through people, there are always conflicts and knocks, and blocks to what we want to do. Most are resolved by changing the contexts around us in some way, or causing other people to change the contexts (which is the same thing since people are part of all our contexts).

So what can seem like 'odd' behaviour can be the result of a long sequence of behaviours trying to solve or resolve life problems. People trying to cope with the problems and conflicts of life can have many reasons to fail through no fault of their own, and also many ways they can succeed but in doing this end up getting locked into other behaviours they have created but might not have wanted (many mental health examples in Firestone, 1998). We can never assume that any behaviours only arise from the immediate outcomes or consequences we observe.

Overall, the point I am making is that trying to cope with life is full of conflicts with both resources and people, and there are many subtle and unobvious ways that people deal with the contexts for such conflicts which in turn produce new behaviours that the person might never have done otherwise; and these can then be locked in like social traps. If there are serious problems in coping, or very abstract and difficult to see problems, then any coping difficulties might be exacerbated. They might be exacerbated by becoming chronic, by becoming exaggerated or dramatic, or by becoming a bluff in which backing down does not seem possible.

So, the first suggestions for viewing mental health issues contextually are to look for normal problems of life which can get blocked, knocked about, and then locked into something more serious. Table 4.1 shows some of these, and some hints for broad intervention strategies.

TABLE 4.1 Conflicts in everyday life with some strategies to overcome

Strategy	Intervention ideas
Too much stress in obtaining life resources (resources in a broad sense)	
blockages from resources	work to unblock or find alternative resources, reduce need for this particular resource
limited opportunities	find equal opportunities or ways to avoid blockages; find ways to use alternatives
lacking the life skills needed	identify skills, possibly from others, and train
needs extensive stories to obtain	work with person to reduce need for stories, sharpen stories, make stories more persuasive, make stories less complex and likely to trap, make stories more coherent or consistent
Too much stress in life from social relationships	
social conflicts	resolve conflicts
competing relationships	remove competition and facilitate cooperation and sharing
pressure of image management for social relationships	change or stop image management, or work to create do-able images
lacking the social skills needed	identify skills, possibly from others, and train
serious language confusions from audience pressures	trace audiences for each language or thinking set, change verbal behaviour, or train new verbal behaviour
needs extensive stories to manage competing relationships	trace audiences for stories, work out which parts of stories are necessary or can be pruned, build new parts of stories if needed for relationships, change audiences if needed, provide new or more consistent audiences, make stories less complex and likely to trap
Conflicting ways of obtaining resources	
competing sources	stop competition, find alternative resources, reduce need for this particular resource
competing opportunities	find other opportunities that are less competitive and with less conflict, reduce need for this particular resource
lacking the skills needed	identify skills, possibly from others, and train, train negotiation and conflict resolution skills
needs extensive stories to mitigate conflict	work with person to reduce need for stories, sharpen stories, make stories more persuasive, make stories less complex and likely to trap, make stories more coherent or consistent

(continued)

TABLE 4.1 *(continued)*

Strategy	Intervention ideas
Conflicting audiences and social relationships	
producing strongly conflicting thoughts and thinking patterns from negotiating	train to be ok with conflicting thoughts, train for a consistent story, defuse the conflict of stories, produce a third version of stories
conflicting audiences brought together somehow	prevent audiences being together, work on new stories for both audiences, detach from stories altogether for one or both audiences
lacking the skills needed	identify skills, possibly from others, and train, train relationship skills and conflict resolution skills
serious language confusions arising from conflicting audiences	make stories more coherent and consistent where possible, reduce the need to stories, reduce the ownership of stories, trace and place stories onto the audience's previous responses, not the thinker
needs extensive stories to mitigate conflict	work with person to reduce need for stories, sharpen stories, make stories more persuasive, make stories less complex and likely to trap, make stories more coherent or consistent
Strategies out of control or locked in	
bluff games gone wrong	find out the stakes and reduce, provide more behavioural options, find options to back down and keep face, reduce need, or worry over keeping face
bluff games using relationships (includes double binds)	find out the stakes and why something other than the relationship was not used, find options to back down and keep face, reduce need or worry over keeping face
competition gone wrong	change potential outcomes, stop competition for all parties, find alternative resources, reduce need for this particular resource
social traps escalating badly	find out stakes and provide alternative sources, find out if keeping face is being used as resource and change this, reduce need for the resources involved
lacking the skills needed	find out the games being used and train in skills to mitigate the game, train to recognize games and traps as they are beginning
multiple thoughts produced from strategies which might be conflicting or confusing	trace the audiences for the thoughts about strategies that are worrying, provide new thoughts through 'therapist' as audience, produce third type of story if there are games with two interlocked agents
needs extensive stories to make strategies work	work with person to reduce need for stories, sharpen stories, make stories more cooperative and less competitive or bullying, make stories less complex and likely to trap, make stories more coherent or consistent

Notice what I am trying to do in Table 4.1. *I am avoiding any categorization into mental versus non-mental issues.* We have conflicts and stress and professionals have used the almost irrelevant criteria given earlier for labelling some of these as 'mental health' issues, which I have dealt with in the first three chapters, as have others. While we currently have different professionals and other people to deal with the labelled 'mental' health issues, I am happy for this to be a thing of the past—at least if we can work with Table 4.1 to reduce the suffering, misery, and sadness from life conflicts as much as we are able.

Some examples can be found from research, especially research which spends intensive time with people exploring their contexts. One such study on clinical depression, for example, found that people reported their conflicts and stress (we could just call these 'difficult situations' or 'contexts leading to suffering' maybe) are from the following (Bradley, Woolley, & Clarke, 2011):

- stress and anxiety (from many situations)
- trauma including loss
- relationships
- stress at school or bullying
- 'negative attachment styles'; needs more exploring into the family and other relationships.

Now that we have a broad sketch of the problems in life, we must remember that the details of the issues for individuals and communities depend on all the other contexts and idiosyncrasies (Chapter 2; Guerin, 2016b). Someone born into a life context with few opportunities compared to others, such as being a poor woman in a capitalist economy, will in general have more conflicts to cope with and to strategize. But there is nothing completely predictable in all this because idiosyncrasies abound. That is why we must (1) learn to generate possibilities for analyses rather than try to learn some simple but false facts about people, and (2) engage in intensive contextual observations (Guerin, 2016b).

Broad description of behaviours used to strategize in main DSM disorders

There are many ways to analyse the strategies in life we use for juggling our resources and our relationships and dealing with conflicts (Guerin, 2016b). Rather than go through more schemes, my plan is to briefly outline next what *behaviours* are already known in the main groupings of 'mental disorders' to see whether we can trace the possible strategies for real 'mental disorders' rather than veer off into hypotheticals too much.

So for a first possible analysis I will try to summarize the *actual behaviours* which occur in each of the main diagnoses and 'disorders' of the DSM and then 'backwards engineer' some possible functional strategies. Some of the disorders I have left out because they are peripheral to the important ones here, and because it would take too long. (The hodgepodge of cases that was given to 'mental health' experts towards the end of the nineteenth century to deal with are diverse and are not necessarily even related to each other except through the metaphor of 'mental'. Some 'disorders' are also only there because the early history of psychiatry involved other biological medical diagnoses which morphed into 'mental' diagnoses because no biology could be located.)

The research question will then be: *how can we describe the general patterns of strategic behaviour which might occur in each case, and which allows the diagnostician to separate the behaviours into groups, at least in principle*?

The main behaviours for each of the key disorders are given in Table 4.2. They have been culled from the DSM-5 using only the words found there. Each one gives the sorts of behaviours you would find a person doing, not because they 'have' that disorder and it causes those behaviours, but because they had been sent to a psychiatrist or clinical psychologist and were diagnosed (they are still suffering in either of these scenarios). Not all behaviours are always present of course, and very strict and precise conditions for their appearance are laid out in the DSM listings.

So we now have a listing of behaviours (categorized but out of context) which if observed by a diagnostician might lead to a diagnosis of a DSM mental health disorder. As the diagnosticians will be the first to say, all these behaviours occur naturally in everyday life. But in the presenting cases, something has happened that they have become extreme, disruptive to normal life, harmful, or weird, or that the contexts from which they arise cannot be fathomed. My main criteria is that the persons are suffering or those around them are suffering.

It is worth looking through this list of behaviours out of context. We normally only read them wrapped around the diagnosis and the theories and metaphors that have been used to construct those diagnoses. If you are interested in mental health issues, then these are the observations you will make; *this is what you will see, stripped from the theory, but desperately needing context*. So what you then say (or think) about them as you read them *will be your own theorizing* shaped from or for your audiences. So it is worth observing your own behaviour as you read this table.

TABLE 4.2 The main behaviours for each of the key 'mental' disorders, culled from DSM-5 words. Each one gives the sorts of behaviours you might find a person doing, not because they 'have' that disorder, but because they had been sent to a psychiatrist or clinical psychologist for diagnosis and these behaviours were recorded

Schizophrenia spectrum and other psychotic disorders

Delusions, hallucinations, disorganized thinking (speech), grossly disorganized, or abnormal motor behaviour (including catatonia), and negative symptoms

Bipolar and depressive disorders

Common behaviour associated with *depression*:
* sad, empty, or irritable mood, accompanied by somatic and cognitive changes that significantly affect the individual's capacity to function, moodiness that is out of character, increased irritability and frustration, finding it hard to take minor personal criticisms, spending less time with friends and family, loss of interest in food, sex, exercise, or other pleasurable activities, being awake throughout the night, increased alcohol and drug use, staying home from work or school, increased physical health complaints like fatigue or pain, slowing down of thoughts and actions

Common behaviour associated with *mania*:
* increased energy, irritability, overactivity, being reckless, or taking unnecessary risks, increased spending, increased sex drive, racing thoughts, rapid speech, decreased sleep, grandiose ideas, hallucinations, or delusions

Anxiety disorders

Excessive fear and anxiety and related behavioural disturbances, panic attacks, phobias, agoraphobia, generalized anxiety

Obsessive-compulsive and related disorders

Recurrent and persistent thoughts, urges, or images that are experienced as intrusive and unwanted, repetitive behaviours or mental acts that an individual feels driven to perform in response to an obsession or according to rules that must be applied rigidly, dysfunctional beliefs, an inflated sense of responsibility, the tendency to overestimate threat, perfectionism and intolerance of uncertainty, over-importance of thoughts, and the need to control thoughts

Adjustment disorder (stress-related)

Unable to adjust to or cope with a particular stressor like a major life event, sadness, hopelessness, lack of enjoyment, crying spells, nervousness, anxiety, worry, desperation, trouble sleeping, difficulty concentrating, feeling overwhelmed, thoughts of suicide

(continued)

TABLE 4.2 *(continued)*

Dissociative disorders

Disruption of the normal integration of consciousness, memory, identity, emotion, perception, body representation, motor control, and behaviour

Feeding and eating disorders

Persistent disturbance of eating, or eating-related behaviour that results in the altered consumption or absorption of food, significantly impairs physical health or psychosocial functioning

Disruptive, impulse-control, and conduct disorders (notice more abstract words are being used here)

Problems in the self-control of emotions and behaviours, unique in that these problems are manifested in behaviours that violate the rights of others and that bring the individual into significant conflict with societal norms or authority figures, opposition behaviour, intermittent explosive behaviours, emotions (anger and irritation) and behaviours (argumentativeness and defiance)

Personality disorders (notice that more abstract words are being used here)

Enduring patterns of inner experience and behaviour that deviates markedly from the expectations of the individual's culture, is pervasive and inflexible, has an onset in adolescence or early adulthood, is stable over time, and leads to distress or impairment

Some more specific disorders have behaviours or abstracted 'patterns' making up the 'personality' issues. These include chronic patterns of:

distrust and suspiciousness such that others' motives are interpreted as malevolent

detachment from social relationships and a restricted range of emotional expression

acute discomfort in close relationships, cognitive or perceptual distortions, and eccentricities of behaviour

disregard for, and violation of, the rights of others

instability in interpersonal relationships, self-image, and affects, and marked impulsivity

excessive emotionality and attention seeking

grandiosity, need for admiration, and lack of empathy

social inhibition, feelings of inadequacy, and hypersensitivity to negative evaluation

submissive and clinging behaviour related to an excessive need to be taken care of

preoccupation with orderliness, perfectionism, and control

Examples of analysing simple possible strategies in the main DSM disorders

We now have the observable behaviours of the DSM but still grouped into the diagnostic categories. Before removing those categories to see what functions we can find hidden, I will simplistically and tentatively link the broad symptoms to possible *normal* life strategies to cope with the situations in Table 4.1.

This is just a first attempt and I do not value this very much as a product, but going through this might be of value, especially to help stop us all lumping the behaviours into groupings of 'disorders' again.

Table 4.3 now has the main DSM 'disorders' along with some suggested life strategies which might have been original contexts for the behaviours appearing innocently, but which got out of control ('locked in'). These are all 'normal' strategies we use in everyday life, but which in difficult situations (Table 4.1) can get out of control and locked in.

TABLE 4.3 The main DSM 'disorders' with some strategies that might have been functional in the original 'normal' contexts before getting 'locked in'

Behaviours in 'disorders'	Possible strategic uses of component behaviours originally
Behaviours seen commonly in 'schizophrenia'	Perhaps originally to entertain in social relationships, shaped by people in relationships, shock people, to gain attention, avoidance and escape from contexts, keep people at bay, to stop evaluation and challenging, stop people reacting in the standard ways, avoid or escape dealing with thoughts from conflicting audiences, used to generate stories, excuses, reasons, explanations, etc., using bizarre or abstract talk
Behaviours seen commonly in bipolar (manic)	To impress people and manage self-image, manage reputation, to get things done, to avoid silence, to block thinking, to deal with conflicting audiences by showing that you are doing, saying, and thinking things for all audiences, to keep people at bay, to stop evaluation and challenging, shock people
Behaviours seen commonly in depression	To gain sympathy, attention, and getting things done, avoidance and escape from contexts, to manage self-image, to deal with conflicting audiences by doing none of what is suggested and trying to avoid conflict thereby
Behaviours seen commonly in anxiety	Avoidance and escape of contexts, removal of fear used strategically, phobias used strategically for getting people to do things, used as stories, used for image management, to shock people, to gain sympathy or attention
Behaviours seen commonly in obsessive-compulsive	Avoidance and escape of contexts, responding to conflicting audiences, used as stories, used for image management, to block thinking, to deal with conflicting audiences by showing that you are doing something, trying to say or manage the conflicting thoughts from conflicting audiences

(continued)

TABLE 4.3 *(continued)*

Behaviours in 'disorders'	Possible strategic uses of component behaviours originally
Behaviours seen commonly in adjustment disorder (stress-related)	Avoidance and escape of bad contexts, to gain sympathy, attention and getting things done, maintaining face in a bad situation, fitting with stories
Behaviours seen commonly in dissociative disorder	Trying to say or manage the conflicting thoughts from conflicting audiences, avoidance and escape from contexts, to manage self-image, keep people at bay, to stop evaluation and challenging
Behaviours seen commonly in feeding and eating issues	Used strategically for getting people to do things, used as stories, used for image management, to shock people, to gain sympathy or attention, to support stories and image management strategies
Behaviours seen commonly in disruptive, impulse-control and conduct disorders	To impress people and manage self-image, manage reputation, originally to entertain in social relationships, idiosyncratically shaped by people in relationships, shock people, to gain attention, avoidance and escape from contexts, keep people at bay, to stop evaluation and challenging, avoid or escape dealing with thoughts from conflicting audiences

Six common contexts for 'mental health' problems which can be rethought as normal life strategies

There are a few other conditions in the DSM diagnostic approach that need analyses first in terms of strategies of everyday life. Assuming that the DSM is not built on thin air, and I certainly do not believe that, we must analyse where these other conditions arise from—what contexts and strategizing have made them a common problem across people.

I will analyse six of these conditions in a speculative way—using backward engineering possibility analysis (Guerin, 2005, 2016b). These are all common contextual outcomes for, or properties of, the 'mental health' behaviours, so it is worthwhile analysing them even if tentatively.

Impairs normal functioning

Most professionals are aware of this, but the impairment of normal functioning which is part of all diagnoses (even 'sudden onset' disorders), is not necessarily a *result* or *effect* of a 'mental disorder' but can also be part of the normal life contextual strategizing that is taking place—whether for good or bad. That is, the impairment could be part of an original working out of contexts (Table 4.1) such that:

- stopping normal functioning is better than continuing as things are
- stopping occurs as an effect of other behaviours but then is a better outcome overall than functioning in the normal way
- stopping occurs as an effect of other behaviours but then becomes a strategic trap that is difficult to rescind.

Along these lines there are many possibilities which need checking in real cases, but this 'strategizing by stopping normal functioning' by no means takes place in every case. It does suggest, however, that just trying to resume normal functioning ('Just get over it!') is not going to work since the new functioning has either been strategized or is an effect of current contexts. So those current contexts will need changing before some sort of normal functioning returns (but probably in a different form).

So some possibilities for *the strategic role of stopping normal functioning put in context* might be these:

- it is non-strategic but is a *negative* effect or consequence of other conditions because the person will:
  - miss out of resources
  - miss out on chances to change their contexts
  - break useful links to resources and social relationships
  - disrupt social relationships that were positive and might have been helpful.

- it is a strategic effect which is in some ways *positive* for the person's overall actual predicament because:
  - it escapes from normal life (which tells us something about the 'normal' contexts for that person)
  - it leads to extra attention for the person which can be strategic in many ways that might need checking
  - it might avoid specific other negative activities or conditions, not the whole context
  - it disrupts negative social relationships, demands and roles, which might be 'more functional' within their context
  - so any sign of a return to 'normal functioning' becomes a resource to utilize for other strategies (a way of getting people to do things, a way of getting affection, etc., by promising normal functioning).

There are other difficulties in using 'functioning' as a criterion, especially so widely throughout the whole DSM—almost all the mental health 'symptoms' are not so bad until they affect 'normal functioning'. I will come back to this in Chapter 6 and compare it to the criteria of 'being irrational' in determining insanity in the early days of psychiatry.

Over long duration

Another common context for the DSM is that the behaviours have been occurring over an extended period. Most diagnoses have something like this in the DSM fine-print: 'and has been present for at least six months'. This again might not only be an effect or consequence of the situation but might also be a strategic part of the context—for good or bad.

Some possibilities for *the strategic role of the behaviours occurring over a long period put in context* might be these:

- it is a non-strategic but *negative* effect or consequence because:

  o it can become further embedded in the conflicts and make more difficult to exit
  o there is more time for other social traps to click in
  o it can lead to other consequences which are negative or make difficult to exit later
  o there are difficulties maintaining face after an extended period
  o there are difficulties maintaining stories about yourself after an extended period
  o there are difficulties building new face after an extended period
  o there are difficulties building new stories about yourself after an extended period
  o people now rely on, and have built their strategies around, that person's extended context (other people rely on them now).

- which is in some ways *positive* for the person's actual predicament because:

  o new contexts can arise through others over that time
  o new shifts in major contexts can occur
  o accidental changes can occur.

Comorbidity

Another context which can be strategically involved in 'mental health' behaviours is comorbidity. This refers to having many 'disorders' or problems at the same time. Almost every listing of the DSM has a section on common comorbid issues, and usually also some ways to differentiate them from the 'disorder' being discussed.

However, in terms of behaviours-in-contexts, the comorbid problems are always part of the context and somehow involved with each other, especially if you remove the metaphor that each 'disorder' is distinct and exists as some

distinct substrate (Chapter 1). In terms of contextual or ecologically thinking, they should be seen as linked problems which should not be separated.
Even if they arose from very distinct contexts in the person's life, they will
become part of every other context's strategic conditions in any case.

In terms of reality, there also appears to be far more comorbidity than
the DSM recognizes, so the attempts to say that the DSM disorders are
distinct, and the usually weak criteria given to separate them, means we
should treat them all as just behaviours together. Every listing of a disorder
in the DSM has multiple common comorbid problems, and requires very
detailed instructions to force them to appear as distinct labels, and this also
puts doubts on the usefulness of doing this merely to prop up the 'distinct
disorders' metaphor of Kraepelin.

In terms of analysing the strategies of contexts, comorbidity can be part
of useful or less useful strategies for dealing with 'mental health' problems.

- it is a non-strategic but *negative* effect or consequence and so:

  o   it can make exit more difficult
  o   it can complicate any one analysis
  o   if drugs (medical or recreational) are comorbid they usually muddy
      other behaviours and makes more difficult to deal with them.

- it is strategic and *positive* for changing this person's contexts because:

  o   it makes better ecological sense to handle all at once
  o   it might have been tried as a solution so it can give us clues
  o   you can work separately for small gains
  o   it sometimes works like a log-jam and might find key-logs rather
      than dealing with everything.

Personality

Another general strategy is for a person to make some strategies part of their
chronic behaviour pattern, in the way we label as someone's *personality*.
A large range of these dysfunctional 'personalities' are listed in the DSM and
the only real rationales given are that they are not part of the social norms
of a culture and that it is a pattern of strategies that appears early in life and
is enduring. Of course, these arise from the life contexts of those people,
and *this might look like a 'personality' trait to casual observers but only because the
contexts in which that person lives have remained static.*

Making a strategy into a 'personality', whether intentional or not, can
also be a useful strategic manoeuvre for the person themselves, depending on their life problems. This is another use of the discursive strategy of

categorization—'self-categorization' (Edley & Wetherell, 1997). What this means first, is that there is a strong *strategic* difference between sometimes behaving in a way that is useful and taking that behaviour as a regular and seemingly essential part of you and your life. The point here is that this can be strategic even if the person does not realize. It depends on your life contexts and especially social relationships, and being able to cope with the collateral effects if locked in.

A second property of 'personality' would seem to be that the person carries on this pattern *regardless of the contexts they are in*. This can be deceptive, of course, as people often appear to do this but in reality what they are doing is to completely limit the number of different contexts they get into at all. They also can have strategies to downplay or escape anything in new contexts they happen to land in. So there are a few possibilities already but some of these behaviour patterns can also involve a disregard or lack of attention to contexts at all, as part of an avoidance or escape strategy which has become chronic for them and is seen now as part of their 'personality'.

A third strategic use of 'personality' comes from sociological research. Spending time in communities shows that what psychologists call personality as an 'internal disposition' can be real but is instead a *social role* in a community or family. There are functions for working in communities and people 'take on' the roles and in a sense assume a personality whether or not they wish to do this (Davis & Schmidt, 1977; Gerth & Mills, 1954; Klapp, 1949; Mills, 1963; Vicary & Westerman, 2004). We can certainly see some of the social roles when we bother to look very closely at families (Laing & Esterson, 1964). This should not surprise us too much given that behaviour arises from social context.

The last general strategic feature of a 'personality' is that it can also be a discursive device or strategy for a person (Edley & Wetherell, 1997). Their self-described 'personality' can be used discursively in all sorts of ways. It can, for example, be used strategically as an excuse or reason in a story justifying to an audience why they are doing something not in a 'normal' way ('I did that because that is who I am'; 'I have always been a happy-go-lucky person'). It can be a way to avoid giving details of oneself in a conversation by just referring abstractly (we say superficially) to your self-described 'personality'.

I will not go through all possible strategies because personality characteristics are many and varied, and too idiosyncratic. They are lumped into three groups by the DSM with behavioural similarities, however.

The questions we must ask looking strategically at the 'personalities' are these:

- what might behaving in *odd* or *eccentric* ways do strategically, both positive and negative, in both everyday life and in a life where it has been locked in or is chronic
- what might behaving in *dramatic, emotional,* or *erratic* ways do strategically, both positive and negative, in both everyday life and in a life where it has been locked in or is chronic
- what might behaving in *anxious* or *fearful* ways do strategically, both positive and negative, in both everyday life and in a life where it has been locked in or is chronic.

This opens up a wealth of avenues for better contextual observations, especially when the more detailed DSM listings are pursued. The other thing to learn from these is that if the resource and social environments do not change then the behaviours can be enduring, especially if the person's strategies are shaped to stay within confined contexts. This then follows similar paths to the comments above about patterns over long durations.

Historical

A lot of the diagnoses refer back to historical events in people's lives: a traumatic event, a family constellation, a lack of something. Certainly historical events are important but so is the argument that something contemporary must be maintaining the persistence of influence—there was no biological substrate changed by the events that 'cause' effects now. I have also gone through some problems when analysing historical contexts in Chapter 2, and it would be worth reviewing that material.

Rather than pretend to answer this question one way or another, the analysis must do two things. For example, in some cases a bad event will so change all the contexts for a person that they will not be able to recapture those original contexts (through no fault of theirs) because all their resource networks and social relationships have become altered after the original bad event and they are in new territory. So the historical event will be a major influence on how their current contexts are arranged: for example, they are now in relationships with people whom they would not have been otherwise. The analysis perhaps could delve into whether current changes are wanted in order to get back to an imagined (which is verbal, so find out who is the audience shaping this?) former state, or whether the historical events have launched the person into a series of contexts that are also bad and need changing in and of themselves.

On the other hand, the idea of '*strategic usurpation*' (Guerin, 2016b) suggests that if strategies are patterned in some way because of the present contexts then that pattern can be used as part of other strategies—which makes analysis very difficult. So in the present case, a bad historical event can be used in stories for narrative effects (Chapter 3) because they will affect listeners, *whether or not* there is actually still a bad effect from these bad events. This can be done in a totally innocent unknowing way or, in the worst case, as an 'intentional' strategy to get what you want by 'using' something (your bad life event) to which people will react strongly.

So the real point is that history is important but difficult to analyse and needs a lot working through and trying out possibilities. Simply saying 'All my troubles stem from this bad event when I was young' can be correct in a roundabout way (as described in general above), or be an example of usurpation as part of another strategy (in either a crass or a complex way).

Unwanted and uncontrollable

Another key feature of behaviours and their contexts that gets them classed as 'mental health' is when the person calls them 'unwanted' or 'uncontrollable'. This seems simple perhaps, that something is happening (usually said to come from inside the person) which is affecting them badly and they did not intend that and do not want it to occur. This is especially common for thinking (which from Chapter 3 should already make us suspicious that it is not simple) in the form of what are usually called 'intrusive thoughts'.

I will say more about this in Chapter 6 but I would like to start rethinking some of the points here. If our behaviour arises from external contexts then in one sense all our behaviour is 'unwanted', 'uncontrollable', and 'intrusive' since it arises outside of us. The real questions then are: 'unwanted compared to what' and 'unwanted in terms of which of your audiences'?

Looked at fresh in this way, having thoughts we do not want, or which are intrusive, is no different in principle—but only in principle—to casually visiting a car-yard and then a few hours later finding ourselves locked into a contract that we did not actually want and we have now spent thousands of borrowed dollars on a new car. It is no different in principle to watching a sports match and finding yourself getting angry and starting to talk back at the television, even though you never wanted to get involved. It is no different in principle to driving on a freeway, missing your exit and finding yourself having to drive back along small roads for some kilometres to get to your destination. All these examples show how *all* our behaviour is shaped by our external contexts and we can end up doing novel, unwanted behaviours without thinking or verbal planning. They are all unwanted or intrusive behaviours.

Two points from this. First, in this sense *all our thoughts are intrusive* since we do not decide or choose to think them—they are shaped by our audiences (Guerin, 2016a, 2016b) and 'pop into our heads'. Second, those thoughts which we normally call intrusive or unwanted therefore must have some *other* special properties different to any other thoughts—but all our analysis is saying is that the special property is not their intrusiveness.

To investigate these special properties in the contexts for thinking we should look just as we would when investigating the contexts in the case of buying a car without any intention. For the intrusive behaviour of signing an 'unwanted' car contract, I would probably look first at the social context of the salesperson's behaviour, and second at the buyer's language use around image management and their self-image audiences. In particular, I would look for conflicting or contradictory audiences for their self-image talk if (1) the behaviour has been shaped by the salesperson but (2) the buyer is now saying (verbal behaviour shaped by one or more of their regular audiences) that they did not intend that to happen. The 'unwantedness' is likely due to conflicting audiences—I say I want one sort of car but the salesperson shows how this expensive car would be good for my self-image.

Once we see all our behaviours as the same in principle—whether doing, saying or thinking—then we can proceed in the same way but for intrusive thoughts we would look for very specialized contexts (Chapter 3). In particular, the most common answer to my earlier question of 'unwanted compared to what' is that there is at least one audience shaping the intrusive thought and at least one audience punishing that intrusive thought. In reality, it is usually more complex than just this, but this is a good place to start your analyses.

What you need to do in practice is to try and 'catch the audiences' for those different thoughts. If you are talking to someone about 'intrusive thoughts' you can watch the person talk and observe as responses to different prior audiences click in, and sometimes you can notice a slight change in their intonation, expressions, breathing, way of talking, or other small behaviours (Carey, 2008; Erickson, Rossi, & Rossi, 1976; Guerin, 2016b). Then you can explore who that talk was aimed at or arose from and even have them talk back to each audience (Passons, 1975).

The behaviours found in any of the DSM disorders

With Table 4.2 of this discourse analysis of the DSM, I cut, pasted, and assembled all references to the actual behaviours, symptoms, or 'complaints' (Bentall, 2006) occurring in the main DSM descriptors. While I listed them in their original disorders, most appear across all labelled 'disorders' and there was huge overlap between disorders that is played down in the DSM text.

For our first look at these behaviours of 'mental health' in a more novel way, Table 4.4 has all the behaviours found but now in an *alphabetical* sequence, thereby making the list independent in which disorder the behaviours were observed. I have listed them in alphabetical order to help readers get away from seeing them as grouped into metaphorical clusters based on some supposed disease, chemical imbalance, or brain substrate (implied still in Table 4.2).

TABLE 4.4 The behaviours found in the DSM descriptions put into an alphabetical sequence, thereby making the list independent of disorders, in order to help reverse the intense categorization learned from the DSM

acute discomfort in close relationships	generalized anxiety	opposition behaviour
affective instability	grandiose ideas	orderliness preoccupation
agoraphobia	grandiosity	overactivity
anxiety, appear anxious or fearful	grossly disorganized or abnormal motor behaviour	overestimating threat
appear dramatic, emotional, or erratic	hallucinations	over-importance of thoughts
appear odd or eccentric	hallucinations or delusions	panic attacks
argumentativeness	hopelessness	perception disrupted from normal
attention seeking	hypersensitivity to negative evaluation.	perfectionism
being awake throughout the night, decreased sleep	identity disrupted from normal	perfectionism preoccupation
being reckless	impulsivity	phobias
body representation disrupted from normal	increased alcohol and drug use	preoccupation
cognitive or perceptual distortions	increased energy	problems in the self-control of emotions that brings the individual into significant conflict
concentration difficulties	increased physical health complaints	racing thoughts
consciousness disrupted from normal	increased sex drive	rapid speech
crying spells	increased spending	recurrent and persistent thoughts

defiance	inflated sense of responsibility	repetitive behaviours applied rigidly
delusions	intermittent explosive anger	repetitive mental acts applied rigidly
desperation	intermittent explosive behaviours	restricted range of emotional expression
detachment from social relationships	intermittent explosive irritation	sad mood, sadness
disorganized thinking	interpersonal relationships instability	self-control problems that bring the individual into significant conflict
disregard for the rights of others	intolerance of uncertainty	self-image instability
distrust and suspiciousness of others' motives	intrusive and unwanted thoughts	sleeping troubles
disturbance of eating, or eating-related behaviour	irritability	slowing down of thoughts and actions
dysfunctional beliefs	lack of empathy	social inhibition
eccentricities of behaviour	lack of enjoyment, loss of interest in pleasurable activities	somatic changes that affect the individual's capacity to function
emotion disrupted from normal	memory disrupted from normal	spending less time with friends and family
empty mood	moodiness that is out of character	staying home from work or school
excessive emotionality	motor control disrupted from normal	submissive and clinging behaviour
excessive fear and anxiety	need for admiration	suicide thoughts
feeling overwhelmed	need to control thoughts	unable to adjust a particular stressor
feelings of inadequacy	negative symptoms	worry
finding it hard to take minor personal criticisms	nervousness	

A useful activity is to look through these repeatedly and imagine the myriad of life contexts within which any one of these might arise as a strategy to cope with stress and conflicts. Stare at them, and begin to stop your thinking from automatically assuming metaphors of disease clusters and labels, and try instead to put them into groupings based on coping behaviours within bad everyday contexts. These are our raw material of analysing and changing mental health (at least divorced from observation).

As another thought experiment, randomly pick two or three from this list and try to imagine a (realistic) life context in which both might be functional initially. They might then get locked in and be difficult to change (because of the bigger context) but can you imagine how they could have arisen together?

Start to deconstruct how you label, observe, and think about all the behaviours on this list. Remember my earlier point in this book—if you name or label you stop observing what is going on in the further details of the context and real life. *And then your label looks more and more certain, but only because you have stopped observing and analysing and do not see the contradictions and diverse details anymore.* What labelling or groupings do you think of while gazing through this listing? What everyday behaviours do you think of that relate to these ones which were listed because they were 'dysfunctional' in some contexts?

Then try to observe these behaviours with ecological thinking instead, in the here and now, as behaviours-in-bad environments which are trying to deal with things, or which might have worked once but not necessarily anymore (Table 4.1). How might they be strategic, in a positive way for the person behaving or their social relationships?

Then try next to imagine these arising as your own behaviours, first as innocuous or everyday behaviours, and then as more severe. When have you ever done a lesser version of these behaviours? What contexts in your life gave rise to them: social, economic, cultural, lack of opportunities, lack of resources? What contexts in your life might give rise to them in the future? What are they strategies for? What do they do? How might they then get locked in and become difficult to change without major context changes in your life?

Contextualizing the behaviours found across all of the 'disorders'

The next analysis attempts to group the behaviours of Table 4.4 into groupings based on the behaviours and their strategies themselves rather than any diagnostic theory. There are nine main categories suggested and these are listed in Box 4.1.

Box 4.1 DSM behaviours put into possible functional groups

1. Very general behaviours
2. General changes to mood presentation
3. Unusual actions
4. Social relationships problematic
5. Thinking and talking problematic: General
6. Thinking and talking problematic: Specific
7. Thinking and talking problematic: Identity talk
8. Thinking and talking problematic: Talking about social relationships
9. Thinking and talking problematic: Anxiety and fear

Before I add some functional details of Table 4.3 to this list, a few general observations. The first three contain behaviours which occur in many contexts of life. They are common and often non-problematic. This means they need to be contextualized very carefully, since they might be irrelevant to the suffering of the person. The third category of behaviours has some that are less common in everyday life, and can appear unusual but not always out of the ordinary.

The fourth category has seven groupings with it, and shows various ways that people relate to one another. In these cases, they are done in a way that raises the likelihood of a mental health diagnosis. But even here, they occur for many people and are not excessively problematic in real life.

The last five groups all involve language use—talking or thinking behaviours. These are in different 'themes', most of which will be obvious. It is interesting to note the ubiquity of these, since it was pointed out earlier that language use is a behaviour for which the contexts are almost never really known by those behaving. And this is our very definition of 'mental' disorders.

Talking about self or image is interesting, and in Chapters 5 and 6 I will discuss how in modernity self-image and identity have probably become more important, and hence more problematic. The other point to mention is that there were surprisingly few behaviours of issues arising from how people talk about their social relationships. There were other problem behaviours with respect to relationships, seen in the fourth grouping. But perhaps there are few issues of talking or thinking about relationships only because they get solved by other professionals and do not become a major issue. (Some are in fact listed in a section of the DSM called 'Other conditions that may be a focus of clinical attention' but it is stated that these are not mental health disorders.)

In Table 4.5 we now have the DSM behaviour groups above put with details of the possible contextual strategies from Table 4.3. This table is not meant as a new diagnostic device. All the entries are merely suggested possible strategies for how those behaviours might be linked in multiple ways to life events around resources or social relationships and the problems which can be associated with these (from Table 4.1). There must be many, many more and, in a way, every person's story will be different and every combination of contexts will produce different behaviours which look the same. But it is not the topography or the microphysics of the behaviour which is important—it is the way the behaviour is entwined in the life situations

TABLE 4.5 DSM behaviours grouped into possible contextual strategies with details from Table 4.3

Behaviours	Possible consequences and strategic effects
Very general behaviours	→ could be strategic for problems with resources, social relationships or both (anything in Table 4.1)
crying spells desperation feeling overwhelmed unable to adjust a particular stressor being awake throughout the night; decreased sleep; sleeping troubles disturbance of eating, or eating-related behaviour somatic changes that affect the individual's capacity to function spending less time with friends and family staying home from work or school negative symptoms attention seeking increased sex drive increased alcohol and drug use	avoidance, getting attention, escaping from having to do something, might be remote audiences not present, trying to exit altogether from problems, trying to shake up or drastically alter current contexts so new solutions appear but getting locked in

General changes to mood presentation

affective instability

emotion disrupted from normal

empty mood

excessive emotionality

hopelessness

moodiness that is out of character

lack of enjoyment, loss of interest in pleasurable activities

restricted range of emotional expression

sad mood, sadness

→ could be strategic for problems with resources, social relationships or both

strategic to change other people, avoidance of people's directives and requests, getting attention, escaping from having to do something, might be remote audiences not present, trying to shake up or drastically alter current contexts so new solutions appear but getting locked in

Unusual actions

appear dramatic, emotional, or erratic

appear odd or eccentric, eccentricities of behaviour

disorganized or abnormal motor behaviour

motor control disrupted from normal

being reckless, impulsivity

increased energy

increased spending

overactivity

repetitive behaviours applied rigidly

strategic to change other people, avoidance of people's directives and requests, getting attention, escaping from having to do something, might be remote audiences not present, trying to shake up or drastically alter current contexts so new solutions appear but getting locked in

Social relationships problematic

(placed into seven groups that seem allied)

1. detachment from social relationships
   lack of empathy
   social inhibition

   solving relationship problems by withdrawal, avoidance, and escape

2. acute discomfort in close relationships
   interpersonal relationships instability

   multiple and conflicting audiences and relationships

3. submissive and clinging behaviour

   avoidance of problems by letting or making others solve them

4. argumentativeness
   defiance
   opposition behaviour

   solving relationship problems by voice, bluff, or disregard

(continued)

TABLE 4.5 *(continued)*

Behaviours	*Possible consequences and strategic effects*
5. irritability 　intermittent explosive irritation 　intermittent explosive anger 　intermittent explosive 　　behaviours	part of bluff strategies, avoiding, or escaping other, stories to tell other audiences unrelated to those present,
6. disregard for the rights of others	gaining resources without negotiation
7. self-control problems that bring significant conflict 　emotional self-control problems that bring significant conflict	'self-control' not shaped from audiences strong enough, or multiple contradictory audiences in conflict
Thinking and talking problematic: General (placed into four groups that seem allied)	→ language use involves past and present audiences
1. slowing down of thoughts and actions 　concentration difficulties 　consciousness disrupted from normal 　memory disrupted from normal 　perception disrupted from normal	avoiding audiences, escaping from voices of audiences, strong contradictory audiences leading to avoidance and escape, over-powering audiences, messing up concentration, lack of audiences altogether in other cases
2. racing thoughts 　rapid speech	strong contradictory audiences leading to over-thinking, over-powering audiences leading to over-thinking, behaving to stop or block challenges from audiences or to escape their talk, trying to impress for image management possibly in cases
3. disorganized thinking 　cognitive or perceptual distortions 　preoccupation	strong contradictory audiences leading to multiple contradictory verbal responses, over-powering audiences messing up verbal responding, poor skills in managing thoughts, responding so as to disengage listeners and avoid social interactions
4. intolerance of uncertainty 　repetitive mental acts applied rigidly	strategically attempting a make a single story fixed to cover all talk about life or one portion, trying to fix thoughts to either suit audience or avoid them, trying to block multiple contradictory audiences by fixating on one

Thinking and talking problematic: Specific

delusions
dysfunctional beliefs
intrusive and unwanted thoughts
grandiose ideas, grandiosity
hallucinations
recurrent and persistent thoughts

real events for everyone but can be made into stories to tell strategically, scare people and keep them at bay, stories to tell about self-identity, way of talking and thinking to avoid or escape from engaging with audiences

Thinking and talking problematic: Identity

(placed into four groups that seem allied)

1. identity disrupted from normal
   self-image instability

2. hypersensitivity to negative
   evaluation
   finding it hard to take minor
   personal criticisms
   feelings of inadequacy
3. need to control thoughts
   perfectionism preoccupation
   orderliness preoccupation
4. inflated sense of responsibility
   suicide thoughts
   body representation disrupted
   from normal
   increased physical health
   complaints
   disturbance of thoughts and
   talk about eating, or eating-
   related behaviour

→ all have situations in which stories about self have taken on too much importance because of strong audiences or weak alternative resources
stories about self not working with audiences, multiple contradictory audiences, new audiences needing new strategies, bluff games with self-stories out of control
protecting stories for one audience by avoiding other audience responses, not managing to please all audiences

protecting one story by trying to cut off all other thoughts

specific parts of stories become strategized with audiences and problematic

Thinking and talking problematic: Talking about social relationships

(placed into two groups that seem allied)

→ few behaviours mentioned in DSM although extensive in real life; perhaps because if there are problematic stories about other people then these issues are dealt with in other ways with other 'experts'—the 'cause' can easily be seen. So they are not classified as 'mental health' issues. If the problems are talked and thought about as problems of 'self' which cannot be seen as easily (the audiences are hidden) then these become 'mental health' issues

(continued)

TABLE 4.5 *(continued)*

Behaviours	Possible consequences and strategic effects
1. distrust and suspiciousness of others' motives	possibly using one audience strategically in stories for the other audiences
2. need for admiration	possibly establishing the resource basis of audiences
Thinking and talking problematic: Anxiety and fear (placed into three groups that seem allied)	
1. nervousness worry generalized anxiety anxiety, appear anxious or fearful excessive fear and anxiety agoraphobia panic attacks	meta-worries about stories to tell others later, anxiety over who stories are for even, strong audiences expecting certain behaviours and stories,
2. phobias	possibly for stories, meta-worries about more specific stories to tell others later
3. overestimating threat	shaped by audiences for dramatic stories

which is important; the strategies of resources and social relationships that make up the ecology of each individual and group.

What I would like to see come from Table 4.5 are a series of case studies carefully tracing as far as possible these *behaviours* for individuals through their resource and social relationship contexts (Guerin, 2016b), both everyday and when presenting clinically. These would provide new examples for this table but showing more intricate paths through the strategies. They would avoid being placed into groups of 'disorders' since there is no substrate for this except the external world contexts.

These case studies would be best carried out not by psychiatrists and psychologists, however, and not with their own clients (Rose, 1962). Such case studies would need people trained in research skills from social anthropology and sociology rather than from current psychology or medicine, since the research methods of the two latter realms are not geared for observing contexts properly, and have not been for many decades (with some exceptions). For example, their gold standard of research (randomized double blind) is not much use for contextual observations, unfortunately, and neither is exploring a person's contexts by talking to the person in an office for one hour. Likewise, doing gold standard research with a carefully selected group who have a diagnosis with little comorbidity, treated in a university clinic, and outliers removed from the sample, is also not much help.

Post-DSM: reinventing old models of 'mental health' behaviours

Having deconstructed the DSM into constituent behaviours, where does this lead us? I have three initial suggestions, which are not very satisfactory or original but which will be useful when a lot more effort is put into observing and documenting the contexts for people's behaviour, and allowing any amount of idiosyncrasy. The suggestions are not much use on their own— they do not constitute any sort of useful theory, for example (and I do not think that is even something we want anymore). What they do is to push practitioners and researchers towards getting more of the story in individual cases (but which might be family or community stories; see Chapters 7 and 8) and not focus on clustering the behaviours into 'diseases' like the DSM does. Any clustering will be idiosyncratic and arise from structural patterns in the contexts and the strategies in those contexts.

The three initial broad suggestions:

- 'mental health' behaviours arise from attempts to deal with difficult situations which cause suffering, distress, and misery, but they sit alongside other behaviours which attempt solutions and not as a special group (Table 4.1)
- which behaviours occur depends only on the actual contexts and strategies of that context
- like any behaviours in life, they can become 'locked' into the person's contexts and 'lifestyle' and be difficult to change, for good and bad.

Hardly original but I will spell this out more now by drawing on the deconstruction of the DSM in this chapter.

We have now looked at ways of observing and analysing the common contexts in which human behaviour arises. We have done this for all behaviours, including talking and thinking which are a little special. I then went on to suggest possible functional analyses of the mental health issues found in the DSM and elsewhere—to see if we can make more sense of the behaviours, symptoms, or complaints arising with suffering than assigning them to some diagnosed inner demons we cannot even observe. Table 4.5 is a first start on this.

As a broad next step I would like to re-consider 'mental illness' situations as ones in which a person is suffering but the suffering appears to be arising from nothing connected with their body or their immediate surroundings. If I am sneezing and have a bad headache then my suffering is probably from a flu. If I am sad because I cannot go to see my friend in a park as we arranged because of my flu, then this suffering arises probably from my social contexts and strategies of my life plan, but this seems to be clear to me. There is a clear 'resource' (in my broad sense) and it is being blocked (Table 4.1), but I can follow skills of recovery to soon change this (text the friend, visit them as soon as I am able, send them a gift). If instead I was to get a text from another friend to say that the friend I was going to meet said they were glad they did not have to see me that day, then I have a more complex intrigue of social contexts and I need different skills to manage these relationships: is the person I was going to meet being two-faced to me; is the second person lying; have I misjudged these relationships; what might the second person be after if they were lying; who else might be involved in all this and for what resources; are they testing my friendship; or in fact do they think that I am lying about my flu as an excuse?

These conflicts and strategies are all the stuff of life (Table 4.1) and how we juggle our resources and our social relationships to get a life, but a key thing to notice is that there are skills and support available from others to get through these conflicts, even if this means losing out in the short term but getting on with some other strategy. In general, with such conflicts you also have a good idea of what resources are at stake and who are the main people involved. You know where your suffering is coming from. These contexts are not hidden from you.

(Note that so far I have talked about *individuals* in difficult situations but of course it is more common that conflicts involve groups of family or friends. Here the whole group suffers as a group, and we could even realistically talk about group 'mental health' issues if they are hidden. So, for example, Indigenous peoples everywhere have suffered badly through no fault of their own as groups inflicted with colonization, but notice, however, that this is kept separate from 'mental health' but only by artificial definition and exclusion. Mental health is usually *only allowed to refer* to the suffering of one individual. But if the suffering is out in the external contexts, as I propose, then we could change this.)

There are other situations, however, in which there is a conflict of resources, people, or both, but for which we cannot easily get out of the situation (whether you gain or lose resources in the resolution). This could be because of a complex situation with conflicting but equally important contexts, or from a situation of not knowing what is happening. Most of the time in life we suffer but also find ways through such situations, especially with the support of others. We have suffering and sorrows but we get through them.

If we now go back to the beginning of Chapter 1, and the top of this chapter, we can summarize now the rethinking about *what makes those contexts we name 'mental illness' seem special*. We know now it is not because they

TABLE 4.6 Scenarios in which behaviours might be named as a 'mental illness'

- the contextual problems giving rise to the suffering are not clear
- the contextual problems giving rise to the suffering are hidden in some way
- the contextual problems giving rise to the suffering disrupt our life so we do not function
- the suffering from the contextual problems disrupts our life
- there are multiple social relationships or resources but they are contradictory or conflicting as they are:

  o balanced evenly
  o mutually exclusive with punishments attached for doing the opposite
  o long-term versus short-term conflicts

- contexts cascade for other reasons and become a social trap
- someone outside sees our behaviour and does not understand the contexts operating

have a brain disease or something at their base—they arise from our contexts like any other suffering and pain (Chapter 2). We also know now that they are not characterized by hidden, inner thinking, or unconscious problems, since our thinking issues also arise from our external contexts (Chapter 3). As I have been hinting along the way, I think there are several scenarios in which we then label behaviours as a 'mental illness'. Table 4.6 finally lists some of these more explicitly.

One scenario is that the contextual problems giving rise to the suffering are not clear to the sufferer or not known at all by anyone—we are suffering but there is nothing obvious we can see that can be fixed, but it is still very real in our world. For example, we just keep crying each day and do not know why. Another scenario is that the problem, or even the suffering itself, disrupts our lives and we can no longer function in ways that we or the rest of the world (or psychiatrists) call our 'normal' ways—our usual economics of relationships and resources is no longer working. Another scenario is when we know there are multiple resources of social relationships or resources but they are contradictory or conflicting and are either balanced or are mutually exclusive with punishments attached for doing the opposite (double bind scenarios are one example; Laing & Esterton, 1964). A final scenario I have seen is when someone is behaving within their contexts with some suffering and they know what is going on, but to someone outside of those contexts the behaviours look unusual and so they are still named as 'mental illness'—that is, they are labelled this merely because an *outsider* cannot understand the contexts.

Summary

- life is full of difficult situations (Table 4.1)
- we each have very different contexts even for similar-looking difficult situations
- we can respond in functional ways to those difficulties if our training or the context allows this; we do this all the time
- if there are no functional strategies known or able to be enacted then a range of options can still be done, such as the myriad of escape strategies, but they can have short- or long-term negative effects
- most of our attempts to cope with difficult situations succeed or we can get help from friends and communities, financial advisors, social workers, lifestyle coaches, bank loans, religious or spiritual leaders, etc.
- there is no special category of 'mental behaviour' in all our attempts to cope with difficult situations, only in the sense that behaviours which have difficult-to-observe contexts (we cannot easily see where they arise from; Table 4.6) have been labelled that for around 200 years and given rise to a new set of 'experts' in the last 150 years (so-called 'mental health' experts) but who focused on medical approaches to these cases because of their background
- from these difficult-to-observe contexts one person might engage in more 'psychotic' looking behaviours to cope and another in more 'depressive' looking behaviours to cope (Table 4.2), but which of these happens will depend on the contexts they arise in (Table 4.5), not any predetermined clustering from a (purely metaphorical) disease of the brain
- so there should be, and indeed is, considerable overlap in 'mental health' behaviours (Table 4.4); so in the previous example there can be *both* psychotic-looking *and* depressive-looking behaviours engaged, perhaps at different times as the person tries new 'solutions' to their difficulties
- a good option is to explore every context as if it will be different since these broad and simplistic strategies give no real information and are clustered using topographical features which is unsatisfactory
- similar looking 'mental health' behaviours can therefore arise from very different 'difficult situations' and similar 'difficult situations' can produce very different 'mental health' behaviours
- every 'mental health' behaviour will depend on the exact possibilities in those contexts and the range of skills the person already had to deal in certain ways.

We therefore need to focus on the suffering, the behaviours leading to suffering (actions, talking, and thinking), and the situations in which these behaviours arose. This will eventually not differentiate between 'mental' and non-mental suffering, and we will have more general practitioners with some experts for specific situations—but not for specific disorders. This needs a lot more time and effort than the methodologies of the past. We do not need specialists for hidden contexts versus not hidden contexts—all practitioners need to deal with both.

This suggests, therefore, these extra points as well:

- a lot of the 'mental health' behaviours will start at a younger age when a child is coping with many new difficult situations but without many of the skills that might be necessary, and they are trying different solutions from a short list, especially if they have little support
- when a person faces a very new context in life (perhaps sudden or traumatic), new 'difficult situations' are likely to arise
- many dysfunctional attempts to cope with difficult situations fail but the difficult situations disappear over time anyway and there are no further issues (we get over it)
- learning more and more skills, and especially flexible life skills, probably helps overall through any difficulties (Guerin, 1994; Neacsiu, Rizvi, & Linehan, 2010)
- the typical (Table 4.4) problem behaviours need to be checked for idiosyncratic contexts and strategies for that person and their situation alone; it will be tempting to generalize again
- most of those difficult contexts will be also be difficult to observe without more time and effort by practitioners, however, which is the only reason why they were referred to as 'mental' in the first place
- any clustering of 'mental health' behaviours (Table 4.2) arises from similar functional patterns in their contexts and strategies (Tables 4.3, 4.5) rather than from centres of disease
- finally, as a heads up, we will also see in Chapter 5 that *modernity* has exacerbated many of these problems:

  o modernity has new and complex difficulties, especially through the effects of capitalism and the large percentage of strangers involved in our lives (work, school, bureaucracies, etc.)
  o new difficulties also mean there are few tried and tested skills that can help people to cope

o   there is weakening of family ties through capitalism so fewer skills are taught (relegated to schools and more strangers) and less assistance in dealing with difficulties that occur

o   having to strategize with strangers 90 per cent of the time rather than people who might be more responsible or have some obligations towards you is problematic and with little human history for guidance

o   because there are few interdependencies and little shared personal history in modernity, difficult situations with all of the strangers involved in our lives will now commonly arise from contexts that are inherently difficult-to-observe, hence more problem behaviours are getting referred to as 'mental health' now.

References

Bentall, R. P. (2006). Madness explained: Why we must reject the Kraepelinian paradigm and replace it with a 'complaint-orientated' approach to understanding mental illness. *Medical Hypotheses, 66,* 220–233.

Bradley, H., Woolley, C., & Clarke, D. (2011). *Reflections on depression: The lived experiences of people with a history of depression.* Berlin: Lambert Academic Publishing.

Carey, T. (2008). *Hold that thought! Two steps to effective counseling and psychotherapy with the method of levels.* St Louis, MO: Newview.

Crowe, M. (2000). Constructing normality: A discourse analysis of the DSM-IV. *Journal of Psychiatric and Mental Health Nursing, 7,* 69–77.

Davis, M. S., & Schmidt, C. J. (1977). The obnoxious and the nice. *Sociometry, 40,* 201–213.

Edley, N., & Wetherell, M. (1997). 'Jockeying for position': The construction of masculine identities. *Discourse & Society, 8,* 203–217.

Erickson, M. H., Rossi, E. L., & Rossi, S. I. (1976). *Hypnotic realities: The induction of clinical hypnosis and forms of indirect suggestion.* New York: Irvington.

Firestone, S. (1998). *Airless spaces.* South Pasadena, CA: Semiotext(e).

Gerth, H., & Mills, C. W. (1954). *Character and social structure: The psychology of social institutions.* London: Routledge & Kegan Paul.

Guerin, B. (1994). *Analyzing social behavior: Behavior analysis and the social sciences.* Reno, NV: Context Press.

Guerin, B. (2005). Combating everyday racial discrimination without assuming racists or racism: New intervention ideas from a contextual analysis. *Behavior and Social Issues, 14,* 46–69.

Guerin, B. (2016a). *How to rethink psychology: New metaphors for understanding people and their behavior.* London: Routledge.

Guerin, B. (2016b). *How to rethink human behavior: A practical guide to social contextual analysis.* London: Routledge.

Klapp, O. E. (1949). The fool as a social type. *American Journal of Sociology, 55,* 157–162.

Laing, R. D., & Esterson, A. (1964). *Sanity, madness and the family: Families and schizophrenics.* London: Penguin Books.

McGruder, J. (2001). Life experience is not a disease or why medicalizing madness is counterproductive to recovery. *Occupational Therapy in Mental Health, 17,* 59–80.

Mills, C. W. (1963). The competitive personality. In *Power, politics and people: The collected essays of C. Wright Mills.* New York: Oxford University Press.

Neacsiu, A. D., Rizvi, S. L., & Linehan, M. M. (2010). Dialectical behaviour therapy skills use as a mediator and outcome of treatment for borderline personality disorder. *Behaviour Research and Therapy, 48,* 832–839.

Passons, W. R. (1975). *Gestalt approaches in counseling.* New York: Holt, Rinehart and Winston.

Rose, A. M. (1962). A social-psychological theory of neurosis. In A. M. Rose (Ed.), *Human behavior and social processes: An interactionist approach* (pp. 537–549). Boston, MA: Houghton Mifflin.

Vicary, D. A., & Westerman, T. G. (2004). 'That's just the way he is': some implications of Aboriginal mental health beliefs. *Australian e-Journal for the Advancement of Mental Health, 3,* 103–112.

5

MENTAL HEALTH IN MODERNITY

Before going on to more specific analyses of particular cases in the next chapters, I believe it is important to look at a broad contextual analysis of the 'normal' Western populations living in 'developed' countries. This is needed *only* because they are the origin, and still the basis, of our accounts of what is 'normal' and 'abnormal' mental health in the DSM, most psychiatric and psychological theorizing, and elsewhere. Most other groups in the world are assigned to special clauses about 'cultural' differences which tell us nothing.

But here I want to examine some special properties of living in Western modernity which are unique to these societies around the world and unique to almost every human group in history. It is the DSM which is 'culturally' special, not the rest of the world! In particular, the big change we will see for mental health is the move from having 90 per cent of our everyday relationships and resourcing working through family or kin—people who are related and accountable to us both directly and through other kin—to having 90 per cent of everyday relationships with strangers who have no family ties or accountability except through even more strangers (Chapter 2).

In terms of history, the way that people live in modern developed societies is relatively new, untried, global for the first time, and not yet fully tested. That is, in capitalism we are still making life up as we go along. We will look at some of the main contextual factors which shape the forms of 'mental illness' that arise. But please, this is not meant—as the DSM does—to define these as the standard, baseline or normal context for life on Earth, to be then compared to 'others' in later chapters. I am putting it here because the mental health literature and profession has been constructed almost entirely around Western, mostly white middle-class populations, and I am trying to deconstruct and rethink that from many different angles in this book. So to say it again, in terms of both history and the contemporary world, it is the Western populations living in modernity which are 'culturally' unusual, not the rest of the world, which has been mostly family- and community-based and cooperative.

From 'then' to modernity: the changes in contexts

Armed with the rethinkings of mental health so far in this book, we will now examine some generic contexts of living in modernity, since most psychology and psychiatry are built from this without explicitly naming it. I have already emphasized that this is new and that we are still making it up. There are no historic exemplars of how to deal with the problems, conflicts and stresses being thrown at people by modernity. These ways of living will reappear later in Chapter 8 on Indigenous mental health, but the difference there will be that Indigenous peoples of the world had these suddenly and brutally thrust upon them by force and this produced even more problems, conflicts, and stresses for them.

The broad changes in social relationships for modernity

Many years ago our ancestors hunted and gathered or else settled in one place and grew crops and raised animals. They almost always did this in large extended families formed into cooperative communities. Life was not a perfect utopia, and I imagine that gathering berries all day long could become quite boring, unless a fun group did it together. The best way to organize these groups of people over a long time was through family ties and through religious and other social formations that used resource and language strategies to keep people wanting to be together. Again, it was not all love and peace but there were families which cooperated together on the whole and succeeded in getting food and a sustainable life, usually with some forms of (loose) religious practices to hold all the families together, especially during crises (Crone, 2013; Johnson & Earle, 2000). Again, these control methods were not perfect and people suffered and people prospered. But that was life.

Thanks to capitalism, industrialization, urbanization, and a huge population growth, our normal relationships have changed markedly over the last few hundred years. I want to emphasize this. We are living totally different lives now to even 200–300 years ago, and I do not mean because we have smartphones and they did not, but because of how we work our basic lives in terms of juggling resources and social relationships. The point I will be making is that because of this our conflict situations (Table 4.1) are very different and hence our mental health is very different.

Formerly, our resources or consequences in life came primarily or even exclusively through our family and extended families. Now the bulk of resources and consequences (in terms of frequency) come from people who are strangers, acquaintances in networks, and other non-kin. This is not bad in itself, and certainly has some positive outcomes, but the properties for how this works are very different. Humankind has never had a situation in which the majority of people spend the majority of their time involved with strangers and acquaintances who are not known to their kin and are not accountable to their kin. Let that sink in.

So our contexts are very different to 'olden times' even though they have the same general outlines. Yes, we still need to get resources, but we do it through gathering and hunting money, and most of us do this by working for strangers (not family) who give us money which because of our broader social system (based around strangers) can be exchanged for food that some other strangers (not family) have raised or gathered (they use the money from us to do the same). Would those bored berry-pickers wish they could do our jobs for money instead of gathering berries? Maybe, but which would you prefer? Our jobs are mostly boring so far as I can glean and disconnect us from family, although we often find a good bunch of fun work colleagues that make it happier. But working at a job is not a perfect utopia, especially working for strangers, surrounded by strangers, and you do not get to keep or use what it is you produce—it gets sold for a profit which goes to the capitalists.

With this kind of new social system, how do we hold people together? Clearly, family is not as important in this new social system because we work and get what we need from strangers and without any family help. Family now rarely get involved in other family members' work. Our broader communities are now huge (using only the inner city, there are about 400 cities of over 1 million people now). Religious groups are less help holding these together, although on a smaller scale they might succeed; but religions are also not very much use anymore (on the whole) in helping us get our resources, which primarily come through strangers who are not church members. In fact, churches mainly work now to help out the people who are not doing very well in capitalism. *This means that the ubiquity of money as the main life resource is the only thing holding most people in relationships now, apart from a few family members.* That is sad in most ways.

All of these changes in context impact on everything else in our lives, and so also affect *the overall quality of our lives.* We still have to get our food and resources but this is done differently: '[Walt] Rostow must have been among the first to perceive that the culmination of human social evolution was shopping' (Sahlins, 1999, p. iv).

You should remind yourself of the social properties of working and getting resources and consequences from strangers (Table 2.2). When you think about these social properties in your own life you will see good and bad. What is important is that *the strategies and life paths we take on in modernity are spelled out by these social properties of strangers.* They also affect and undermine our attempts to be closer to family members. Also, whereas in kin-based families there is usually some education about how to behave with the different family members, we do not have this for stranger relationships: 'What do you do if a stranger sits next to you on a bus and then starts talking about their spouse in bad terms, and asks your advice?' *Few of us are ever given much training in how to work with these stranger social properties of modern life.*

We now rely in most social relationships on working through contractual relations with strangers and acquaintances rather than through family obligations and commitments, and this affects even the *'mental health' contexts.* For example, how do we now see ourselves and our value to anyone, what is our worth, our self-identity? With large extended families and tight communities you had a place in which to prove your worth, and a forgiving family which allowed mistakes and changes over time. These were never perfect or unbiased, nor violence-free of course. But now we are faced with so many strangers involved in what we do—people we have not known before and who have little accountability to us or the people we know, and especially not to our family. They could move somewhere else far away at any time. Any accountability with strangers must work through other strangers in a regulated system—primarily police and law courts. And how many friends and work colleagues will help us when we are down and out?

In family- and community-based groups, who were you afraid of and who could protect you from these people so you were not left in situations leading to mental health issues? You might have been afraid of certain family members but you were told about them and protected by other family members: you always had family around you. Now, in modernity, we all need to be wary or scared of anonymous strangers or groups of strangers you have never met and about whom you know nothing. Sometimes you do not even know where they are, and you just get a letter telling you that you are in trouble. Think about how much you really, truly know about the people you work with and perhaps spend all day with. How much obligation to you do they really have? We do not even have family members protecting us from other unsafe family members in frequent cases.

One final point about the general changes in social relationships in modernity: it might be thought that modernity ushered in a new era in which our behaviour was much less determined by social relationships, since most people we deal with are not closely involved in our affairs or are related to us. However, this libertarian idea is very misleading, I believe. Relationships between strangers are certainly *different* from relationships among kin-based communities, but they are still strong relationships (albeit different ones) and, more importantly, our resources still very much come from these (stranger) relationships, as they previously did from family.

The relationship problem in modernity is that we are now dependent upon strangers for most of our resources but it is less clear what is required of us to maintain those relationships (compared to family cooperatives), and so much of our behaviour now has to go into these sorts of activities: maintaining reputations, personal image management, being up with the latest and the greatest, impressing people, keeping up on Facebook, knowing what we should know and a few things no one else does, showing off, finding out about the people around us we do not know just in case they are unsafe, and acting in ways that gain the attention of people who otherwise have no other (i.e. family) interest in you. Because it is unclear what is even required of us to fulfil these goals, this means, in fact, that *we might now spend **more** effort on social relationships than earlier forms of society*, rather than less, but in very different ways.

So, the argument is that far from being freer of other people and more distant and independent, as modernity strengthens and as kin-based communities lose their influence, we in modernity have probably become far more dependent on others but dependent more upon whims and fads and fashions guiding us through multiple stranger relationships rather than the more direct or obvious resource implications found in closely structured families and communities. In terms of analysis, we must look for different sorts of social influences on everyday life, but social influences nonetheless. Different types of social influences now resonate as our contexts for acting, talking, and thinking.

Changes in resource distribution (economics)

The other directly related major change in modernity which affects our mental health behaviours has been the economic system, from the smaller, local cooperative economies which followed widespread subsistence and gathering, to the current capitalist, neo-capitalist, or neo-liberal systems, with many mixtures (Salisbury, 1970). While such changes are almost never considered within traditional psychology as being important, Chapter 2 suggested that the whole rationale of capitalism affected people's contexts hugely. This also therefore changed their 'psychology', the resources, the distribution of resources, and much more.

I will not go through all the changes for people's behaviour since some has been presented in Chapter 2 and more elsewhere (Guerin, 2016). Basically, all the parameters of how we juggle our relationships and our resources change with capitalism (Table 4.1). Just to give some flavour for this, however, there are at least five parts of analysing the modern capitalist economy which can change the contexts for our acting, talking, and thinking:

- accumulation of capital as a key life resource (including strategically using the 'power' from people wanting access to your capital)
- competition or entrepreneurship as basic to modern social exchange of resources (whether or not they are essential)
- work and labour as marketable resources (the only exchangeable resource for many people unless you have capital)
- the operation of bureaucracies to organize contractual (stranger) exchanges, even between family and friends now
- the effects on people from having money as almost the sole exchange medium.

There are other broad effects of capitalism as a system to live within, but these five alone completely change the playing field for how we live our lives. Contractual relationships with strangers alone have changed the way we live and interact with people, not just strangers but how we interact with our families. (I read a case recently of a couple who could not attend their friend's wedding because of last-minute baby-sitting issues. The 'friends' later sent them a bill for the cost of their not showing up at the wedding. While people were aghast, this makes perfect sense through stranger-relationship logic.)

So events can only happen in our life contexts if they are profitable for someone else, and our lives are laced with competition among strangers who have little or no obligation or responsibility to others. We can only function if the contexts include gaining and spending money. Instead of a wide range of actions and outcomes, we are made to focus on one main outcome—money. This focuses us upon employment, saving money for everything we need, etc. And as per the previous heading, this all gets focused 90 per cent (+) of the time through strangers. Find any event in your life and analyse the contexts—you will find the effects of capitalism.

I will, however, list 25 more direct changes in context that give rise to modern behaviours and thinking. Each of these can become a source of issues and conflicts for a person's world (Table 4.1) which can then become a noticeable 'mental health' issue, or play a strong role in those issues. They are also issues that to the most extent are new. We have not had centuries of trying to deal with the side-effects of capitalism and how people can cope with their new worlds, the new forms of stress, and the suffering caused. Capitalism also has subtle ways of blaming the individual (a concept it promotes) for their own suffering, and this plays a big role in the study and practice of 'mental health'. So these are all effects on people that can turn into new mental health issues, or new variations of old issues. And because they cannot easily be seen (originating in the very economic system), they are likely to be classified as 'mental health' issues rather than physical health or social work issues.

To help start this, Table 5.1 presents a few possible suggestions of such impacts from these 25 social properties of capitalism. They need to be enlarged with case study examples that have sufficient context to make better sense of them. But it is hoped that Table 5.1 will be a start.

TABLE 5.1 Effects of capitalism on behaviour and the properties which constrain our lives in modernity

Effects of capitalism on our lives in modernity	Behaviours that can be shaped by these effects
1. Relies on a stable social system to maintain the monetary system	• if we try to work outside the system it is extremely difficult • need to maintain 'normality' to ensure the resources keep being available • many anxieties over monetary system not working: 'What if credit cards suddenly stopped working?'
2. Those using money must stay within the monetary system for the money to be able to do things (have value)	• dependency on money • poor learning of skills to obtain resources without money • dependency on getting things done through using money • if outside monetary system then unable to build relationships with most people • if you do not have money you can be shut outside the main networks of social relationships

(continued)

TABLE 5.1 *(continued)*

Effects of capitalism on our lives in modernity	Behaviours that can be shaped by these effects
3. *People develop good knowledge of the behaviour of money rather than the behaviour of people*	• ignore relationships for maintaining monetary position • social skills honed primarily for maintaining monetary position • singular resource (money) holding relationships together • learn competition divorced from any social relationship obligations • learn to view people through singular outcome
4. *Parties in monetary transactions can complain about the value given for an exchange since the dollar value is arbitrary*	• anxiety over purchasing since all transactions will involve profit to the other and uncertainty about 'real' value • use extra monitoring needed for purchases • use of informal contacts to verify purchases • addressing transactions afterwards must involve more strangers • constant feeling like the other person cheated you
5. *If conflict occurs then higher authorities can be brought in such as police and courts, thus removing the exchange from being an interpersonal exchange*	• conflicts require further strangers involved • any monetary exchange is not between two people but involves the police and the law potentially • you must use monetary rules because you are within the system
6. *The same item is exchanged (money)*	• we become more focused on the one resource • we know less about the variety of resources available in the world and in our lives • we can flexibly strategize with money since it is abstract and the major exchange item
7. *Can be used to prevent any social relationship*	• money is abstract and based in stranger relationships and contracts so no other social relationships required for exchange • can live without human contact if you have money • can live on takeaway food • makes secrecy and anonymity easier • if you do not have money you are more reliant on relationships

8. *Promotes individualism*	• main focus is on money-for-resources instead of family and friend relationships-for-resources • reduces need for social relationships if you have money since economic networks can suffice for resources • fewer children required for resources • life focuses more on 'self' and relations to economic networking • promotes the compartmentalization of activities in life • allows participating in separate life domains (compartmentalization) without needing consistent social relationships across those domains
9. *Promotes nuclear families*	• life resources come through strangers and money and not family networking • families and especially large families are not required and can be an encumbrance • large cooperative groups not required • fewer children well-educated better outcome than large families
10. *Promotes dispersal of families*	• less need to remain near to family • need to pursue contracts with strangers for resources wherever that might be • produces more transient and itinerant life strategies
11. *Facilitates indirect types of exchange*	• allows many types of exchange too difficult with physical items • allows flexible strategies for resources including abstractions
12. *Allows action at a distance* (Weber)	• can exchange resources and do things to people over distances • especially with modern technology, but the abstraction of money also encouraged the development of such technologies
13. *All types of services can become valued* (Weber)	• because money is abstract, with enough money almost any objects and events can be valued and bought • human lives can be valued in different ways in terms of money
14. *Facilitates hoarding, as a means of offsetting future risk* (Weber)	• easy to hoard money if current resources are met • can accumulate great wealth (unlimited in principle) if physical resources are not actually accumulating

(continued)

TABLE 5.1 *(continued)*

Effects of capitalism on our lives in modernity	Behaviours that can be shaped by these effects
	• little physical space needed to hoard money • money can be set as a number if the social system is stable
15. *The transformation of all economic advantages into the ability to control money* (Weber)	• the ability and skill to accumulate and control money becomes paramount in life • knowledge of money and stranger relationships (contracts) paramount
16. *Allows small groups to become independent of the larger society if they are wealthy enough* (Weber)	• if groups have money they can become independent of other relationships • minorities can therefore be less oppressed if they have money • this means, however, that dominant people in capitalism will work strategically to stop minorities accumulating capital
17. *Allows individuals to become independent of groups and society, thereby facilitating forms of individualism and individual personality* (Simmel)	• promotes individualism and the ideas of people as independently functioning organisms, ignoring the stranger relationships • the ideas of people being self-contained individuals has promoted many other ideas and ideologies
18. *Allows interactions devoid of any other social relationship* (Simmel)	• can develop stranger relationships in most areas of life without involving other relationships • stranger contracts can be made obligation-free outside of the contracted activities so no further social interaction is required • no further relationships obligations are required beyond the contract
19. *Encourages single-obligation contracts and interactions* (Simmel)	• means that we can focus people in our lives into single-resource outcome compartments if needed • we can partition our lives into safe areas with little overlap • we can exit from relationships easily if money is paid or contracts ended
20. *Promotes rational calculation, which has both good and bad effects* (Simmel)	• knowledge of money and monetary valuations in all areas of life encourages calculations within and between relationships • shapes rational, mathematical, and logical thinking • history of exchanges become less relevant and historical and social obligations less relevant

21. *Is the basis for abstract thinking* (Simmel)	• easy to forget that money is abstract and is a social relationship with strangers • money and exchanges can be easily strategized in abstract learning systems unlike physical resources • resources and social relationships can become independent of the physical reality so this shapes more abstract thinking
22. *Gives freedom to do what you like—if you have money* (Simmel)	• if you have money you can become 'free' in many ways, although illusory since the money is tied to a stable social system in the long run • can become independent of familial, cultural, and societal patterns
23. *Makes most of life substitutable* (Simmel)	• the different areas of life can be made independent and can be substituted more easily • money can flexibly substitute for almost any resources so they can be exchanged
24. *Produces a blasé attitude which makes life dull and grey* (Simmel)	• if you have money the 'freedom' and substitutability can become boring • social relationships and resources can become 'meaningless' since they can be bought and exchanged in so many ways • you can also be bought and exchanged by others if thinking this way • fun and excitement becomes solely reliant on money and not a skilled repertoire
25. *Quality disappears to some extent because money is only quantity*	• actions become unidimensional as quantity and the only distinctions to be made are the costs • this promotes artificial ways of making distensions to appear as quality (but illusionary) • becomes difficult to judge social relationships and resources because only monetary comparisons can be made and not other judgements of 'quality'

Changes from increased impersonal relationships and neo-liberal bureaucracies

One of the clearest things to come from analysing the effects of capitalism is that even our closest relationships are now permeated with strangers. This means that the majority of our exchanges with people occur through verbal, contractual relations, whether formal or informal. The most formal ones are through bureaucracies and the services which run our lives through governments.

The argument below will be that we need to look at these contexts for many of the behaviours labeled as 'mental health' issues. We basically have a large part of our lives and futures put into the hands of people we do not know and who have no obligations to us personally. We do not know them and only have recourse through other strangers. The contexts leading to our behaviours in these situations are therefore likely to be frequently hidden, and will also be classified as 'mental health' problems if 'normal' functioning is messed up, which bureaucracy often does! This broad picture is the source of many mental health effects of bureaucracy and the stress from not knowing and not being in more control.

The work of Max Weber on bureaucracy related social systems and the increasing rationality-driven Western society to the development of bureaucracies and the 'typical' bureaucrat. The systems arose from running everything 'rationally' for the most effective systems of dealing with large numbers of people. Every little facet is put in verbal rules which are followed, by an amazing assumption that we can document all of life into a verbal system of rules.

The following is what Weber (1947, p. 333) saw as the basic bureaucrat produced by the organization necessary to have a functioning bureaucracy:

1. They are personally free and subject to authority only with respect to their impersonal official obligations.
2. They are organized in a clearly defined hierarchy of offices.
3. Each office has a clearly defined sphere of competence in the legal sense.
4. The office is filled by a free contractual relationship. Thus, in principle, there is free selection.
5. Candidates are selected on the basis of technical qualification . . . They are appointed, not elected.
6. They are remunerated by fixed salaries in money . . .
7. The office is treated as the sole, or at least the primary, occupation of the incumbent.
8. It constitutes a career. There is a system of 'promotion' according to seniority or to achievement, or both. Promotion is dependent upon the judgement of superiors.
9. The official works entirely separately from ownership of the means of administration and without appropriation of his position.
10. He is subject to strict and systematic discipline and control in the conduct of the office.

(Weber, 1947, p. 333)

What this all means is that the major people running our lives (government, work organizations) are following written, abstract rules and end up treating us all in an impersonal way. Clearly, these systems are asking for things to go wrong, and they do, especially more modern forms (Ritzer, 1996, 1999). This also adds to the increase in language use over other forms of interaction in everyday life which we saw earlier coming from capitalism directly. Both of these combined support the Matrix of words that we live in (Chapter 3).

In discussing the dysfunctions of bureaucracy, for example, Merton (1957; also Guerin, 1994; Sennett, 2006) suggests three common ways that these systems fail:

- they follow codes and rules but when thing are different or change, bureaucrats are not sure what to do, meaning there is less creativity and innovation
- more effective ways of achieving organizational goals can be overlooked because of red-tape and rules followed too closely
- the impersonal (stranger) relationships can lead to friction with clients.

What this means for individuals is that there is a lot of conflict and stress generated through these impersonal verbal forms of running people's lives (Table 4.1). They are interactions with strangers and we have no recourse except through complaints to other strangers who are following similar impersonal rules. Hummel (2014) takes us through many of these extremely common experiences of everyday life, when battling against the systems. It is a large part of everyday life in modernity in fact, because your resources are coming through these systems (Braedley & Luxton, 2010; Harvey, 2007).

So, whereas our ancestors might have gained resources through gathering berries and hunting, we go, as I have said earlier, to the shopping mall to 'hunt' for resources. Now resources are distributed and made available in the first place only through impersonal, stranger relationships over which we have little control and with whom we have no other connections by family or friends by which we might influence or control this distribution. Hence, a major source of stress and conflict in modernity comes through the bureaucratic and organizational systems run by strangers for our benefit using written, abstract rules—neo-liberalism. We will see more of this in Chapters 7 and 8.

Mental health in modernity: strangers and the generalized other

We have now seen some of the main changes in modernity which affect the very core of our lives, and how we suffer from stress and conflicts, and how these are different to earlier times in human history. The main focus, of course, has been on the properties of stranger relationships and their ubiquity in modernity, and how these properties permeate our lives. They lead to the changes we saw earlier and the increasing use of words over other forms of interaction and engagement with our contexts. In other words, they actually create the language Matrix we live in (Chapter 3).

The points that now follow summarize the broad historical and socio-logical material put into the terms of Chapters 2 and 3, especially on social relationships and economic contexts as we have seen in this chapter (Guerin, 2016). These are some strands that myself and others believe are directly related to modern mental health:

- The role of kin-based communities and even smaller family ties have been hugely reduced through capitalism, neo-liberal bureaucracy, colonialism, and industrialization.
- We now deal with many, many more stranger relationships than people did in the past; they are probably the most frequent relationship for most people.
- Religious belief, practice and therefore informal social organizations in Western countries have been weakened.
- These three points were brought about by the 'Western' capitalist economic system itself and the reduction (for many reasons) of both self-sufficiency and bartering; we have lost skills to engage with our environment since our skills are honed on what pays a salary and because we purchase the labour of others to make up for the skills we have lost.
- At the end of the 1800s there was growing recognition by medical personnel that some suffering (soon to be defined as 'mental health disorders') was related to neither physiology nor to obvious conflicts and issues with family as before, and these formed the basis of a new(ish) field of psychiatric disorders.
- At the end of the 1800s there was recognition of what might now be listed as 'Generalized Anxiety Disorders' (GAD) and generalized depression, called neurosis, hysteria, melancholia, and other names which also did not arise from physiology or family conflicts; the origins were not clear and seemed to require a new discipline called 'psychiatry'.
- In the early 1900s, sociologists began talking about a determining force (context) for individuals in modern societies which they called the 'generalized other'; people were now acting with respect to a generalized other of society rather than specific family members or community authorities as before.
- The fields of psychiatry and psychology *were created* to deal with these cases when the contexts for behaving were no longer obvious (Rose, 1996, 1999); they did not just evolve from pastoral care.

- I am saying that all the above points are related events; they were all part of bigger changes in Western society moving to a full capitalism and bureaucracy-run society and they gave rise to different and new forms of what were now called 'mental health' issues.

What these first points are saying is that there have been major changes in our basic societal contexts and opportunities, at least for those living in Western capitalist urban societies in 'developed' countries. If we think first back to the earlier paragraphs we can see that the social contexts and consequences have changed from primarily being family, community, and church to strangers and acquaintances in bureaucracies and workplaces. For the stranger relationships, there is little real obligation or monitoring between those involved; that is, a property of strangers and acquaintances is that they frequently do not have contact among each other—your friends do not know your family well and your workplace acquaintances with whom you spend so much time do not mix with your friends and family either.

For me, this means that there will be a lot more thoughts 'popping into our heads' which arise from, and involve, strangers and acquaintances—more than ever before in history. We will be thinking thoughts mainly about resource relationships with unaccountable strangers now instead of family and family conflicts. This is greater now not only compared to those in kin-based communities, but also compared to those who lived prior to the 1950s and certainly prior to the 1900s. The differences in social, cultural, monitoring, and secrecy properties are huge and will also apply to our talking and thoughts. Conflicts (Table 4.1) will be difficult to resolve within stranger relationships as will any problem behaviours that arise from things happening in the relationships. We either give up or call the police; either is stressful.

So welcome to the twentieth and twenty-first centuries. So much of our lives, relationships, and resources are tied up with, and networked by, people we do not really know, and people who in turn do not know each other or our families; and they are not easily accountable to any of those others. There are many good and fun relationships of course, but there are so many unknown relationships to worry about, including strangers, dangerous random strangers, anonymous strangers in bureaucracies, and anonymous strangers in charge of organizations (Kafka wrote of these well). This is, I speculate, the origin of both the force on our thinking, talking, and actions which was called the 'generalized other', and the vague feelings of anxiety, doubt, and depression or hopelessness that plague us all in modernity (Cooley, 1909; Foucault, 2009; Gerth & Mills, 1954; Giddens, 1990, 1991; Janet, 1925/1919; Leonard, 2016; Mead, 1934; Meyer, 1948; Sennett, 2001; Smail, 2005; Swindle, Heller, Pescosolido, & Kikuzawa, 2000).

In modernity, then, we deal most frequently with non-kin, and just a few friends and family. If you look at Table 4.1 again you might begin to see that the issues, coping strategies, and stresses from those strangers are much more difficult to deal with because we need to work primarily in words (contractual relations), there are no clear social processes, and there is little that is concrete. People often have difficulty with stranger conflicts because they do not know how to persuade strangers or deal with them in contractual ways.

Technically, any stress or conflict from acquaintances, strangers, and work colleagues can be dealt with by Human Relations people, psychologists, counsellors, police, or law courts, but they are also acquaintances, strangers, and work colleagues who do not know each other in our life either, so there is little consequentiality or consequences on them other than those more formal, bureaucratic pathways, which are often more stressful.

This in turn, I believe, is one main root for the contemporary widespread modern depression and anxiety. Indeed, it seems to me that *everyone living in modernity now has both generalized depression and anxiety; how we deal with these differs among people but that we have them is not in question.* The sorts of 'mental health' issues that would have arisen in kin-based families would have been solved by the many people in the extended family who knew all about you and your history. This does not mean it was always perfect—it was often not—but it meant there were clearer ways of doing things to resolve problems and stresses.

In modern society it is less clear how to solve problems with the people in our life we are forced to interact with, who do not know anyone else in our life who might gain leverage in negotiation, and who can ignore any pressure from us. This is worse, however, because according to sociologists, there are also pressures from 'generalized' others who we cannot even identify. At least in a kin-based community, you usually knew who was doing what to whom. Now, for example, we sort of know that our job is under threat and that our partner is being influenced by some people in a way we are unsure about, but we do not know who those people are or what to do about it. The result for me of all this? *Generalized depression* and *generalized anxiety.* Here I believe 'generalized' means 'coming from strangers' and difficult to see the contexts in which they arise.

As an interesting half-way point in this history, to help give these historical ideas more concrete links to mental health, think of around the late nineteenth century and early twentieth century and until about the 1950s or so. The large extended family networks working cooperatively were very much gone by this time or at least devalued, and a patriarchal system existed in many 'developed' countries, at least for wealthier families, in which the father and husband now had societally ordained power (due to the workings of capitalism) to do what he liked to run a household.

In a kin-based community and family system there would be many other relatives who could and would intervene when individuals had stresses and were not coping (even intervening with elders), and this was also a niche the churches could help with if the families were members—remember that during most of this period there were no official or paid counsellors, psychologists, or psychiatrists, just key people in families and church pastoralists (read some George Eliot). So everything revolved around the father and husband in the family; and relatively isolated nuclear families, isolated from extended family members and stranger social groups, could also run a young person's life and cause difficulties in coping (e.g. Laing & Esterson, 1964).

My point is that the same contexts rarely apply nowadays, given the changes in parental, family, and societal relationships. We are far more likely to be worrying about conflicts to do with strangers, a few close friends, acquaintances, and anonymous bureaucracies than with our wider family (of course there are exceptions), even if we love our family members the most. There are still very strong patriarchal contexts, of course, but these now work through the privileges of male strangers and less from male family members (Chapter 7).

The (speculative) point here is that worry over conflicts in kin-based communities would have usually had a concrete family person or group as the focus. There could be situations in which you know that 'someone' in the community is doing something to mess with you but you do not know who it is, even a coalition, but in general with all the family monitoring going on, you would know concrete people to worry over and think about. So many of the situations in Table 4.1 would not have occurred so frequently.

Now enter the late twentieth century. As emphasized above, our lives, relationships, and resources all involve people we do not know, and people who in turn do not know each other and have little obligation to each other. We need to remember these contexts when considering the mental health of people living in Western, urban, developed countries. Such people (including myself!) are not culture-free, history-free, context-free, relationship-free. We are not 'people without a history' (Wolf, 1982). We are not the normal, unblemished standard models and everyone else is 'cross-cultural' or immigrants or Indigenous. There are very clearly defined social, political, economic, historical, and social contexts in which we live that are relatively new and untested, and from which all our behaviours, talking, and thinking arise. *We are the new people on the global block and the DSM only applies to a small range of the people in history.* What this means for this book is that our 'mental illness' behaviours, talking, and thinking, therefore also arise from those contexts so these economic and social relationship contexts need to be described and taken into account when dealing with mental health issues.

Summarizing mental health issues in modernity

I want to finish this chapter by making the main points very clear so they can be examined and expanded or changed. This is important for what follows in the book because the general underlying sentiment in psychiatry and psychology is that our mental health disorders were born in time immemorial and have been nicely packaged in the DSM. Any other 'cultural' groups are doing something a bit weird or different so we have to 'factor in' some cultural adjustments to the otherwise individualist (i.e., capitalist) diagnoses of mental illness. I really want the reader to see how wrong this is. Indeed the opposite is more true.

So we need to be clear that what we call mental health in this modern era is new and restricted, and stems explicitly and directly from people's attempts to cope with the massive changes to social relationships and resource distribution (economics), and from having to do this without much guidance because we have not tried this all before in history. The capitalist and bureaucratic systems also mean that so much of life we cannot understand and will never understand because it is abstracted and generalized. And so we are all trying desperately to deal with life situations that not only have little history in which people might have learned some good solutions, but for which there are no real answers anyway except to change the larger systems, which is unlikely to happen soon. And families cannot really help us anymore in the way they once could. This is the real context for mental health in modernity and the DSM is not wrong but is just a tiny Band-Aid in all this (Smail, 2005).

I wish to summarize here some suggested possible ways that modernity leads to modern mental health problems. Table 5.2 presents these suggestions.

TABLE 5.2 Possible links between modernity and modern mental health issues

- People are mostly in stranger relationships without further obligations to help at all so little support available
- Control has become abstract so there is (generalized) anxiety over what will happen
- There is understandable helplessness from the systems running resources and economics (sharing of resources)
- Depression from lack of control of outcomes and helplessness to change anything
- Depression from abstract and monetary social relationships
- Anxiety of finances since abstract systems are controlled by capitalists
- Anxieties of relationships because of changes and new forms of social relationships with unknown obligations and responsibilities

- No familial set of consequences (previously all behaviours had two sources of consequences)
- Anxiety from intense and embedded competition between people even when resources are not really in conflict, encouraged by capitalist system
- Modern abstract (stranger) relationships have no strong permanence since no social or moral obligations, so fewer real attachments
- Modern abstract (stranger) relationships built on conspicuous consumption unrelated to anything in real environment
- Behaviour almost all abstract and verbal and not related to engaging with our environments, either social or ecological

Summary

I will finish by trying to set out in summary the full argument of how I now see 'mental health' in the context of everyday Western living after we include the changes which have occurred in modernity. The way we now 'talk about mental health' becomes a modern phenomenon.

- In life, there are always problems and conflicts, and almost all can be traced to *scarcity of resources*, if resources are thought of in a complex and nuanced way and not simplistically. Because most of our resources come through other people, *most of our life problems arise in our social contexts*. Most problems are therefore interpersonal or community-based.
- For most of these problems and conflicts we have many ways to deal with them, or through sneaky strategies or just giving up on having resources; we can overcome the problems and keep on living about the same as before. So, if their car breaks down, most people can arrange some solutions by getting it fixed or doing without a car for a while. Buddhism, for example, has always stressed the neat solution of *just wanting less*.
- There have always been serious problems, however, that people cannot deal with easily. If your land was attacked and your houses burned down and food supplies destroyed, this would be difficult in the extreme. You might die. You might give up totally and die. If in modern life there is a traumatic event of great magnitude which shatters your 'normal' way of life, this can similarly make coping very difficult.
- In traditional kin-based communities there would still be a number of kin who would help you (if you also had previously helped and reciprocated) to overcome these most difficult problems. There was almost always support if you did likewise.
- Although, in traditional kin-based communities if your problem involved going *against* the community and family in some way there was probably little other support and your chances would not be good for getting a solution.

- My key point here, however, is that for all these sorts of problems in old times, both big and small, people could actually *observe* the obvious or salient contexts which led to the problems: drought, raiders from the north, floods, community members themselves with their cultural rules to follow, plagues, etc. You could mostly 'see the enemy'. You knew where the problem lay. Even in cases like a plague or drought, you could see what was happening in a concrete way, despite not having words to talk about how it came about. You knew the groups of people or the environment which were responsible for your troubles.

- This still occurs today when we have problems because our neighbours will not turn their music down, our land agent is demanding more money, our kids keep failing at school, our money does not pay for everything, we lose our credit cards, etc. We can observe the contexts in which these problems are arising quite easily and either solve the problem or be unhappy about things and keep complaining. We suffer, but life can go on.

- In all times, old and current, there would also have been some problems so bad and unsolvable that the people involved would just give up and stop behaving in any way that might serve to get things back on track as they had been. They might behave in ways that just served to escape the contexts and did not try to solve anything, or in ways that did not make sense if you believed the goal was to get back to how things were. These people have just given up, as it were, or begun acting strangely.

- In such cases, kin-based communities often kept people these on and supported them still, so there would be a place for them, or those people could have left that really bad situation to try and make up a new life elsewhere. They could go to the badlands, become a nun or 'village idiot', or run away to sea as a sailor or pirate.

- Now enter modernity. This is difficult to get across, but we are now living in a world of social relationships and economic contexts that have never happened before. We are in the process of making up new ways of living and surviving. We cannot claim that we are doing things based on what our ancestors did because the world has totally changed from anything that has gone before. There are no precedents and our old ways of living cannot be used (we cannot go back to kin-based subsistence farming until there is a revolution).

- Since the beginning of the 1800s or so people have been living in *new social contexts* in which the majority of people they deal with, interact with, or spend time with, are strangers with no obligations outside of abstract rules. Strangers have special properties not just because we have little commitment to them initially and so little real responsibility towards them, but also because they in turn have no commitment to our family and friends, so they cannot even be held responsible by the other people in our life.

- Since the beginning of the 1800s or so people have also been living in *new economic contexts* in which the majority of people have to get their resources through strangers and networks of abstract strangers doing activities that they have little control over and for which they do not keep the products of their work. They get money to use to buy their resources but those same abstract strangers mostly control what resources are available. The societies also have huge stratifications and division of labour so that people only have opportunities for certain social relationships and certain work (to obtain our resources).

- So, most of what we do is now shaped by people we do not know, have little consequence or responsibility to, and our families and friends do not know them either. Humans have never been in these social contexts before because strangers were rare, and we are still making up how we can handle all this. This has come about through our new economic systems.

- For the present discussion, the point is that we now have enormous shaping pressures on us from a myriad of strangers and structures in modern society, people we do not know and who do not have any real commitment to us. Moreover, they are not concrete and observable in the way that our real communities and families were observable and concrete. They are abstract in actual practical terms.

- Around the 1800s, then, people started getting pressures, stresses, crises, and problems which were shaped in contexts by people they could not see and who might not be an actual person in any event. Kafka and de Chirico did good jobs in an artistic way of portraying some of these amorphous forces that can block us. We cannot pin-point them but they are very real nonetheless (read case-studies of Freud, Janet, etc.).

- There are two other historical events that I have argued are related to these changes in social and economic contexts from modernity. First, around the turn of the 1900s, sociologists began describing new pressures and shaping in modern society by 'generalized others'. They were amorphous pressures which now control our behaviour to a large extent, and have very different properties from the family, civic, and church leaders who controlled behaviour prior to that.

- Second, during these same times we see the development of the brand-new psychology and psychiatry disciplines, which are now there to deal with people who have *problems, suffering and issues for which there were no obvious or salient contexts*. This is what is new. Some people now cannot deal with their lives and there is no obvious or observable problem context, such as local economic woes, a drought, a noisy neighbour, etc. There are similarly people who cannot cope or find solutions at all and develop ways of behaving which are no longer trying to resolve things, ways that look 'crazy' or 'maladaptive' and we again cannot see any obvious context for this. They can then get locked into those patterns.

- But what is different now is that the contexts leading to these strange ways of behaving can no longer be seen, even by psychologists (those who just sit in their offices at least). They are now vaguely thought of as due to 'societal' pressures, 'familial' pressure, but are said to originate 'inside' people as either brain problems or else that brand new invented category—*'psychological' problems* (Rose, 1996, 1999).

- Here, finally, we come to 'mental health'. In the way I have outlined, we can see that 'mental health' issues are just extensions of any other behaviours and ways of life, they are just conflicts around people and resources, but the term is now invented purely for modern situations in which there is no observable 'problem person' or context to deal with, there are only 'generalized others' as the problems but they are virtual or abstract, and the ways of totally escaping and giving up are more difficult and have more impact.

- This is why I have said that psychology can be characterized as a discipline which deals with the dumping ground of problems in people's lives for which there is no easily observed contexts from which the problems arise. But they are problems and suffering created by modernity, neo-capitalism, neo-liberalism, bureaucracies, and our current way of life with ubiquitous strangers, even though saying this does not make them any less painful. But it might give us clues to help in new ways.

- Those who cannot continue to cope with these pressures are now labelled as having 'mental health' issues. Some just succumb, while others behave in 'strange' ways in their strategic attempts to avoid certain paths or find a new path. These have always been the options but now we cannot see what leads to this.

- The third historical change is that we now have two big, common, new sets of symptomatic behaviours which are called 'generalized depression' and 'generalized anxiety'. Almost everyone in modernity now suffers from these amorphous pressures and stresses from the very nature of our social relationships, but there is no easily seen 'enemy' to tackle (sometimes labelled abstractly as the 'black dog').

- So the key difference for a contextual view is that people do not *'have'*
depression or anxiety disorders; instead, *they are living in modern contexts which*
are depressive or anxiety-inducing in ways that have not occurred in human
history before. They are not coping well with the new, modern unobservable conflicts (Han, 2004).

- We have only been led to think of these as existing 'inside of us' because
they are coming from generalized contexts which have arisen from the
capitalist, modern world with its preponderance of stranger relationships
which have little interpersonal commitment or responsibility. We know
there are pressures and stresses, and we know our behavioural options get
severely blocked, but we cannot observe the source of these in a concrete
way. As described in Chapter 1, these get attributed to something internal or essentialistic to the person (or ethnic group, as we will see later).

- We cannot easily observe the nature of these pressures, stresses, and
blockers, not just because we are observing badly and non-contextually,
but because they are new and they are generalized and abstract to talk
about. So, people who suffer most from these contexts are *not* poor
observers, weak, or stupid; they are trying to live in maladaptive contexts which do not show their face and which provide no easy solutions,
and for which we have no precedents to follow for solutions.

- So, to answer the original question, I see 'mental health' issues as a
recently named phenomenon arising from the massive changes in social
relationships through massive changes in the economic context of
modernity (forms of neo-liberalism and capitalism). The links between
these are real. They appear different to other life problems (about noisy
neighbours and lapsed rent payments) only because they arise from contexts spread across a whole society of strangers working together but
giving no individual commitments or help.

- Historically, because these maladaptive contexts could not be seen
they were initially attributed to events 'inside' us and conflicts between
unconscious and ego, and the like, and called 'mental' issues—a term
that only indicates their difficult to observe external contexts rather than
revealing a secret new location.

- They are solvable problems and conflicts, however, but they must be
seen in the broader context that *our social and economic relationships are no*
longer nurturing good environments for most people, and people can no longer
resolve their conflicts easily in the modern world. This gets worse every year.

- *'People do not "have mental illness"; people live, and have lived, in envi-*
ronments that do not support healthy behaviours.' And we now have some
brand-new unhealthy environments.

References

Braedley, S., & Luxton, M. (2010). *Neoliberalism and everyday life*. Montreal: McGill-Queen's University Press.

Cooley, C H. (1909). *Social organization*. New York: Charles Scribner's Sons.

Crone, P. (2013). *Pre-industrial societies: Anatomy of the premodern world*. London: Oneworld.

Foucault, M. (2009). *History of madness*. London: Routledge.

Gerth, H., & Mills, C. W. (1954). *Character and social structure: The psychology of social institutions*. London: Routledge & Kegan Paul.

Giddens, A. (1990). *The consequence of modernism*. Oxford: Polity Press.

Giddens, A. (1991). *Modernity and self-identity: Self and society in late modern age*. Oxford: Polity Press.

Guerin, B. (1994). *Analyzing social behavior: Behavior analysis and the social sciences*. Reno, NV: Context Press.

Guerin, B. (2016). *How to rethink human behavior: A practical guide to social contextual analysis*. London: Routledge.

Han, C. (2004). The work of indebtedness: The traumatic present of late capitalist Chile. *Culture, Medicine and Psychiatry*, *28*, 169–187.

Harvey, D. (2007). *A brief history of neoliberalism*. London: Oxford University Press.

Hummel, R. P. (2014). *The bureaucratic experience: The post-modern challenge*. London: Taylor & Francis.

Janet, P. (1925/1919). *Psychological healing: A historical and clinical study*. London: George Allen & Unwin.

Johnson, A. W., & Earle, T. (2000). *The evolution of human society*. Stanford, CA: Stanford University Press.

Laing, R. D., & Esterson, A. (1964) *Sanity, madness and the family*. London: Penguin Books.

Leonard, S. (2016). Introduction. In S. Leonard & B. Sunkara (Eds.), *The future we want: Radical ideas for the new century* (pp. 1–12). New York: Metropolitan Books.

Mead, G. H. (1934). *Mind, self, and society from the standpoint of a social behaviorist*. Chicago, IL: University of Chicago Press.

Merton, R. K. (1957). *Social theory and social structure*. New York: The Free Press.

Meyer, A. (1948). *The commonsense psychiatry of Dr. Alfred Meyer*. New York: McGraw-Hill.

Ritzer, G. (1996). *The McDonaldization of society*. Thousand Oaks, CA: Pine Forge Press.

Ritzer, G. (1999). *Enchanting a disenchanted world: Revolutionizing the means of consumption*. Thousand Oaks, CA: Pine Forge Press.

Rose, N. (1996). *Inventing our selves: Psychology, power, and personhood*. Cambridge: Cambridge University Press.

Rose, N. (1999). *Governing the soul: The shaping of the private self* (2nd Ed.). London: Free Association Books.

Sahlins, M. (1999). What is anthropological enlightenment? Some lessons of the twentieth century. *Annual Review of Anthropology*, *28*, i–xxiii.

Salisbury, R. F. (1970). *Vunamami: Economic transformation in a traditional society*. Melbourne: Melbourne University Press.

Sennett, R. (2001). Street and office: Two sources of identity. In W. Hutton & A. Giddens (Eds.), On *the edge: Living with global capitalism* (pp. 175–190). London: Vintage.

Sennett, R. (2006). *The culture of the new capitalism*. London: Yale University Press.

Smail, D. (2005). *Power, interest and psychology: Elements of a Social Materialist understanding of distress*. London: PCCS Books.

Swindle, R., Heller, K., Pescosolido, B., & Kikuzawa, S. (2000). Responses to nervous breakdowns in America over a 40-year period. *American Psychologist, 55*, 740–749.

Weber, M. (1947). *The theory of social and economic organization*. Oxford: Oxford University Press.

Wolf, E. R. (1982). *Europe and the people without history*. Berkeley: University of California Press.

6

BELIEF AND RATIONALITY, SOME THOUGHT DISORDERS, AND SELF-IDENTITY

The cases below of more specific contexts are not new theories or answers. They are meant to be triggers to have people—especially practitioners in 'mental health'—rethink what might be going on in such situations, what they are observing and what else they *could* observe. It tries to show how practitioners might observe and integrate more context into their thinking and their interventions. All I wish to do is to make some suggestions from a contextual approach as to where they might start looking for the relevant contexts in some tricky situations where people are suffering. We are no longer looking (or hoping) to find the answers in the brain, to uncover a disease substrate that can be fixed (Chapter 1), or get a more refined cognitive metaphor to show understanding. The answers are out there in the client's environment, especially in their social relationship strategies.

I wish to delve a bit more closely into three topics which need a good deal of rethinking. As always, these are not my original thoughts but stem from many earlier thinkers although I will not stop to give lots of references. To do this I have selected three areas in which the contexts for acting are very difficult to see and have a huge history of philosophers and psychologists looking for the wrong solution (usually internally and inside the head). It will be no surprise, if you have digested Chapters 3 and 5 that these will mainly be to do with talking and thinking—the contexts for language use. This is the area of cognitive therapy and cognitive behaviour therapy, but we are going to approach the three topics in a different way. Much of what I will say also echoes thinking in areas such as postmodernism and social constructionism, and indeed, I have learned a lot from them. But I wish to make this into a form which gives us observable (potentially anyway) contexts we can look for and research—not just more words. Postmodernisms and social constructionisms do not always do that.

The three areas, each important in mental health, are belief and rationality, thought disorders, and the sense of self or identity. These are important to analyse (and find somewhere observable to look) for mental health and therapies.

Beliefs, rationality, and delusions

We saw in Chapter 3 that both talking and thinking are shaped by our audiences, which can be many. We also saw in Chapter 5 that in modernity there has been a huge shift in audiences, something I will come to later in this chapter. I now want to treat beliefs and rationality in the same ways, and this coincides with many views within the areas of postmodernism and social constructionism.

Beliefs

People's beliefs follow in a similar way to attributions (Chapter 3) both in the cognitive modelling and in the contextual analysis. The cognitive models typically have beliefs being a sort of guiding storage of things we assume to be true based on our picking up and processing information like an amateur scientist. The metaphor is then that people 'possess' beliefs inside them (in a memory storage) which they can report as memories—'I believe that China is the most powerful country in the modern world.' More of a problem is that the beliefs are then said to cause our behaviour—I do X because of my belief Y.

But an even bigger problem with such models is that it then makes perfectly logical sense to infer that in order to change someone's beliefs we must present evidence or arguments that the belief is wrong, and that this will then change a person's belief. But this is the basis for so many misguided attempts at changing people's beliefs (Guerin, 2005). A further problem is that it also makes perfect sense with the cognitive modelling that a person will act in accordance with their beliefs (unless there is a strong opposing force somewhere), and that they will act and talk *consistently* with their reported beliefs. The problem is that people do not do this very much. People are frequently inconsistent; and people rarely do what they say even when they give really good reasons.

So given these problems, it is important to refocus a person's reporting of their 'beliefs' into their social contexts, but beliefs are difficult uses of language to analyse and occur in many different functional contexts. Indeed, there are several ambiguities and contradictions even in normal usages of the word 'belief'. Pouillon (1979/1982) pointed out how we often use the term when, in fact, we are *not sure* of something; that is, it can be used as a hedge or mitigator (in discourse analysis terms; Chapter 3; Guerin, 2016b). Compare the effects on you as a listener when you hear these: 'Lima is the capital of Peru' to 'I believe Lima is the capital of Peru.'

So for discursive and contextual analysis beliefs are ways of talking rather than inner possessions or states, which means they are part of our rhetoric and strategy to organize and strategize our lives (Edwards, 1997; Guerin, 2004; Hayward, Awenat, McCarthy Jones, Paulik, & Berry, 2015; Potter, 1996; Potter & Wetherell, 1988; Putcha & Potter, 2002). So thoughts about 'beliefs', such as self-image beliefs, the 'core beliefs' of RET (Bernard, 1981; Ellis, 1994), or the uncontrollable and distressing worry which is central to GAD (Wells, 1995), can be understood by contextually observing and describing the social and cultural contexts in which they have been uttered and the consequences they have had on audiences (Guerin, 2016a).

Beliefs as language use shaped by audiences. The real questions for researching 'I believe X' become: who are (and were) the people shaping this use of language; who are (and were) the audiences for this; how does it fit into the other social strategies for this person or group, their life patterns, relationships, etc.; what does it do to the listeners? (what do they now do, or what do they stop doing?); how do you handle multiple and conflicting audiences for this (conversational repairs, hedging); is it being 'rehearsed to say' or 'repeated from before'?

Observed contextually, beliefs are therefore just events in which we say things. No different to saying anything else, except in their specific social properties and effects. Like all things we say, the main property of any talking is that it only does something in the world by affecting other people. My beliefs about cats cannot affect a cat except through a person sometimes. My beliefs about poverty cannot affect the world or resources except through people.

This can even go further, that *my beliefs about myself cannot affect me except through other people.* (This idea also comes from sociologists such as George Mead.) My behaviour is not controlled by my beliefs, but can be by the consequences of those audiences who shape my beliefs. Beliefs do not control behaviour.

So, beliefs are not about the structure of the brain or cognitive processing. They are all about the historical and current structuring of social relationships and the conversational strategies for doing this. So when we hear someone saying that they believe X, we need to observe all the social contexts, which is rarely done in psychology except by discourse analysts. These are some useful questions:

- Why call it a belief in this instance: 'I believe that . . .'? Why not 'an opinion' or 'an attitude' or 'something I thought of' or 'something person X believes'?
- What does calling it a 'belief' do to the listener? What are, and have been, the consequences?
- What different effects on listeners would come from calling it 'an opinion' or 'an attitude'?
- Who was the audience for this? Who has been an audience for this in the past?
- What did the listeners do, and what have listeners done previously?
- What if they had said it was their opinion, or attitude, or some thought that merely popped into their head—what would those have done to the listener differently?
- What would happen in the social strategy going on if you said the opposite belief? How would your life social relationships and strategy change if you stated the opposite?

Contextually, these are all better questions to ask and observe than whether the belief is 'true', whether the speaker 'truly ruley' (worse—'authentically') believes it, or whether they have evidence or proof for it (which also becomes part of their rhetoric or social inference). Whatever the exact effects on different listeners and life situations, calling it your 'belief' changes the social game. For example, how someone might subsequently challenge your new 'belief' is likely to affect their social relationship with you, meaning that often people are *less likely to challenge* you if you call it your belief, unless they are much higher status or want to shake up the relationship or break it off.

So, because beliefs arise from social shaping embedded in the social and cultural contexts of our life, we can start to see why it is so hard to change what people say they believe? There is no paradox here. Simply, there are many social events that powerfully shape your *stated* beliefs and *how you state them in different contexts*. Likewise, just presenting evidence does not ever mean someone will change their stated beliefs—it depends on the value to them of the other social contexts in which they typically say those things and how the 'beliefs' are being used strategically there.

Consistency in beliefs. This further means that having *consistency* in what we say, and between what we say and what we do, or what we say on two different occasions, totally depends on the social contexts. The strategic value in one context of keeping a dubious but consistent belief in the face of challenges might be less problematic to a speaker than appearing to be weak or inconsistent. Or it might be of more strategic value to change beliefs in another context and potentially appear inconsistent than to try and maintain the same beliefs with two contrasting audiences. Consistency in speaking, then, is also shaped socially—it arises in social contexts.

The *real questions for consistency* then become these:

- What is the value (consequences) in conversations and in social relationships of appearing consistent?
- What happens in conversations and in social relationships when we appear inconsistent?
- Does consistency really matter when people are dying?
- The world is not consistent, things and events are fluid and in flux, so why do we try to appear consistent?
- In what contexts can appearing *inconsistent* lead to good consequences (such as presenting an identity of being a flexible person)?

All these new ideas spring forth if you can start to think of beliefs as nothing essential or 'core' or 'inner' or even clearly defined, but just as things we say that are shaped by other people's consequences and the contexts in which we are raised and live. This might seem a weird way to think about beliefs, and it is not recommended for everyday conversation, but it follows from discourse analysis and contextual analysis and it helps with therapeutic outcomes.

Rationality

We have seen that not just our 'beliefs' but also the consistency of our beliefs is socially shaped. We can take this further, however, and look at rationality and logic also. This is very pertinent to mental health since in the early days, insanity was assumed to apply to people acting 'irrationally' (Foucault, 2009; Rose, 1999). If you acted 'irrationally', then you were insane. In these modern DSM times (Chapter 5), 'not acting functionally' as seen in the DSM is the equivalent of 'being irrational', where 'functional' nowadays means in a 'normal' Western lifestyle manner with a job and small family, and obeying rational economic principles.

But the logic about rationality and logic itself needs to be examined more closely, especially within economic thought (Chapters 2, 3 and 5). Following from Chapter 3, everything about rationality and logic is still about the learning and the use of language systems, whether talking or thinking. I wish to suggest another category use instead of the usual dichotomy of rational/irrational:

> *Being rational is not so much about following logic as it is about rejecting other external social shaping of our language use.*

Let me illustrate by some different uses of acting 'rationally'.

- Being rational as following the course of action with the best outcome. If there is a choice between 10 and 20 dollars, only someone irrational would choose the 10 dollars. If I am hungry and there is food in one jar and no food in the other, the rational thing would be to pick up the one with the food.
- Rational as following the best verbal instructions available. If you told me that a stove is hot and yet I still touch it, then I would be acting irrationally.
- Rational as not being swayed by mere opinion and custom. If the 'evidence' shows that garlic does not cure warts, then it is irrational to suppose it does or to continue to put garlic on warts just because your grandparents told you it works.
- Rational as acting with a (verbal) knowledge of the reasons or causes of why you are doing the action. If I tried baking bread with ground rice just to see what happens, then I am acting irrationally. If I know (verbal) that yeast makes cakes rise by giving off gas, then I am acting rationally if I try using yeast to make bread rise.

From a contextual point of view we can see some problems immediately. Most of these points depend upon having (certain) verbal knowledge of some events before or after acting. From Chapter 3 it was clear that all language use is maintained (at least initially) in social contexts, therefore what is rational or not will depend upon the verbal communities and your life experiences with these communities (trust), not certainty of words (Guerin, 2016a).

I hope it can be seen that *acting irrationally is always a case of strong alternative social consequences* (dementia aside, but perhaps even then). If there is a choice between 10 and 20 dollars, I would be irrational to choose the 10 dollars. However, this depends on the social contexts, which are totally ignored (indeed, excluded from consideration) in these examples. It could be that if I took the 20 dollars then people would think I am greedy and I could lose many other useful social and economic consequences in the future because of doing that. Which, then, is being irrational—ignoring the social effects and future social outcomes or losing half the money?

So judgments of what are the rational and 'irrational' choices requires a thorough knowledge of *all* the person's contexts, not just the one in focus currently, and especially the social ones. For this reason anthropologists and sociologists have been very careful and wise to observe and analyse in great detail the social context of so-called irrational behaviours (Abbink, 1993; Beattie, 1970; Durkheim, 1951/1897; Evans-Pritchard, 1976/1937). In fact, they also make the point that there are no irrational behaviours, just ones with culturally different outcomes to ours. Everything is done 100 per cent for the consequences (Guerin, 2016a).

To put this boldly, if you wish to categorize behaviour as being *irrational* or *non-functional* (DSM), this really means that you have not properly investigated all the contexts! And you just cannot say 'Oh, those social reasons do not count.'

So, as was hinted in Chapters 2 and 5, *the whole Western capitalist system is predicated on a purely economic rationalism which ignores the value or consequences of alternative social, cultural, and other contexts which might be more important in that person's life.* We must begin to fully realize the costs of having such a rational-ism implanted for a few hundred years: because the way in which European 'civilization' came to be 'rational' was by preventing families and communities from shaping people's thoughts and behaviours. Thinking had to come from mathematical or other representations or models of the world, and it did this by ignoring other ways behaviour is shaped. (Doing *this* is irrational, actually.)

While in some domains of life this exclusion might be advantageous, such as science, *paying attention to and cooperating with family consequences gives access to many more long-term beneficial outcomes which rational thinking cannot understand because they have been excluded.* Rejecting influence from the social world certainly brought some discoveries but left tragedy in its wake as well, since large family and community structures were rendered impossible when rationalism took over economics.

In a broader (or wiser) view of life, paying attention to and following your family and community *is far more rational* in terms of other practical and social outcomes. The only exception is if you fully engage with a capitalist system of rational economics. This is especially so, we are learning only now in the twenty-first century, in the life domains of: engaging with our ecolog-ical environment; reducing conflicts among people; and having supportive social environments to prevent that those types of individual suffering we currently call mental health. To put my point most bluntly:

The opposite of rationality is not madness, but socialness.

If you are not behaving in ways considered 'functional' by the DSM, then that is not because you are mad but because other social and cultural conse-quences are shaping your behaviour (100 per cent) which the diagnostician is missing. You might be suffering, but not from a 'mental disease'. This is where we got to in Chapter 4, but now we are here through another route.

Delusions. Briefly, analysing delusions follows from the two sections above, and can serve as an example of how this might go in a clinical case. If someone states a belief that is clearly not correct by anyone else's account, it is not the best approach to consider them insane, suffering a brain problem, or having a cognitive dysfunction. Clearly from the above, speaking delusional comments can still have all manner of (100 per cent) effects on audiences.

If we follow what was said in Chapter 3 about the functions of stating beliefs but substitute 'delusions' instead, then telling 'delusions' can be unrelated to *convincing* the audience, but instead relate to contexts of: entertaining the listener; getting the listener to like you; getting the listener just to listen to you; getting the listener just to pay attention to you; getting the listener to do something unrelated to what is being said. The trick is to extrapolate from these to come up with possibilities as to in what contexts someone is telling delusional thoughts, and refusing to admit they are delusions.

As functional examples, delusions can also be a good way to ward people away, or increase social isolation from perhaps some groups of people. As listed above, they can also start out as entertainment for increasing friendships, or be a way to end them or control them. They might be part of keeping a friendship even if I have doubts about the beliefs that person wants me to agree with. Like the section on 'intrusive thoughts' below, a lack of other critical voices might shape delusional statements.

What is clear in all this is that there are social relationships or audiences shaping and maintaining the delusions. This can incorporate the attributional accounts (Merrin, Kinderman, & Bentall, 2007; Rankin, Bentall, Hill, & Kinderman, 2005; and see Chapter 3 for the social basis of attributions; or Guerin, 2016b), and the rule-governed behaviour accounts which also assume a social basis to this form of language use metaphor (Monestès, Villatte, Stewart, & Loas, 2014). They are different metaphors for observing the alternative social contexts for people making delusional statements. The social basis might also be seen in the account of using reality testing for people with delusions, that they strongly resist giving up their delusional beliefs and this resembles more of a social game of playing off the strength of contradictory audiences (therapists) than anything else (Guerin, 2016b, Chapter 10).

Thought disorders and the social contexts of welcome and unwelcome experiences

In Chapter 3, I approached thinking in a new(ish) way, by considering it as just the same as other language behaviours we have learned to use in context but which are not said out loud. This led to some interesting properties (also Galletly & Crichton, 2011):

- Thoughts are 'language responding in context' so the contexts for thoughts *must* be social ones—our relationships, audiences, people.
- There can therefore be multiple, concurrent 'thoughts' happening all the time.
- Thoughts can be conflicting and contradictory without a problem normally.
- If we have contradictory thoughts it is because we have audiences who have shaped us in opposite ways.
- But if the audiences were to meet there could be problems.
- Thoughts therefore arise like any behaviour from our life contexts.
- We need to focus the analysis of thoughts on the audiences which have shaped those thoughts and how that plays out in all our other life strategies and situations.

All the 'mental health' issues of thinking can be rethought in these ways, and they show some new ways to approach treatment as well.

From intrusive thoughts to unwanted thoughts

I mentioned in Chapter 3 that with a contextual view all thoughts are intrusive—we do not decide to have thoughts and we do not control how those thoughts unfold. The thoughts appear in contexts according to training and the confluence of all the other contexts currently present.

So the thoughts which are commonly called 'intrusive' are not a problem leading to suffering *because* they are intrusive. We could therefore use a variety of names for what we commonly call intrusive: uncontrollable thoughts; unwanted thoughts; unstoppable thoughts. In fact, for idiosyncratic cases they might have unique properties. But in general I use '*unwanted thoughts*' since that characterizes them for me best. Some unwanted thoughts are ok, such as music getting stuck in your head when it is pleasant, but the major 'thought disorder' cases are not pleasant and lead to suffering and other unwanted changes in parts of the person's life.

So, what might be some contextual suggestions for unwanted thoughts that lead to suffering? Table 6.1 has some suggestions which can be explored in real cases, whether clinical or everyday.

These are only a few suggestions and there must be many more for every case. If you have unwanted recurrent thoughts about bad outcomes the anxiety can lead to other consequences which need to be dealt with, for example.

How might we go about stopping the unwanted language responses? There are many ways and most have been highlighted in clinical work in different contexts, so not much is new. Once again, though, the really new

TABLE 6.1 Some suggestions to explore when having unwanted thoughts which lead to suffering

---

- the thought might be the one and only thought in your social contexts and so be unwanted since it is all you can think (this will also tell us something about your limited social contexts)
- the thought might be a 'demanding' thought: it is thought as if you are saying something emphatic or someone in your social contexts is being demanding of you in saying it
- the thought might be a strong statement or demanding thought and there are no others currently from your social contexts to counter it or cool it down (typically we learn other thoughts to counter any strong thought—this is identical to the ever-present *challenges* outlined in Chapter 3 and Guerin, 2016b)
- there might be no other thoughts currently resonating with audiences to put it into perspective so you begin to 'believe' this thought you have and no other thoughts stop this
- you might have a life strategy of telling people thoughts as a social relationship builder and therefore some single thought can become overpowering because strong audiences shape it
- you might get two strongly contradictory thoughts which can be a problem if coming from two strong audiences you want to keep, so they become repetitive and unwanted (although only a problem if those audiences come together)
- you might have two strong thoughts that feed each other, meaning that if you get a 'counter thought' against the first one from an audience you have in one context, the second strong one counters that and leads you back to the first, and thence in a loop, over and over (feels as if your thoughts go round and round in circles and get nowhere)
- the 'intrusive' thought comes from a generalized (see Chapter 5) audience so it does not get a reality check very often or at all, and it just keeps resonating; often just doing new things produces new thoughts and words (for new audiences) and so stops the unwanted thoughts (we say that our thoughts get a reality check but this means we get new audiences)
- a problem in modernity is that we get resonating thoughts from 'generalized other' or 'stranger-society' audiences; these are often *critical* of us but we do not concurrently get the multiple, supportive extra resonant thoughts we would get when a friend or family audience is critical (we do not even know who it is coming from in our modern society); so the 'societal critical' thoughts can be overly intrusive and take on huge unwanted significance when they should not (e.g. 'People think of me as fat'—who are these 'people'?)

---

part is focusing a lot more on past and present *audiences* for the thoughts and what the consequences might be for saying the thoughts.

Table 6.2 presents a few suggestions for stopping the unwanted thoughts, but check first whether this is a wise thing to do. If there are important audiences strongly shaping your client to say certain things repetitively, and the

TABLE 6.2 Suggestions for stopping unwanted thoughts

- do not try to just stop them or punish them, as that can backfire; trying to stop them requires an audience which then also shapes saying the thought over again
- flooding the thought or trying to repeat many, many times until the audience's influence reduces, the new audience (the one encouraging you to flood) re-shapes, or the events lead to new thoughts (ACT therapy has many techniques they call 'cognitive defusion' to do this—Guerin, 2016b, p. 218)
- focus on observing and acting more than thinking and talking; get out of the 'talking' contexts altogether (like mindfulness, mediation, and Zen training); this is why learning new behaviours for acting (even if they are unrelated to the problem) can be useful (DBT: Neacsiu, Rizvi, & Linehan, 2010)
- learn to think multiple possible things rather than fixed ideas or beliefs or opinions; have multiple audiences and voices most of the time so a single one is not powerful (the audiences shaping that is, not the thought itself)
- not always a good idea but build some strong, reality oriented and challenging thoughts from new audiences (like RET) to counter any unwanted thoughts that get repetitive, but it might not hold when therapist–audience leaves
- learn about the audiences for the unwanted thoughts, and even have the thoughts talking to other thoughts or to people (like Gestalt therapy does)
- get new audiences for new possible ideas, and this is often the best thing about a therapist

client in their context usually does not report these out loud, then treat them as important thoughts (despite being annoying or leading to suffering). *You need to focus on changing the relationships with those audiences rather than stopping the thoughts.* If I have a recurrent thought that I have not visited my dying grandmother in hospital then it would not be wise to arrange to just stop that thought. The thought is being shaped by important audiences, and therefore probably needs to be acted upon and not ignored or stopped.

Thinking and hearing voices

There has been much confusion about the clinical phenomena of hallucinations and hearing voices, despite good attempts to change the conceptions (Basu, 2014; Fernyhough, 2016; Leudar & Thomas, 2000; Longden, Corstens, Escher, & Romme, 2012; Romme, Escher, Dillon, Corstens, & Morris, 2009). Analysing thinking in the way of Chapter 3 (Guerin, 2016a, 2016b) means that we are *always* hearing voices whether out loud or not. Hearing voices can be seen as just an extrapolation of thinking more generally. We have thoughts 'pop into our heads' even if the contexts (consequences, people) are not present at that time. If there is a context of consequences (relationships, economic, etc.) we will be having 'background' thoughts all the time about them, like hidden conversations not spoken. A thought about someone who is not present can occur anytime depending upon their consequences, and we do not need to look for a salient 'trigger' in the local context. Sometimes the thinking is localized in a context so it appears more like we actually hear it; other times they come and go (depending upon the context, of course) very fleetingly.

So, like 'intrusive thoughts', the hearing of voices is not a problem in itself—it is happening all the time. This is not meant in a spooky way, like hearing disembodied voices when they are not there, but meant in the same way that we can do air guitar without an actual guitar in our hands, hit with a tennis racket when there is no ball, or a good mime. No more than that.

The clinical problems, therefore, with hearing voices must arise from other aspects, the hearing of voices are unwanted or are leading to suffering of some sort. We should again look to the contexts mentioned earlier for the appearance of unwanted thoughts to find the contexts for unwanted hearing of voices. Some people who hear voices also report that it is other people's reactions and discrimination that cause their suffering.

For example, if most of us have a sudden bad context, like we were about to be fired by our boss, we could have a thought 'pop into our heads' of 'We should kill him!' For the majority of us, luckily, we would have other audiences in our lives for that thought to be challenged or laughed at, and not go any further. The properties mentioned in Table 6.1, however, might make that a bad hearing voice scenario, if we cannot stop hearing that same bad thought. We then begin to think further that we really mean that thought, or really believe that thought, or really are that thought. The point, though, is that it is not the hearing voices *per se* that is the problem, but what develops out of hearing voices (like Table 6.1).

The problem is that the idea of 'hearing voices' has had a negative perception in its history, since people did not talk much about the 'normal' voices in their heads (thinking) but only talked about hearing voices when there was a problem—especially when the voices were unwanted by the individual or their groups. But using these voices in positive ways also has a long history, and borders on many forms of prayer, spirituality, and healing. Many religions, for example, accept that people hear the voice of their particular God talking to them, either as an outside voice or as an 'inner' voice. This is seen as a positive thing rather than a mental illness.

I think there is a lot more we can explore in the future about the positive outcomes of having many audiences shaping many voices (language responding with saying out loud). Having multiple voices probably gives us stability since no one voice will predominate (Herbert, 1969). Decisions can be made by thinking (verbalizing) the problem and attending to the different voices (you might recognize who some of the shaping audiences were).

Issues of 'self' and identity

The last topic has to do with the many issues which are talked about in mental health as issues of self, selfhood, identity, etc. There are two parts of this from a contextual analysis: what a person *does* and has accomplished, and how a person *talks* about themselves (includes thinking of course). These two can potentially have little or nothing to do with one another, but both are intricately bound up in our social and cultural contexts.

Self and self-identity

The analyses from Chapters 2, 3 and 5 suggest that self or identity is constructed primarily with language use, to portray ourselves in certain ways to gain resources or relationships (Guerin, 2016b). Identity is how we talk to people about ourselves and show ourselves to others. It is not done for fun (although it can be) but is strategic, to position ourselves for making our lives actually work—to get the resources and social relationships we need or want for ourselves and our families and communities. But identity statements can be checked, so limits are usually drawn as to what can be said.

In earlier times your 'identity' came very much automatically from your family and your life position (see contemporary kin-based communities, Myers, 1991), but with the advent of modernity (late 1800s), when the majority of our relationships shifted to strangers (non-kin), *the social properties or logic of identity also changed* (Chapter 5). On the one hand, you now need to try harder to convince strangers as to your place in the world and what you can do and what you should receive, but it is also now more difficult for strangers to check what you say about yourself so you can invent more if you are persuasive. As one more example of strategic context, strangers can ignore what you say about yourself or disagree and there is no network of family to back up what you say—they can ignore you with impunity.

Because of these new social properties of living in stranger relationships, *we now actually need to spend more time constructing our identities and positions in this modern world*, to get what we need. This often seems (especially to older generations) like time wasted on paraphernalia, talking about ourselves incessantly, accessorizing, obsessively finding out what others are doing, posting on social media, and constructing stories about ourselves to give other people. Even those who think they do not worry about or spend time on self-identity are actually spending time presenting this very image to others.

So, the sad thing is that with the advent of modernity and the colonization by capitalism of all the things we need in life, we all *need* to do a lot of image-presentation and self-identity talk in some form or another (Bauman & Raud, 2015). But this is recent and a direct result of capitalism and the changes occurring in modernity with social relationships.

In reading the creative, fictional literatures of the period 1800–1950 you can see the rise of these new self-identity behaviours, when our resources for life stopped coming through family and *was replaced by having to convince strangers about who we are and why we should get what we need* (for jobs, reputations, relationships, kudos). Even marriage became less about your family and more about presenting yourself in a way to convince strangers and their families to commit your lives together in some ways. But even more telling, achieving concrete outcomes—what you have actually done in your life that is good—became less important than using rhetorical skills to convince people who you are and what you deserve.

The real analysis for self and identity, therefore, lies in observing and documenting the life strategies that engender the statements and actions about self that occur (Myers, 1991). There is nothing authentically self, it is all constructed. However, it is not randomly constructed either; it is built from the life contexts and what is available and what needs to be done and said to gain resources. And we are limited by our opportunities.

Self-control

The sense of self arises also from the sense that what we do follows from what we think and say, but Chapter 3 suggested that this is artificial as well. It also follows from a sense that we control our selves and have a core, whereas if there is a core, it is a core of external stable social relationships. Our stable sense of selfhood is based on a stable set of social and cultural relationships. As mentioned above, however, this has been eroded in modernity because we need to build so many relationships with strangers who cannot provide stable interconnectedness between all our social relationships that family and kin-based communities were able to do.

The problem as I see it with thinking and re-thinking 'self-control' is that it mixes many complex issues about which people make huge assumptions blended with passive acquiescence to common sense. So you do not need to rethink one or two fundamental issues about human behaviour and experience, you need to rethink many, and all at the same time.

The basic starting point is that the experiences we have during 'self-control' seem very real, and they are. I am just arguing that how we think about it and attempt to change it are just not right yet. But it is vitally important to get the thinking right because so many interventions and therapies are based upon a naïve metaphor of self-control, and most are not working. If they do work, we do not really know why, so any extensions then do not work.

Table 6.3 lists what I believe are the main issues of 'self-control' that need a radical re-thinking. It takes a long time but if you can re-jiggle your thinking about all of these, you will get to a better understanding of the experiences and origins of 'self-control' (and be even more super cool than you are already, be like Zen Masters, Yoda, and Master Shifu). And more

---

TABLE 6.3 The main issues of 'self-control' which need a radical rethinking

- we are taught from birth that we have self-control which works and this has gone through centuries in different forms (as have the ideas that the Earth is flat, the sun revolves around the Earth, and particles exist)
- 'self-control' is actually based mainly on social and historical contexts but these are usually hidden and very difficult to observe
- the common methods of observation fail to 'see' the contexts involved in the experience of self-control; we are not yet attending to and measuring the right things—the consequential audiences for what we do and other social relationships
- the whole idea of a 'self' also needs re-thinking as well: it is not about an inner person but external social contexts in our lives and our image management to maintain social relationships (even sociologists agree)
- we are wrongly taught instead that thinking occurs inside us, it originates from our 'self', and is private
- acquiescing to the usual ways of thinking about self-control also allows people to blame the victim, so there are conspiracy reasons why these views are so prevalent in a liberal, individualistic society ('Poor people just cannot control themselves when they get money'; 'Obese people just have no self-control with food, it is their own fault')
- but we do not actually control our thoughts, they just 'pop into our head' as we say, arising from the contexts we are in (this way of thinking is very difficult to change, but examine your own thoughts when they arise and judge whether you actually *made* them be thought or they just appeared—'all thoughts are intrusive thoughts')
- we do almost everything we do without needing to talk or think about doing them (this way of thinking is also extremely difficult to change, that our actions are *not* controlled by words, thoughts or rules)
- however, we *do* talk or think about what we do *all* the time, and a lot (yes, the experience is real) but this talking and thinking are for other people and image management; they are not for controlling what we are actually doing at the time; they are about how we will talk about our actions later and make excuses or make good stories out of what we are doing, etc.

---

importantly, changing your own behaviours will improve because you will not be straining your nerves to engage your 'will power' and then blaming an–inner-*self* when you fail.

'Self-awareness' is also contextual and external

What is called 'self-awareness' is also not about a real inner core of authenticity. Just talking about yourself is not self-awareness, not even when talking as if to yourself about yourself alone in your room (Guerin, 2001).

Talking about yourself is really about influencing your various audiences (social context) to see you in certain ways (usually in good ways, except for metalheads, bikies, and goths). Talking about yourself is just like talking about your friends except that you have other information. This applies equally when *talking about yourself to yourself* (that is, thinking about yourself is shaped by others, paradoxically).

Real self-awareness instead would be all about: being able to describe the contexts that engender your own actions; being able to describe in detail the various things you do and the thoughts you think, as multifarious, contradictory, and situation-specific as these might be. It would be about describing in detail the historical, social, economic contexts in which you have found yourself in life, and how these strategic contexts link to the various things you do, what you say, and the thoughts you think. If you can do this you will gain true self-knowledge and self-awareness, *but you will have to learn much of this 'self-awareness' from other people and from detailed inquiry of externalities, not from navel-gazing and talking about yourself to yourself alone in your room.*

To hopefully make this clearer, think about trying to analyse everything you can about one of your friends and write a biography: the social, cultural, historical, economic, and opportunity contexts that have given shape to all the things that friend does and thinks and says, the strategies they developed through life with the people and resources that were available to them. To do this, you would need participant observation, a lot of time, a lot of questioning, talking to people, reading records, etc. You would not, however, sit in your room and ruminate and talk to yourself about your friend. (Writers even go out and do research for the *fictitious* characters they portray, let alone material for biographies.)

The comparison I am trying to make is that if I now ask you *to do the same for yourself* as you did for your friend, *the methods should not be different;* you should not sit in your room and ruminate on your true inner being or your navel, which merely builds new persuasive words around a new image of yourself, or perhaps constructs how you would like to be viewed by people.

True self-awareness, paradoxically perhaps, requires you going outside and analysing everything you can about your own social, cultural, historical, economic, and opportunity contexts that gave and will give shape to all the things you do and think and say, the strategies you have developed through life with people, and resources that were available. You would need participant observation of yourself (observing and recording systematically what it is that you actually do, say, and think all day and the contexts in which they occur), a lot of time, a lot of questioning, talking to people, reading records, etc.

Summary

- 'Beliefs', such as self-image beliefs, the 'core beliefs' of RET, or the uncontrollable and distressing worries which are central to GAD, can be understood by contextually observing and describing the social and cultural contexts in which they have been uttered and the consequences they have had on audiences.

- In modernity, 'not acting functionally' can be seen in the DSM as the equivalent of 'being irrational means you are insane', where 'functional' nowadays means in a 'normal' Western lifestyle manner with a job and small family, and obeying rational economic principles.

- Being rational is not so much about following logic as it is about rejecting other external social shaping of our language use; acting 'irrationally' is always a case of strong alternative social consequences, as is acting 'non-functionally'.

- If you wish to categorize behaviour as being irrational or non-functional, this really means that you have not properly investigated all the contexts.

- The whole Western capitalist system is predicated on a purely economic rationalism which ignores the value or consequences of alternative social, cultural, and other contexts which might be more important in that person's life but do not enter the equations.

- The opposite of rationality is not madness, but socialness; one is about resources, one about social relationships.

- Identity is how we talk to people about ourselves and show ourselves to others; it is not done for fun but is strategic to get the resources and social relationships we need or want for ourselves and our families and communities; but identity statements can be checked so limits are usually drawn as to what can be said.

- Therefore, with the advent of modernity (late 1800s), when the vast majority of our relationships shifted to strangers (non-kin), the social properties or logic of identity also changed.

- Because of these new social properties of living in stranger relationships, we now actually need to spend more time constructing our identities and positions in this modern world, to get what we need; this happened when our resources for life stopped coming through family and was replaced by having to convince strangers about who we are and why we should get what we need (for jobs, reputations, relationships, kudos).
- Just talking about yourself is not self-awareness, not even when talking as if to yourself about yourself alone in your room; talking about yourself is really about rehearing ways to influence your various audiences to see you in certain ways.

References

Abbink, J. (1993). Reading the entrails: Analysis of an African divination discourse. *Man* (N.S.), *28*, 705–726.

Basu, H. (2014). Listening to disembodied voices: Anthropological and psychiatric challenges. *Anthropology & Medicine*, *21*, 325–342.

Bauman, Z., & Raud, R. (2013). *Practices of selfhood*. London: Polity Press.

Beattie, J. H. M. (1970). On understanding ritual. In B. R. Wilson (Ed.), *Rationality* (pp. 240–268). Oxford: Basil Blackwell.

Bernard, M. E. (1981). Private thought in RET. *Cognitive Therapy and Research*, *5*, 125–142.

Durkheim, E. (1951/1897). *Suicide: A study in sociology*. Glencoe, IL: Free Press.

Edwards, D. (1997). *Discourse and cognition*. London: SAGE.

Ellis, A. (1994). *Reason and emotion in psychotherapy*. New York: Birch Lane.

Evans-Pritchard, E. E. (1976/1937). *Witchcraft, oracles, and magic among the Azande*. Oxford: Clarendon Press.

Fernyhough, C. (2016). *The voices within: The history and science of how we talk to ourselves*. London: Wellcome Collection.

Foucault, M. (2009). *History of madness*. London: Routledge.

Galletly, C., & Crichton, J. (2011). Accomplishments of the thought disordered person: A case study in psychiatrist–patient interaction. *Medical Hypotheses*, *77*, 900–904.

Guerin, B. (2001). Individuals as social relationships: 18 ways that acting alone can be thought of as social behavior. *Review of General Psychology*, *5*, 406–428.

Guerin, B. (2004). *Handbook for analyzing the social strategies of everyday life*. Reno, NV: Context Press.

Guerin, B. (2005). *Handbook of interventions for changing people and communities*. Reno, NV: Context Press.

Guerin, B. (2016a). *How to rethink psychology: New metaphors for understanding people and their behavior*. London: Routledge.

Guerin, B. (2016b). *How to rethink human behavior: A practical guide to social contextual analysis*. London: Routledge.

Hayward, M., Awenat, Y., McCarthy Jones, S., Paulik, G., & Berry, K. (2015). Beyond beliefs: A qualitative study of people's opinions about their changing relations with their voices. *Psychosis*, *7*(2), 97–107.

Herbert, F. (1969). *Dune messiah*. New York: G. P. Putnam's Sons.

Leudar, I., & Thomas, P. (2000). *Voices of reason, voices of insanity: Studies of verbal hallucinations*. London: Psychology Press.

Longden, E., Corstens, D., Escher, S., & Romme, M. (2012). Voice hearing in a biographical context: A model for formulating the relationship between voices and life history. *Psychosis, 4*, 224–234.

Merrin, J., Kinderman, P., & Bentall, R. P. (2007). 'Jumping to conclusions' and attributional style in persecutory delusions. *Cognitive Therapy and Research, 31*, 741–758.

Monestès, J. L., Villatte, M.., Stewart, I., & Loas, G. (2014). Rule-based insensitivity and delusion maintenance in schizophrenia. *Psychological Record, 64*, 329–338.

Myers, F. R. (1991). *Pintupi country, Pintupi self: Sentiment, place, and politics among Western Desert Aborigines*. Los Angeles: University of California Press.

Neacsiu, A. D., Rizvi, S. L., & Linehan, M. M. (2010). Dialectical behaviour therapy skills use as a mediator and outcome of treatment for borderline personality disorder. *Behaviour Research and Therapy, 48*, 832–839.

Potter, J. (1996). *Representing reality: Discourse, rhetoric and social construction*. London: SAGE.

Potter, J., & Wetherell, M. (1988). Accomplishing attitudes: Fact in racist discourse. *Text, 8*, 51–68.

Pouillon, J. (1979/1982). Remarks on the verb 'To believe'. In M. Izard & P. Smith (Eds.), *Between belief and transgression: Structural essays in religion, history, and myth* (pp. 1–8). Chicago, IL: University of Chicago Press.

Putcha, C., & Potter, J. (2002). Manufacturing individual opinions: Market research focus groups and the discursive psychology of evaluation. *British Journal of Social Psychology, 41*, 345–363.

Rankin, P., Bentall, R., Hill, J., & Kinderman, P. (2005). Perceived relationships with parents and paranoid delusions: Comparisons of currently ill, remitted and normal patients. *Psychopathology, 38*, 16–25.

Romme, M., Escher, S., Dillon, J., Corstens, D., & Morris, M. (2009). *Living with voices: 50 stories of recovery*. London: PCCS Books.

Rose, N. (1999). *Governing the soul: The shaping of the private self* (2nd Ed.). London: Free Association Books.

Wells, A. (1995). The metacognitive model of GAD: Assessment of meta-worry and relationship with DSM-IV generalized anxiety disorder. *Cognitive Therapy and Research, 29*, 107–121.

7

CONTEXTS FOR SOCIETAL OPPRESSION

Being female, poor, or with a refugee background

In the last two chapters I will look more closely at the mental health contexts of a few select groups of people—women, poor, refugees, and Indigenous peoples. However, defining them by these groups does not mean that the issues are about that group of people *per se*. The issues are about *the contexts for those groups of people*, most of which are not under their control and occur through no fault of their own.

What the next two chapters are about

Having said that, we will find that all these groups have historically had their suffering blamed on something about themselves—their essence, their genetic makeup, their race, their 'inherent' characters, etc. This is the same story we heard in Chapter 1 (Table 1.1): the contexts that give rise to the suffering for these groups are not easy to observe, especially when professionals are not motivated to look, and so their suffering is blamed or explained by some abstract characteristic about themselves. That the categorization of these groups in the first place is discursive or socially constructed, a *language event*, is also forgotten.

This also means that the research and interventions for these groups of people, to reduce their suffering, have been looking in the wrong places. We can see people in pain, but we cannot see the contexts or sources of that pain, so we assume it is something inherent in those people as a group, and they need changing. This is the same wrong reasoning that formed the vast construction of 'individual' characteristics assigned to those suffering in isolation, which I tried to rethink in Chapters 4 to 6. Here, however, instead of the abstract constructs of 'mental disorders', we have abstract constructs about the whole group that is said to be the source of the suffering: 'Women are weaker'; 'Gay men have a hormone imbalance'; 'Slaves are lazy'; 'Indigenous peoples are not rational'; etc. But every time a researcher has actually gone looking for the real contexts of the people in these groups, the contextual sources can be found, unlike Kraepelin's brain lesions.

Given these three points—the groups suffer because of common contexts, they have usually been assigned a group characteristic to 'explain' the issues, and the research and interventions are erroneously based on the second point and measuring the wrong things—my goal will be to loosely explore the full contexts for a few of these groups of people. This is not to answer all the questions, but to get the reader, and hopefully researchers, to start looking in new places for the contexts from which arise the stress, anguish, and suffering which we see all too clearly, and without blaming this on the victimized groups.

What the next two chapters are not about

While there are literatures and research on some of these groups, it was not worthwhile reviewing a lot of that material (which I have done, nonetheless, but not here). Almost all this research automatically assumes the DSM diagnoses, as part of the very conception and methodology of the research, and then proceeds to correlate the diagnoses with *abstract* features of these groups (Jorn, 2006). All of this is completely divorced from the life contexts of the people in those groups, and loses both the contexts and the diversity.

If, for example, you look up 'mental health and women' you will find a lot of data about which diagnoses of 'mental health diseases' women get more than men. You will find a lot of statistics about prevalence rates of DSM diagnoses and *speculation* about how women got those diseases more than men—the factors that might have led to those diseases. Some look to societal factors that differ between men and women but, sadly, a lot draw the speculation from 'biological' differences between men and women. In particular, there is a huge and very unsophisticated emphasis on menstruation, pregnancy and post-partum depression, and menopause, to explain almost any difference in 'odd' behaviour. While these are certainly issues which do not occur for men, and can certainly cause suffering, the whole context for women is being ignored when focusing on these. And, moreover, *how women deal with these three events in life could be a result of how they are in general treated by men and society, not a result of those events themselves.* This is the history problem we saw in Chapter 2. If we provided a better social context for women in society then these three events might not lead to any issues except positive ones.

So, my point is that while we can learn some things from the typical literature search of these topics, we are not learning about the contexts for women nor about the specific behaviours involved in the sense of Chapter 4. We need to get to the stage of describing the specific behaviours rather than 'disease syndromes', and describe the contexts in which the specific women live. This chapter is to commence that work but I will not get very far.

As one example, a very good review of research studies by Fryers, Melzer, and Jenkins (2003) found that eight of the nine good studies they located showed a strong correlation between some measure of social inequality and common mental health disorders. But the measures of inequality were broad (occupational status, standard of living) and the measures of mental health were all standardized DSM questionnaires or interviews (GHQ-12, Diagnostic Interview Schedule; see their table 2). This is useful but any connections between the two will always be guesses or interpretations if further contextual observations are not made.

My question, therefore, for these next two chapters is not 'What causes mental illness for these groups of people?' The question will be 'What are the hidden contexts for some groups of people, people who share similar contexts with those in their groups, and what is hidden and so gives rise to the "mental health" behaviours are recorded?'

A final word about what these chapters will not be about. I am limiting this discussion to a few select groups, which does not mean that other groups are not also important. This is done because of space limitations and the limits of my experience with groups. Moreover, within these groups I will only be raising some of the contexts that are probably important.

Think of my role here as showing you a few examples of how the hidden contexts behind some *group labels* lead to suffering for which the origins are not clear ('mental'). This is a goad for you to take all this further into the details and to other groups I have not covered here (e.g. Carr, 2005; Riggs & Treharne, 2016). There is just so much diversity in all this that a full story can only be made in very specific details for specific groups of people. My bland statements about these 'groups-in-general' are only useful to show you the way to do more specific analyses and interventions with the very specific people you are working with.

What we will find

There are, of course, and luckily for us, good researchers and good practitioners who have looked for the contexts behind the group labels

(Chapters 7 and 8) as well as the DSM labels (Chapters 4 to 6). We will find some of the same contexts re-appearing but also some new ones. In particular, where particular types of suffering *seem to occur for everyone in such large groups* we will likewise discover *large societal structures, patterns or contexts* which give rise to those sufferings (Smail, 2005, 2012), not something built into thousands of those persons.

In Chapter 2 we saw the importance of the *opportunities* available in a person's context—having fewer opportunities greatly changes life in very complex and real ways but which are difficult to see. And fewer opportunities also limits not just what a person might do but also how they might overcome the many conflicts that occur in life, a lack of resources, suffering, and changing their contexts to ones that show more promise of being happy (Table 4.1). And finally, to make matters worse, the majority of situations in which there are reduced opportunities in this world are not of the person's making. People should not be blamed and should not suffer throughout their lifetime just because they were born without rich parents, were born with the wrong colour or body shape, were born into a pre-existing group in society who are given fewer opportunities, or were born in the wrong place on the planet we all share.

Sadly, however, people *are* blamed for these contexts which are not within their control and which mostly pre-existed before they were born, and they suffer for these contexts over which they have no control. So for mental health we come straight into a difficult situation. Some people are born through no fault of their own into difficult situations and conflicts (Table 4.1), and part of the problem is that they do not have the resources or the opportunities to obtain resources by which they might change those difficult situations or solve those conflicts. So they stay in conflict and remain stressed. Further, how this whole system works is very difficult to observe or even analyse, so the situation appears both helpless and hopeless, and everything looks to be wrong with that person—and therefore is called a 'mental' or 'psychological' issue.

Societal oppression

Every society has its own ways of oppressing some of the population, usually with the aim of helping to facilitate resources for either the majority of the people (a nicer interpretation) or just for a powerful minority (more common). The groups vary markedly and I am not going to bother trying to outline most, because that requires idiosyncratic analyses by those who know far more than I do. Many of the groups in Chapters 7 and 8 fall into this category, but even the social exclusion of people through racism or violence has multiple mental health effects (e.g. Kelaher, Ferdinand, & Paradies, 2014). Oppressing some of society to favour either the very rich or the middle-class majority is a hallmark of capitalism, and we saw some of the mental health effects of capitalism in Chapter 5 (Cryan, Shatil, & Piero, 2013; de Soto, 2000; Marx, 1962; Polanyi, 1944; Sandal, 2012; Smail, 2005, 2012; Stiglitz, 2013).

What seems most weird about the mental health effects of societal oppressions is that the link has not occurred to many Western psychiatrists and psychologists. In particular, the DSM has scant regard for such links. The problem, of course, is that the links between mental health behaviours and societal oppressions are multiple, diverse, idiosyncratic, and difficult to observe directly, can be spoken about in alternative and more societally acceptable ways, and finding them is not in the interest of those benefitting from the privileges gained through the lifetime oppression of others. The correlations are well known but the links are just coming to the foreground in research because the more detailed contexts have not typically been observed and analysed (e.g. Fryers et al., 2003; Kelaher et al., 2014; McGibbon, 2012a; Paradies, 2016; Shevlin, O'Neill, Houston, Read, Bentall, & Murphy, 2013).

The links between mental health behaviours and societal oppressions are also mixed in with effects that have nothing to do with mental health directly, including physical health (McGibbon, 2012b). This means that any of those other in-between links can be used as the 'reason' for mental health behaviours. For example, mental illness can be said to arise from poor physical health, when actually the poor physical health is a result of a lifetime of societal oppression (or rather, from the contexts this engenders). I have seen women's mental health 'explained' as a problem because it is said that women focus and even obsess about their looks and attractiveness. But again this only arises from a lifetime of society forcing women to focus and obsess in these ways. But those last steps are not observed in detail so they get left out and the individuals are left to blame.

So, societal oppression has numerous effects as a context of trying to engage in life, and includes stress, depression, chronic worry about everything (economics, all the opportunities contexts), racism, and violence (McGibbon, 2012b; Watson & Eack, 2011).

The life contexts of being a woman

The question for this section, for which a lot of people already know some answers (Williams, 2005) but for which there is scant documentation (or an unwillingness to accept the documentation), is this: what are the different contexts for women that arise from the way society is structured and run (Table 4.1)? What contexts do men typically not have to deal with or stress about? What extra conflicts and stresses do women typically have to deal with, and how do these run their course and give rise to the behaviours that eventually become labelled as 'mental health' issues?

In many places in the world, despite great improvements towards equality, women experience many restricted opportunity contexts compared to men. In most 'developed' Western countries, for example, there has in principle been equal pay for women for many years but, on average, women still earn less than men who do exactly the same job. There are still more men at the top of most job structures, and there are still many more male politicians in parliaments around the world making decisions for everyone. Some of these are a result of the changes being gradual, but many are taking far longer than is necessary. What this means, of course, is that to gain their resources and maintain their relationships, women need to find ways other than money to do them but doing so can engender more conflict and stress (Williams, 2005).

You need to spend time observing and getting a gut feel for this, even for some women, since the links are not always salient in the context (hence they get called 'psychological' or 'mental' as we saw in Chapter 1). From an early age women learn by seeing around them and on media that men do more, get more, have higher positions, higher salaries, etc. Opportunities are fewer in most areas of life, and assumptions are made about what men and women can do regardless of the huge diversity when comparing 3.5 billion people to another 3.5 billion people. (This is actually an absurd comparison to make for any reason and under any circumstances, but I will leave that rant for another day.)

To explain these supposed differences (since the societal contexts from which they really arise are not salient), women face the problem of a large series of stereotypes about their looks and what is good and bad behaviour, as well as specific 'character' stereotypes—they are not aggressive, dependent, easily influenced, submissive, passive, home-oriented, easily hurt emotionally, indecisive, talkative, gentle, sensitive to feelings, wanting security, frequently crying, emotional, nurturing (taken from lists I have found). If you learn more about the contexts for women in their societal life, many of these stereotypes might seem applicable for at least some women. But this is not because 'women' are like that, but because the pressures and stresses they are put in from contexts arising in their societies. For example, women are sometimes said to be 'indecisive' but this can merely be a result of constant life contexts in which men interrupt decision-making for women and overrule whatever a woman might decide anyway, and no matter what they choose they will be less likely to succeed.

The point here is not that these stereotypes are correct but that they arise from society. The point is that cases of these might occur but even when they do, they arise from the many impossible situations of conflict women are made to endure from the way that society is structured through a dominant patriarchy. Your job is to spend more time observing contexts in which women have to live, and learn how the behaviours arise from those social contexts. These abstract 'explanations' for women's 'odd' or 'deviant' behaviours, which are brought about by societal structures, especially forms of patriarchy, but are difficult to observe, go back a long way in Western cultures (Appignanesi, 2008; Arnold, 2008; Astbury, 1996; Briggs, 1996; Demos, 1982; Federici, 2004; Laing & Esterson, 1964; Scull, 2009; Showalte, 1987; Skultans, 1975; Trevor-Roper, 1967).

In terms of social relationships, women around the world have far greater limits and fewer opportunities than males. Women are more likely to have: violence inflicted on them; greater likelihood that the perpetrators will not be held responsible; more people commanding what they do; more likely to be stared at, watched, and judged by strangers; more likely to be interrupted by men; and more likely to receive unwanted harassment.

> We regard the effects of men's violence against women as crucial in understanding women's current psychology. Men's violence creates ever-present—and therefore often unrecognized—terror in women. For instance, this terror is experienced as a fear, by any woman, of rape by any man or as a fear of making a man—any man—angry. We propose that women's current psychology is actually a psychology of women under conditions of captivity—that is, under conditions of terror caused by male violence against women.
>
> *(Graham, Rawlings, & Rigsby, 1994, pp. xiii–xiv)*

So, it is not that women—because they are women—experience mental health more often or differently. The problem is that they are more likely to experience social, economic, cultural, opportunity, and historic contexts very differently and have overall reduced opportunities and hence become more dependent through no fault of their own (Guerin, 2016; Williams, 2005). If there are gender differences, this is from where they arise, and this is what you must go hunting for since they are not obvious to short-term or easy observations—it all looks like the woman's fault.

As a more detailed example, Williams (2005) looked at how the societal inequalities can shape women's behaviour in different ways to men and lead to seemingly inexplicable behaviours which are called 'psychological' or 'mental'. She highlighted these: reduced opportunities to access resources including money, work, and status and value; increased exposure to unhealthy contexts due to devalued and unpaid labour (housework, unpaid child care), relationships with men who have privilege, and more exposure to violent contexts and abuse; and exposure to processes that maintain the current inequalities such as concepts of what it is to be feminine and masculine, what it is to be a 'good woman', maintaining health as a woman, managing anger of men, and being blamed even when a victim. If you consider these as typical contexts for being a woman then analysing the so-called 'mental illness' behaviours will follow from these contexts, not from properties of being a woman *per se*. Therapists can, if they wanted to, ask about these.

The difficult part of observing context then is to reconcile that *observing individual males and females interacting is already replete with societal context, and patriarchy in particular for women*. One way you might like to try thinking about this is to observe the individual behaviours (a bit like Chapter 4), and then think about and find ways to make further observations and answer these questions: what contexts have engendered those behaviours; what contexts have let these individuals carry out this interaction; and a particularly good question to help you see the bigger contexts, *what societal privileges have allowed the man to do certain behaviours and succeed only because there is societal support for what he is doing?*

As an example to help you rethink and observe the societal-within-individual-behaviours, Marcela Ortolan and I collected numerous behaviours commonly carried out by men who are abusive in social relationships with women (Guerin & Ortolan, 2017). We did a number of analyses with these materials but we arrived at some possible groups of functional (for the male) but unwanted (for the female) strategies. For example, there were many behaviours which were all seemingly directed towards getting control of the resources in the relationship and using them for control over the women's behaviour.

The point here is that when analysing these it became clear that the men in these situations cannot just successfully carry out these behaviours as individuals, even though they are physically acting as individuals in the relationships. *The individual-looking strategies only work to gain control because society and patriarchy allow that the man can succeed.* The man is not succeeding in these strategies because of their personal abilities, because they have better ways and better social skills; they are only succeeding in such strategies against the woman because society backs their behaviours and provides punishing consequences for women if they oppose.

For example, under a category of behaviours involving verbal or emotional abuse, there are these three more specific examples: 'Putting her down'; 'Making her feel bad about herself'; and 'Calling her names.' The point is that without the societal endorsement that males can interrupt, override, verbally bully, persist in raising the stakes, and endorse without penalty, most of these men would never be successful in carrying out these strategies. They are not that good actually.

So, it was argued that the functional strategies of the men which appeared in our analyses can only succeed within broader social and political contexts. This means that to analyse the behaviours of domestic violence it is necessary to use broader visions, such as those found in political and feminist analyses. The analysis of domestic violence *must* involve more than just the two individuals behaving. Even what is considered 'private' or 'intimate' behaviours within social relationships is made possible by the patriarchal and capitalist bases of modernity. This sort of analysis requires skills way beyond those taught to psychiatrists and psychologists (Rose, 1962; Weisstein, 1971, 1993).

The societal control embedded in individual actions, talking, and thinking, are what you must learn to observe in your contextual observations over time, rather than a micro-physical description of just what you see in front of you at the time. This is difficult, but that is the very reason, as I keep pointing out, that such behaviours are called 'psychological' or 'mental' and any 'odd' or 'deviant' behaviours labelled as 'mental illnesses'.

Table 7.1 has some contexts that you should consider before trying to analyse the 'mental health' issues of women. But there is a lot more to be done.

TABLE 7.1 Unequal contexts for women which need to be taken into account when trying to understand the issues and suffering they go through

- women have fewer opportunities overall, of all sorts
- women have fewer economic opportunities in particular
- men are supported by society ('patriarchy') to dominate situations
- women less safe and need to strategize for this
- women are expected to have certain appearances more than men
- women have limits on how far they can succeed (called glass ceilings because they are hidden contexts and therefore relevant to mental health)
- women experience more violence towards them whether physical, sexual, or bullying
- women more likely to be watched or monitored by family, friends, and strangers
- women less likely to go higher in positions within work or communities
- women have extensive language categories built around how they should act, talk, and think; what it is to be feminine and how they should look

The life contexts of being poor

Being poor, lower socio-economic status or in poverty have almost always given high correlations with diagnosed 'mental health' disorders (Cochrane, 1983; Evans, Wells, Chan, & Saltzman, 2000; Fryer & Fagan, 2003; McLeod & Nonnemaker, 1999; Meich & Shanahan, 2000; Rank, 2011; Read & Bentall, 2010; Ross, 2000; Walker, Johnson, & Cunningham, 2012; Wise, 2011; Yu & Williams, 1999). The problem is that this alone does not tell us much, and certainly gives few ideas for interventions. As we know from early university level study, correlations can appear strong but arise from different pathways. And like the contexts for being female, this can affect different people and groups differently. Finally, like all the groups in this chapter, the measures have been very abstract indices of 'socio-economic status' correlated with gross mental health abstractions such as DSM diagnoses.

With respect to the embedded societal contexts, there are two main points that have been made:

• There are complex pathways for 'mental health' behaviours to arise from a context of being poor, with two main paths: (1) having the behaviours (from other life conflicts) can lead to loss of resources and hence poverty; and (2) not having enough resources can lead to the behaviours.
• The context of being poor is less about how society views or stereotypes people in poverty (less than for women, for example) and more about basic properties of the economic system and its workings as we saw in Chapters 2 and 5—just being powerless to do things and achieve things because of a lack of resources and lack of privileges and being stressed and in conflicts from this context.

As noted in Chapter 2, the 'lack of resources' is not just the material things but also the social relationships through which we gain resources in life (or 'social capital'; Webber, 2005). The problem for analysis is that there are so many pathways from poverty or 'low economic status' to responding in ways that can be deemed 'mental health' issues. They are serious behaviours but just knowing there is a correlation between poverty and such behaviours helps very little.

Basically, being poor in modernity (Chapter 5) means you will be constantly reacting and in conflict over most interactions you have, since all relationships now involve money and there will be insufficient of this to do smooth transactions (Table 4.1). This can therefore arise from so many sources in so many ways, leading to stress and unresolved conflict situations. This in turn means that many behaviours will be tried and exaggerated in order to succeed, including ones later deemed 'mental health' issues. But in the original conflict situation they might have been the only behaviours that worked initially.

If you refer back to, and read, the papers listed at the top of this section, you can see there are many situations within a 'poor life' that prove difficult—neighbourhood, housing quality, childhood adversity, all forms of opportunities and lack of privileged, access to resources, collateral physical health issues, homelessness, unemployment, and lack of social capital in relationships. Further, while some people become poor within their lifespan, we know from Chapter 5 that most are born in such contexts through no fault of their own, with few ways of avoiding this context.

What this all means is that the behaviours arising from contexts of being poor will be many and subtle, and not captured in broad abstract correlations between questionnaire measures of both context and behaviour (as suggested by Fryer & Fagan, 2003).

Box 7.1

Some of the subtleties were captured in a popular forum by Rios (2015), as '*7 everyday things poor people worry about that rich people never do*':

- We're not planning for the future—we're planning for right now
- We have to make money (and purchases) last as long as possible
- The risk of emergencies and other costs informs almost every decision we make
- Affording shared experiences is a luxury we often don't have
- Getting to work and back home again is often not an option
- We're constantly trying to figure out what we can sacrifice to save money
- Asking for help in this culture is often painful and shame-inducing

---

All these promote extra stress and will produce behaviours that are not likely to make sense to outsiders. This, as the reader should be alert to by now, means they will be attributed to an internal choice or decision which looks bizarre and therefore seen by outsiders as 'mental health' issues (irrational or non-functional). To trace and analyse these more subtle pathways from a large set of poor life conditions to the 'mental health' behaviours that arise

TABLE 7.2 Unequal contexts for poor or low socio-economic status people which need to be taken into account when trying to understand the issues and suffering they go through

---

- the poor have fewer opportunities overall, of all sorts
- the poor have fewer economic opportunities in particular
- mental health symptoms of many sorts can lead to being poor
- the wealthy are supported by society to dominate situations
- the poor are further disadvantaged in modernity because money is expected for any sorts of actions or accomplishments
- the poor will have conflicts and problems in most areas of life because of the capitalist system
- the poor will have restricted social access since social relationships in modernity depend upon capital
- the poor have extensive language categories built around how they should act, talk, and think; what it is to be poor and how they should look
- because of this, there will be a lot of avoidance of situations further exacerbating any other effects

---

needs to be done, therefore, in a very idiosyncratic and community-based way (Fryer & Fagan, 2003).

Table 7.2 tries to summarize some of the contexts for poor or low socio-economic people which must be taken into account when working with behaviours that look like mental health issues. They are likely to arise out of these contexts and not something inherent in the person themselves.

The life contexts of those with a refugee background

This next section will explore some different contexts in which people with a background as a refugee live, and which have (again) commonly been associated (correlated) with mental health issues. As we have seen already, this has usually been done by giving broad abstract measures of the 'context' and then correlating this with questionnaire or standard short-interview measures of mental health based on DSM categories (e.g. Ahearns, 2000; Fazel, Wheeler, & Danesh, 2005; Stafford, Newbold, & Ross, 2010).

So, the review mentioned above, while interesting, interpreted the results as refugees being about 10 times more likely to have PTSD, whereas it should have been interpreted as '10 times more likely to be diagnosed as PTSD' or '10 times more likely to be in situations which produce strategic behaviours which can be diagnosed as PTSD' (Fazel et al., 2005). The diverse life activities and contexts of the 7,000 people recorded, from which arose the abstract symptoms, have been lost. For the validity of the measures it is usually emphasized that the interview schedules are all standardized, but this can also be seen as a loss of validity—any diversity of the participants' lives has been lost in the generalities and standardization and cannot be recovered.

My message from all this is still the same—we must explore the contexts in which these people find themselves, whether by birth or tragedy, and how the behaviours arise from these contexts. This is the time to re-learn the opening statement of this book:

> People do not 'have mental illness'; people live, and have lived,
> in contexts that do not support healthy behaviours.

We have explored some of those contexts for women and people in low socio-economic contexts but now we come to a real mixture of people who find themselves out of their 'normal' contexts (refugees, immigrants), of a wrong race or religion for the country in which they are living (race, refugees), or in another minority situation within the country they now live.

Refugees and their contexts. A lot has been written about the mental health of refugees. As a group, they are extremely diverse and it should be clear that any similar 'mental health' behaviours between these groups arise from many different contexts and social strategies. However, there are some contexts that refugees of diverse backgrounds share, merely because the process of becoming and being a refugee has some similar properties, not because of any essential properties of those people themselves.

I wish to go through just some of the common contexts for refugees. This will not apply to all and every refugee; no claim is made to that. However, these properties are worth checking if you are working with people with a refugee background. Even calling these people 'refugees' labels them as having some intrinsic properties—so they are not 'refugees' but people who have lived through a refugee context in their background at some point. To paraphrase: *people do not have 'refugee-ness'; people live, and have lived, in refugee contexts.*

Refugees are a hugely diverse group, primarily because all they share is the refugee context in their past. But this past is diverse, with people fleeing from wars and conflicts, environmental disasters, and bad economic contexts. The problem again, as we have seen all through this book, is that once they are named as 'refugees', professionals and others begin assuming they know the contexts for that person (purely based on that word 'refugee') and they no longer observe the diversity and real-life complexities.

We can, however, begin by sorting through several contexts that are very common for refugee groups. You should not assume that any people of refugee origin you meet will automatically share these properties, nor assume that they are the only relevant properties or the most important.

The idea is to get you thinking about the contexts or environments within which people live, and have lived, and which might lead to their problems or issues and difficulties coping with their lives (poor mental health).

For people of refugee backgrounds residing in a new country, Table 7.3 gives some of the common contexts you might be likely to encounter. (It would be worthwhile thinking about how you would cope if you were landed into these contexts, all at once.) The key thing to note is that these are not about the people themselves; they are about past opportunities or lack of opportunities. Within these broad changes in contexts there are many idiosyncratic strategies and life paths. So, frequently refugees will have poor language skills in the host country's language, but this is because they have not been expecting to end up in that country and so have not studied or had experience in that language. Despite this, research I have been involved in found that the people speak many languages—most adults could speak about three!

These opportunity problems are wider, however. Whether children or adults, most of what we might consider 'normal' functional activities of life, especially work and education, are disrupted or absent during time as refugees. So most of the children have had their schooling disrupted, although sometimes they get lessons in the refugee camps. It is also typical that the adults end up unemployed due to many reasons, including discrimination, poor language skills in host language, non-acceptance of qualifications, and lack of documents with them. This context means they are likely to end up in government housing and poorer areas of suburbia.

TABLE 7.3 Common contexts you will observe for the diverse range of people with a refugee background

- absent family members
- strong but disrupted social support within communities
- of different cultural histories to the people around
- possibly different religious practices to those around them
- in a position of being a societal minority group
- a history of bad events which have occurred sometime in their (recent) past
- poor or mediocre language skills of host country
- previous strategies of social influence and organization probably do not work outside of their community but possibly inside as well
- living in very new or uncertain life arrangements
- interruptions in schooling and education not recognized
- unemployment and low income (because of other contexts not because they are unemployable)
- poorer housing and neighbourhoods (ditto)
- weak support or explicit discrimination from the outside community
- stronger support within their community

Socially, almost everyone in a refuge community has missing family members: killed, lost, or accepted in another country. Apart from the stress and sadness of this, it also means that families and communities are 'disrupted', in the sense that their normal community structure of people is not present. There might be fewer males, for examples, especially those who have leadership qualities, so running the community has to be developed in new ways. It might also mean fewer elders are there to help guide the young people. So when they report that they are 'missing' their family members this has a variety of contextual effects, not just the sadness that is present.

But it is not just about the previous contexts through which refugees have been exposed. Refugees in a new country also get exposed to new contexts. In our research, for example, we found, as others have, that the children get exposure to these contexts (again, these are generalities):

- observations of new behaviour patterns
- observations of other children not heeding their parents and elders
- easier availability of things prohibited in the community
- the importance of money over family
- a focus on time and time regulations
- better training than parents in the host language
- importance of non-family peers over family
- potential 'romantic' partners outside community.

The other common new context which refugees usually get exposed to are those of a hostile, racist, or discriminatory social environment. I do not have space in this book to look at the 'mental health' contexts of minority groups (see Chapter 6 of Guerin, 2004) but there are mental health affects measured from just being a minority group (Brown, Sellers, Brown, & Jackson, 1999; Ferns, 2005; Miehls, 2011). This can also arise from having cultural practices which are a minority within the society in which you are living, although this already contains many layers of contexts and is more complex than it seems (Kirmayer & Bhugra, 2009).

So the point to learn to observe is that people with refugee backgrounds have had some very difficult and unusual contexts in life to adapt to, and have developed strategies and behaviours to cope, but ones which are often not 'normal', or functional in a Western sense. When diagnosed, therefore, these will lose their contextual salience and, especially with limited exposure to the people's lives, judgements will be made in terms of the persons themselves, their 'race', or their refugeehood as causes.

The special case of PTSD. In my experience a large number of professionals of 'mental health' pretty much take 'refugee' to be synonymous with 'PTSD' and look no further. And because the DSM definition of 'PTSD' is so broad and abstract (Chapter 4), not to even mention its measurement, most of the presenting symptoms or complaints will look like confirmation.

We saw some of the problems with 'trauma-as-cause' in Chapter 2, and we will see more in the next chapter (also Han, 2004). The specific symptoms in the DSM need to be read, but notice that much is vague, much is optional (has 'one (or more) of the following features'), and the symptoms cover almost any behaviours in which the trauma is mentioned.

In all, it is really only saying that a traumatic event has occurred which has affected the life contexts of the person, and this can mean very many different things. It needs to last over a month and 'causes clinically significant distress or impairment in social, occupational, or other important areas of functioning'. But this all occurs in the person's context, not in a disease in their head (or somewhere). What we really need to do is trace the ways that the person's life contexts (relationships, community, economics, opportunities) were altered by their bad experiences, and also trace the behaviours in the DSM to other unrelated sources of stress and conflict. Think back to Figure 2.2.

Working with a community of refugees for many years I observed first hand that professionals jumped to conclusions about PTSD diagnoses. The people had witnessed very bad events, but so had everyone in the community. They did have some of the DSM symptoms as behaviours but there were plenty of other contexts that were bringing these about. For example, many had depressive behaviours but they had many sources for that (see below).

A number of people have made similar points about trauma-related diagnoses, and the overuse of these (Bracken, 2001; Bracken, Giller, & Summerfield, 1997; Bracken & Petty, 1998; Guerin, 2001; Marlowe, 2010; McFarlane & Yehuda, 2000; Salis Gross, 2004; Summerfield, 1999; Zarowsky, 2004). We also saw similar critiques of 'trauma' diagnoses in Chapter 2 (Kirmayer, Gone, & Moses, 2014; Maxwell, 2014; Mohatt, Thompson, Thai, & Tebes, 2014; Paradies, 2016).

While I do not have the answers, it follows from Chapter 2 on history context that a major traumatic event will impact on all a person's contexts. It can change secrecy and trust, the way social relationships function (even with family and close friends), economic contexts, the social shaping of thoughts and intrusive thoughts, etc. (Figure 2.2). Any or all of these can affect other behaviours. For example, in the community I worked with everyone had been through similar trauma so it was accepted but rarely talked about, and was not something particular to a single person in the community or silent because repressed (Guerin, Elmi, & Guerin, 2006). This is why we believed their 'symptoms' of PTSD were arising from other parts of their life, and they told professionals about their trauma only because they were asked to.

But this refugee situation is a very different context to a Western war veteran returning to their former home life: their family will have very little understanding of their traumatic experiences and so they probably keep quiet, leading to further contextual changes in their relationships and economic changes if it begins affecting their life in a bigger way. This means that new ways of working with refugee clients and new treatments are required, and many have been doing this (Briggs & MacLeod, 2008; Carroll, 2004; Eastmond, 2000; McMichael, 2003; Richters, 2014, 2015; Ventevogel, 2015; Ziaian, 2003).

What were the mental health issues in one refugee community? Where does this take us in terms of the context producing the symptoms or complaints labelled as 'mental illnesses'? For this, I will go back to the long-term project in which I was involved (Guerin, Abdi, & Guerin, 2003; Guerin & Guerin, 2007; Guerin, Guerin, Diiriye, & Yates, 2004; Guerin, Diiriye, Corrigan, & Guerin, 2003; Guerin et al., 2006; Guerin & Guerin, 2007; Guerin, Guerin, & Elmi, 2013; Ryan, Guerin, Guerin, & Elmi, 2006).

What we learned I think, in retrospect, was that there were many sources of stress and worry for people in this Somali community (Table 4.1) and the traumas of war were present but not the overarching focus most professionals seemed to assume. Some issues were from social situations, many from economic woes, many from government policy and interference, many were from having to deal with a bureaucratic system that did not ever fit their cases and without the benefit of good English-language skills, and some from family tragedies and family who were not with them (I could tell many of the saddest stories you ever will hear). All were external events which affected them directly in resources and running their lives, or in social relationships and community politics.

From there, there were many subtle and nuanced responses, but which often *resembled*, in general, either our depression/sadness or else our anxiety issues. But what we learned here was that the contexts for these behaviours which resembled what we might call depression and anxiety issues were very different to our (Western, non-refugee) contexts. A PhD student, Juanita Ryan, worked more with the Somali women on their 'mental health' and drew up a figure for her PhD showing how they talked and thought about 'mental health' (Ryan, 2007). (We half-jokingly called this the DSM-S, with S for Somali.) Many of the observable symptom outcomes look similar to the DSM, but the contextual origins were very different, as must be the interventions.

But sadly, like the Indigenous Australians discussed in the next chapter, many of the 'symptoms' arose from difficult events and interactions with governments, bureaucrats, policies, and lack of support. Much of the stress also came from the religious and racial discrimination that was very in-their-face. Much came from missing their absent family members, not just due to the sadness but more from the insurmountable bureaucratic hurdles and rules which prevented them reconnecting with their loved ones who were elsewhere in the world at this stage (McMichael, 2003).

Other stressors leading to 'mental health symptoms' were related to living in a new and often very different society with different practices. Most of the parents were consistently worried about their children in such an environment. Having survived through wars, violence, corrupt officials along the journey, etc., their children were now exposed to many new and seemingly bad influences—even though some of these only seemed bad because the parents did not understand them.

With the groups I have worked with, the parents often stay somewhat isolated from the society in which they now live but the children cannot do this. They at least face exposure through school. They are the ones who often say that they live in two worlds, and have to cope in two worlds, which is another conflict they must face.

The point then, is to emphasize that the 'symptoms' of mental issues are not about some conglomerate of mental disease in the brain or elsewhere but arise from normal stresses and strain and conflicts of everyday life (Table 4.1), ones that are exacerbated for different reasons even if the resulting behaviours looked the same. Like the Indigenous Australians in the final chapter, much of this comes from conflicts around government bureaucracies, bureaucrats, and policies—which should be helping them but the government officials do not listen to or observe the wider contexts in place determining behaviour.

Summary

- Three common points are found for oppressed groups—that the groups suffer because of common contexts, they have usually been assigned essentialistic group characteristics or stereotypes to 'explain' the issues, and the research and interventions are erroneously based on the second point and are measuring the wrong things.

- The goal is therefore to explore the full contexts for these groups of people; we find some of the same contexts reappearing as for anyone but also some new ones, especially societal structure which imposes the same contexts on those people but not others always.

- In particular, where particular types of suffering seem to occur in such large groups we discover large societal structures, patterns, or contexts which give rise to those sufferings, not something built into the brains of thousands of those persons.

References

Ahearns, F. L. (2000). Psychosocial wellness: Methodological approaches to the study of refugees. In F. L. Ahearns (Ed.), *Psychosocial wellness of refugees: Issues in qualitative and quantitative research* (pp. 3–23). New York: Berghahn Books.

Appignanesi, L. (2008). *Mad, bad and sad. A history of women and the mind doctors from 1800 to the present.* London: Virago.

Arnold, C. (2008). *Bedlam: London and its mad.* London: Pocket Books.

Astbury, J. (1996). *Crazy for you: The making of women's madness.* Oxford: Oxford University Press.

Bracken, P. J. (2001). Post-modernity and posttraumatic stress disorder. *Social Science & Medicine, 53,* 733–743.

Bracken, P. J., Giller, J. E., & Summerfield, D. (1995). Psychological responses to war and atrocity: The limitations of current concepts. *Social Science & Medicine, 40,* 1073–1082.

Bracken, P. J., & Petty, C. (Eds.). (1998). *Rethinking the trauma of war.* London: Free Association Books.

Briggs, L., & MacLeod, A. D. (2006). Demoralisation: A useful conceptualisation of non-specific psychological distress among refugees attending mental health services. *International Journal of Social Psychiatry, 52,* 512–524.

Briggs, R. (1996). *Witches and neighbors: The social and cultural context of European witchcraft.* New York: Viking.

Brown, T. N., Sellers, S. L., Brown, K. T., & Jackson, J. S. (1999). Race, ethnicity, and culture in the sociology of mental health. In C. S. Aneshensal & J. C. Phelen (Eds.), *Handbook of the sociology of mental health* (pp. 167–182). New York: Plenum.

Carr, S. (2005). 'The sickness label infected everything we said': Lesbian and gay perspectives on mental distress. In J. Tew (Ed.), *Social perspectives in mental health: Developing social models to understand and work with mental distress* (pp. 168–183). London: Jessica Kingsley.

Carroll, J. K. (2004). Murug, waali, and gini: Expressions of distress in refugees from Somalia. *Primary Care Companion and Journal of Clinical Psychiatry, 6,* 119–125.

Cochrane, R. (1983). *The social creation of mental illness.* London: Longman.

Cryan, D., Shatil, S., & Piero. (2013). *Introducing capitalism: A graphic guide.* London: Icon.

Demos, J. P. (1982). *Entertaining Satan: Witchcraft and the culture of early New England.* London: Oxford University Press.

de Soto, H. (2000). *The mystery of capital: Why capitalism triumphs in the West and fails everywhere else.* London: Black Swan.

Eastmond, M. (2000). Refugees and health: Ethnographic approaches. In F. L. Ahearns (Ed.), *Psychosocial wellness of refugees: Issues in qualitative and quantitative research* (pp. 67–87). New York: Berghahn Books.

Evans, G. W., Wells, N. M., Chan, H-Y. E., & Saltzman, H. (2000). Housing quality and mental health. *Journal of Consulting and Clinical Psychology, 68,* 526–530.

Fazel, M., Wheeler, J., & Danesh, J. (2005). Prevalence of serious mental disorder in 7000 refugees resettled in western countries: A systematic review. *Lancet, 365,* 1309–1314.

Federici, S. (2004). *Caliban and the witch: Women, the body and primitive accumulation.* New York: Autonomedia.

Ferns, P. (2005). Finding a way forward: A Black perspective on social approaches to mental health. In J. Tew (Ed.), *Social perspectives in mental health: Developing social models to understand and work with mental distress* (pp. 129–150). London: Jessica Kingsley.

Fryer, D., & Fagan, R. (2003). Towards a critical community psychological perspective on unemployment and mental health research. *American Journal of Community Psychology, 32,* 89–96.

Fryers, T., Melzer, D., & Jenkins, R. (2003). Social inequalities and the common mental disorders. *Social Psychiatry and Psychiatric Epidemiology, 38,* 229–237.

Graham, D. L. R., Rawlings, E. I., & Rigsby, R. K. (1994). *Loving to survive: Sexual terror, men's violence, and women's lives.* New York: New York University Press.

Guerin, B. (2001). Explanations of bereavement, grief, and trauma: The misuse of both mental and foundational terms. *European Journal of Behaviour Analysis, 2,* 154–161.

Guerin, B. (2004). *Handbook for analyzing the social strategies of everyday life.* Reno, NV: Context Press.

Guerin, B. (2016). *How to rethink human behavior: A practical guide to social contextual analysis.* London: Routledge.

Guerin, B., Abdi, A., & Guerin, P. B. (2003). Experiences with the medical and health systems for Somali refugees living in Hamilton. *New Zealand Journal of Psychology, 32,* 27–32.

Guerin, B., & Guerin, P. (2007). Lessons learned from participatory discrimination research: Long-term observations and local interventions. *The Australian Community Psychologist, 19,* 137–149.

Guerin, B., & Ortolan, M. O. (2017). Analyzing domestic violence behaviors in their contexts: Violence as a continuation of social strategies by other means. *Behavior and Social Issues, 26.*

Guerin, B., Guerin, P. B., Diiriye, R. O., & Yates, S. (2004). Somali conceptions and expectations of mental health: Some guidelines for mental health professionals. *New Zealand Journal of Psychology, 33,* 59–67.

Guerin, P., & Guerin, B. (2007). Research with refugee communities: Going around in circles with methodology. *The Australian Community Psychologist, 19,* 150–162.

Guerin, P., Guerin, B., & Elmi, F. H. (2013). How do you acculturate when neighbors are throwing rocks in your window? Preserving the contexts of Somali refugee housing issues in policy. *International Journal of Sociology and Anthropology, 5,* 41–49.

Guerin, P. B., Diiriye, R. O., Corrigan, C., & Guerin, B. (2003). Physical activity programs for refugee Somali women: Working out in a new country. *Women & Health, 38,* 83–99.

Guerin, P. B., Elmi, F. H., & Guerin, B. (2006). Weddings and parties: Cultural healing in one community of Somali women. *The Australian e-Journal for the Advancement of Mental Health (AeJAMH), 5*(2).

Han, C. (2004). The work of indebtedness: The traumatic present of late capitalist Chile. *Culture, Medicine and Psychiatry, 28,* 169–187.

Jorn, A. F. (2006). National surveys of mental disorders: Are they researching scientific facts or constructing useful myths? *Australian and New Zealand Journal of Psychiatry, 40,* 830–834.

Kelaher, M., Ferdinand, A., & Paradies, Y. (2014). Experiencing racism in health care: The mental health impacts for Victorian aboriginal communities. *Medical Journal of Australia, 201,* 44–47.

Kirmayer, L. J., & Bhugra, D. (2009). Culture and mental illness: Social context and explanatory models. In I. M. Salloum & J. E. Mezzich (Eds.), *Psychiatric diagnoses: Challenges and prospects* (pp. 31–40). New York: John Wiley.

Kirmayer, L. J., Gone, J. P., & Moses, J. (2014). Rethinking historical trauma. *Transcultural Psychiatry, 51,* 299–319.

Laing, R. D., & Esterson, A. (1964). *Sanity, madness and the family.* London: Penguin Books.

Marlowe, J. M. (2010). Beyond the discourse of trauma: Shifting the focus on Sudanese refugees. *Journal of Refugee Studies, 23,* 183–198.

Marx, K. (1962). *Selected writings in sociology and social philosophy.* London: Penguin Books.

Maxwell, K. (2014). Historicizing historical trauma theory: Troubling the trans-generational transmission paradigm. *Transcultural Psychiatry, 51,* 407–435.

McFarlane, A. C., & Yehuda, R. (2000). Clinical treatment of posttraumatic stress disorder: Conceptual challenges raised by recent research. *Australian and New Zealand Journal of Psychiatry, 34,* 940–953.

McGibbon, E. A. (2012a). Oppression and mental health: Pathologizing the outcomes of injustice. In E. A. McGibbon (Ed.), *Oppression: A social determinant of health* (pp. 123–137). Black Point, NS: Fernwood.

McGibbon, E. A. (Ed.). (2012b). *Oppression: A social determinant of health.* Black Point, NS: Fernwood.

McLeod, J. D., & Nonnemaker, J. M. (1999). Social stratification and inequality. In C. S. Aneshensal & J. C. Phelen (Eds.), *Handbook of the sociology of mental health* (pp. 321–345). New York: Plenum.

McMichael, C. (2003). Sadness, displacement, resettlement: Somali refugee women in Melbourne. In D. Barnes (Ed.), *Asylum seekers and refugees in Australia: Issues of mental health and wellbeing* (pp. 135–147). Sydney: Transcultural Mental Health Centre.

Meich, R. A., & Shanahan, M. J. (2000). Socioeconomic status and depression over the life course. *Journal of Health and Social Behavior, 41,* 162–176.

Miehls, D. (2011). Racism and its effects. In N. R. Heller & A. Gitterman (Eds.), *Mental health and social problems: A social work perspective* (pp. 62–85). London: Routledge.

Mohatt, N. V., Thompson, A. B., Thai, N. D., & Tebes, J. K. (2014). Historical trauma as public narrative: A conceptual review of how history impacts present-day health. *Social Science & Medicine, 106,* 128–136.

Paradies, Y. (2016). Colonisation, racism and indigenous health. *Journal of Population Research, 33,* 83–96.

Polanyi, K. (1944). *The great transformation.* New York: Rinehart.

Rank, M. R. (2011). Poverty and its effects. In N. R. Heller & A. Gitterman (Eds.), *Mental health and social problems: A social work perspective* (pp. 44–61). London: Routledge.

Read, J., & Bentall, R. (2010). Schizophrenia and childhood adversity. *The American Journal of Psychiatry, 167*, 717–718.

Richters, A. (2014). Enhancing family and community resilience and wellbeing across the generations: The contribution of community-based sociotherapy in post-genocide Rwanda. *International Journal of Emergency Mental Health and Human Resilience, 17*, 661–662.

Richters, A. (2015). Introduction. *Torture, 24*, 8–11.

Riggs, D., & Treharne, G. J. (2016). Decompensation: A novel approach to accounting for stress arising from the effects of ideology and social norms. *Journal of Homosexuality, 26*, 1–14.

Rios, C. (2015, May 7). Seven everyday things poor people worry about that rich people never do. *Everyday Feminism*.

Rose, A. M. (1962). A social-psychological theory of neurosis. In A. M. Rose (Ed.), *Human behavior and social processes: An interactionist approach* (pp. 537–549). Boston, MA: Houghton Mifflin.

Ross, C. E. (2000). Neighborhood disadvantage and adult depression. *Journal of Health and Social Behavior, 41*, 177–187.

Ryan, J. (2007). *Going 'Walli' and having 'Jinni': Exploring Somali expressions of psychological distress and approaches to treatment*. PhD, University of Waikato.

Ryan, J., Guerin, B., Guerin, P. B., & Elmi, F. H. (2006). Going 'Walli' and having 'Jinni': Considerations in the evaluation and treatment of Somali refugees. Selected as a 'Recommended Reading' in The Mental Health Services Conference 2005 Book of Proceedings: *Dancing to the Beat of a Different Drum*, Adelaide, September 2005.

Salis Gross, C. (2004). Struggling with imaginaries of trauma and trust: The refugee experience in Switzerland. *Culture, Medicine and Psychiatry, 28*, 151–167.

Sandal, M. J. (2012). *What money can't buy: The moral limits of markets*. London: Penguin.

Scull, A. T. (2009). *Hysteria: The disturbing history*. Oxford: Oxford University Press.

Shevlin, M., O'Neill, T., Houston, J. E., Read, J., Bentall, R. P., & Murphy, J. (2013). Patterns of lifetime female victimization and psychotic experiences: A study based on the UK Adult Psychiatry Morbidity Survey 2007. *Social Psychiatry and Psychiatric Epidemiology, 48*, 15–24.

Showalte, E. (1987). *The female malady: Women, madness, and English culture, 1890–1980*. London: Penguin Books.

Skultans, V. (1975). *Madness and morals: Ideas on insanity in the nineteenth century*. London: Routledge & Kegan Paul.

Smail, D. (2005). *Power, interest and psychology: Elements of a Social Materialist understanding of distress*. London: PCCS Books.

Smail, D. (2012). Draft manifesto for a social materialist psychology of distress. *Journal of Critical Psychology, Counselling and Psychotherapy, 12*, 93–107.

Stafford, M., Newbold, B. K., & Ross, N. A. (2010). Psychological distress among immigrants and visible minorities in Canada: A contextual analysis. *International Journal of Social Psychiatry, 57*, 428–441.

Stiglitz, J. E. (2013). *The price of inequality*. London: Penguin.

Summerfield, D. (1999). A critique of seven assumptions behind psychological trauma programmes in war-affected areas. *Social Science & Medicine, 48*, 1449–1462.

Trevor-Roper, H. R. (1967). *The European witch-craze of the sixteenth and seventeenth centuries.* London: Penguin.

Ventevogel, P. (2015). The effects of war: Local views and priorities concerning psychosocial and metal health problems as a result of collective violence in Burundi. *Intervention, 13*, 216–234.

Walker, C., Johnson, K., & Cunningham, L. (Eds.). (2012). *Community psychology and the socio-economics of mental distress.* New York: Palgrave Macmillan.

Watson, A. C., & Eack, S. M. (2011). Oppression and stigma and their effects. In N. R. Heller & A. Gitterman (Eds.), *Mental health and social problems: A social work perspective* (pp. 21–43). London: Routledge.

Webber, M. (2005). Social capital and mental health. In J. Tew (Ed.), *Social perspectives in mental health: Developing social models to understand and work with mental distress* (pp. 90–111). London: Jessica Kingsley.

Weisstein, N. (1971). Psychology constructs the female. *Journal of Social Education, 35*, 362–373.

Weisstein, N. (1993). Psychology constructs the female: Or, the fantasy life of the male psychologist (with some attention to the fantasies of his friends, the male biologist and the male anthropologist). *Feminism and Psychology, 3*, 195–210.

Williams, J. (2005). Women's mental health: Taking inequality into account. In J. Tew (Ed.), *Social perspectives in mental health: Developing social models to understand and work with mental distress* (pp. 151–167). London: Jessica Kingsley.

Wise, J. B. (2011). Homelessness and its effects. In N. R. Heller & A. Gitterman (Eds.), *Mental health and social problems: A social work perspective* (pp. 110–132). London: Routledge.

Yu, Y., & Williams, D. R. (1999). Socioeconomic status and mental health. In C. S. Aneshensal & J. C. Phelen (Eds.), *Handbook of the sociology of mental health* (pp. 151–166). New York: Plenum.

Zarowsky, C. (2004). Writing trauma: Emotion, ethnography, and the politics of suffering among Somali returnees in Ethiopia. *Culture, Medicine and Psychiatry, 28*, 189–209.

Ziaian, T. (2003). Persian women in Australia: Psychological challenges and coping strategies. In D. Barnes (Ed.), *Asylum seekers and refugees in Australia: Issues of mental health and wellbeing* (pp. 163–238). Sydney: Transcultural Mental Health Centre.

8

CONTEXTS OF DEVASTATION
Indigenous mental health and colonization

I watched a video of a large condor being released on a mountain top. It paused, spent time looking around, and then flew off. The camera zoomed in as the bird cruised along the tree-tops and down the side of the mountain. I realized that for the bird, the 'ground' underneath was not ground at all, the 'trees' were not trees, but it was all a learned network of food, shelter, other resources, and social relationships with other birds and predators. It was not a bare terrain or a geographical topography but a living web of foods and relationships with other birds and creatures of the Earth. The bird was not seeing 'things' but was seeing what was *afforded* by that region—in both resources and relationships.

This is how I have also seen Australian Indigenous friends gazing over a bare desert or a mountain range: they are not seeing geographical or physical topologies but they are seeing a living network of resources and relationships, both past and present; they can see stories; they can hear songs. This is their Country and their ancestors and their consequences are in this country. I do not know how exactly they see this, since I am an outsider, just as I am for the condor. But I try to imagine this partly by realizing that they can see the consequences and effects of all their relationships with their people and their resources, past and present, when they look at this desert. What they are seeing would be different without those previous hundreds of generations of inhabitants (60,000 years), as would their current way of life, so if you know the contexts like they do (including historical) then you can literally *see* all this in the landscape.

***

There is a long history in every continent of the world that special services and programmes have been needed for the Indigenous peoples of those lands. These include employment programmes, welfare, community services, psychiatrists, psychologists, and social workers (Alexander, 1984; Lawson & Saltmarshe, 2002). One of the sad themes in this chapter is the constant and almost universal attribution of these problems to something about the people themselves—they are weak, lazy, old-fashioned, unable to learn, uncivilized, resistant, inflexible, unappreciative, etc. Coupled with this has been the European-origin people's fascination for the salient 'cultural' features of Indigenous peoples—an overemphasis on the bits of their lives which stand out as different or exotic (or 'othering' in modern lingo).

So, it needs to be said up front clearly: if you are working with Indigenous people you really need:

• to know all about the colonization of their country with specific, local contexts
• to know about their everyday ordinary lives and practices and not just the salient ones which seem exotic
• to know about their family and community relationships in the many different forms and complexities (usually not the same as Western social relationships)
• to learn this from the people themselves and their stories, not from books or me or policy-makers.

Notice what this really means. We have learned in earlier chapters that (1) mental health focuses on behaviours for which a lot of context is hidden, and that (2) mental health focuses on behaviours that look non-normal, irrational, or dysfunctional compared to Western ways. *The Indigenous situations around the world have serious issues in the extreme with each and every one of these points.*

> But the war goes on; and we will have to bind up for years to come the many, sometimes ineffaceable, wounds that the colonialist onslaught has inflicted on our people.
>
> *(Fanon, 1963, p. 200, 'Colonial wars and mental disorders')*

For example: the effects of colonization have been intentionally hidden as causes by most colonizing governments; non-assimilation to the colonialists' practices of life has been made to look like non-normal or deviant behaviour; not wishing to join in the Western economic and bureaucratic systems is framed as dysfunctional behaviour; professionals have almost no experience of being with the Indigenous people in their everyday lives; and the other big hidden contexts for 'mental health' are the social properties of kin-based family groups and communities (Chapter 2) about which most professionals are ignorant.

There should be no surprise, then, that Indigenous peoples around the world appear to have many issues and need mental health services, given that their whole lives have been uprooted and changed, the populations (and hence families and communities and all that they provided) decimated from both violence and disease, and Western systems of political control and economics forced upon them with few alternative pathways left to run their own lives anymore. What perhaps *is* surprising is the blindness of colonizing populations to the contexts mentioned above and their connection to mental health. In hindsight, this blindness is itself a further indictment of colonization and its devastation.

For me, this is further emphasized because over many decades I have read cases from many places around the world, and worked closely with Indigenous people in a few different places in the world, and it is saddening to see the amazing similarities everywhere in how Indigenous peoples have been affected by colonization and then been referred to Western mental health systems for 'help' (for similarities, start with Moody, 1988). This is true both of how 'mental health' is dealt with, and also in how it is talked about by professionals and others.

For example, having reviewed all the literature on mental health issues for the numerous Australian Indigenous groups, the *chapter headings* of Waldram (2004) for North American groups (focusing on what is now Canada) are scarily similar: the psychoanalyst's aboriginal; measuring the aboriginal; the disordered aboriginal; the construction of aboriginal psychopathology; the alcoholic aboriginal; the depressed aboriginal; the culture-bound aboriginal; the traumatized aboriginal. If I were to write a book just on the mental health of Australian Indigenous peoples, these could be my exact chapter headings. And if you scan them in this way, you can begin to get the idea that these issues are the same across every colonized part of the world and are therefore *a result of the contexts of colonization* and not a result of the characteristics of any Indigenous people or their traditional cultural practices.

So if we go back to the foundation of this book, we can see how this fits: *People do not 'have mental illness'; people live, and have lived, in environments that do not support healthy behaviours.* It should be clear from this, therefore, but has not been in psychology or psychiatry, that *we must carefully explore the contexts of colonization if we want to understand and describe how the 'mental health' behaviours arise for Indigenous people*, not just explore the salient 'culture' and impugned 'essentialistic characteristics' of those people.

This is further compounded because, as you will find when you explore more, many of the problems attributed to 'characteristics' of Indigenous people are actually recent responses to colonization rather than anything present 'from time immemorial'. For example, Indigenous workers are very frequently described as coming from 'lazy races'. But where it exists, the 'laziness' is a reaction to, or a passive resistance to (Scott, 1985), being forced away from family and community and made to work in poor conditions for a violent master. So, many behaviours attributed to indigeneity or cultural practices have actually been more recent Indigenous strategies to resist or just survive the effects of colonization.

So, describing the contexts out of which the 'mental health issues' arise for Indigenous populations is fraught with difficulties. The best solution, of course, and as always, is to work and talk with the people themselves. But this needs to involve the social, colonization, economic, and historic contexts, needs to be very carefully observed and described, and the 'cultural' contexts need even more attention since they have been wrongly described many times in the past and attributions of cause have been wrongly assigned.

One good approach is that of Hunter (2004) who points out that wider contexts are needed to understand and treat Indigenous mental health issues, but he goes a step further and gives examples to make this more concrete— examples of coordinated activity at four levels. He suggested that we must work at four levels to alleviate the problems, noting that the first primarily involves colonization effects:

- Society: Social justice, reconciliation
- Community: Community development/empowerment
- Family/clan: Family well-being and parenting programmes
- Individual: Indigenous therapies, adapted/appropriated therapies (e.g. narrative therapy), and culturally appropriate conventional therapies

To illustrate all these themes of the mental health contexts of Indigenous peoples I will stay mainly with the Indigenous people of Australia. I have no real authority to speak for them but have spent some years working alongside a few different communities and learning what I could from yarning and observation. Sadly, wherever the reader is in the world there will be similar examples easily found, even though the details and names will change, and many of the effects of colonization hidden.

The Australian literature on Indigenous mental health as an example

We saw at the start of the last chapter that most groups surviving under societal oppression have had their mental health studied by giving DSM-based questionnaires or standardized interviews and correlating these scores with abstract measures of their conditions (being female, poor, etc.). The situation is no better for researching the mental health of Indigenous peoples but there are a few twists to the plot.

I will first present briefly what I found when reviewing the large literature around Australian Indigenous mental health, since it illustrates some of the areas that Western researchers have focused on. What this will more importantly highlight for readers, are some blind-spots where *in lieu of describing contextual details of the specific community and kin-based relationships or the effects of colonization as the contexts for the behaviours, abstract verbal substitutions are made.* You can therefore learn from this the skill of spotting when someone is not observing the full social relationship or colonization contexts but is using some discursive subterfuge with abstract language to cover it up.

Broadly speaking, when looking at all the literature there were only four main themes relating specifically to Indigenous Australians' mental health:

- processes in service provision
- specific mental health issues and treatments for Indigenous Australians
- characteristics of indigeneity
- spirituality.

Each of these dodges the issue of community involvement and kin-based relationships as contexts (Guerin & Guerin, 2012), as well as the contexts arising from colonization.

Processes in service provision. There is a sizeable literature about models for processes in service provision and proper consultation processes for Australian Indigenous mental health issues (Bishop, Vicary, Andrews, & Pearson, 2006; Henderson et al., 2002; Powell, 2000; Westerman, 2004). This is not only about mental health, however, and there are large literatures for medical, physiotherapy, occupational theory, social work, and other consultations (e.g. Nelson & Allison, 2007; Street, Baum, & Anderson, 2007). If one looks to other colonized countries, one will find similar models; there are also large literatures on better consultation with other diverse ethnic groups (Lee, 2007).

The basic idea is to find ways to make 'normal' (Western) service provision more acceptable and appropriate for Indigenous people. This can vary from using local languages to employing Indigenous people as mental health workers. Less frequent are: attempts to take the services to the Indigenous people instead of them having to travel to 'mainstream' services; the use of traditional forms of healing within the 'mainstream' services; or seriously including contexts of community and family in the whole process. And rarely are the contexts of colonization included;

for example, decolonization workshops are almost never seen as a treatment option of 'mental health' issues, which they should be (Guerin, 2010; Moeke-Pickering, 1998; Wanganeen, 2001, 2011).

The main idea, therefore, is that mental health consultations need to take into account the ways of diverse Indigenous peoples, so it is important to develop consultation models that 'fit' with the clients' perspective. If family is vital to people, then allow, or even welcome and encourage, family to take part in the health consultation. If the community has strong gender differentiation then develop a system in which male clients will be seen by a male professionals and female client by a female professional.

While most of this is becoming standard, if not in practice then at least in mission statements and visions of consulting professionals, there are a lot of issues that are not usually discussed. Much of the 'fit' with the clients' perspective is superficial, and does not really delve into any contexts except superficial 'cultural' differences. While service provision for Indigenous peoples most often depends strongly on the community contexts, these are not often investigated and rigid or stereotyped ideas about communities are often used (examples in Taylor & Guerin, 2010). A common problem is that consultation is made with Indigenous communities but no effort is made to find out what a 'consultation' would mean for the communities; so typically a Euro-centric 'community meeting' is set up which is then poorly attended.

Service provision models and recommendations are therefore important when working with Indigenous clients but by themselves these models do not engage a critical understanding of how mental health and well-being are contextualized by social relationships on the ground, nor do they attempt to influence or improve the actual treatments for 'mental illness' (see Taylor & Guerin, 2010, for more).

Specific mental health issues and treatments for Indigenous Australians. The second area in the Indigenous mental health literature for Australia involves papers reporting on specific mental health issues affecting Indigenous Australians (Brady, 2004; D'Abbs & Brady, 2004; Nagel, 2006; Petchkovsky et al., 2004; Phillips, 2003). This is different, however, to what we saw in the last chapter, where DSM measures were primarily used. As for Indigenous groups elsewhere in the world, the literature almost exclusively focuses on alcohol, drugs, petrol sniffing, comorbidity, suicide, depression, loss and grief, stolen generations, relapse, psychosis, dementia, gambling, women, men, and youth.

Although the issues are not unique to Indigenous Australians, the implication is made that these are 'Indigenous problems' rather than contexts from colonization. More critically, any underlying external community contexts such as the impact of colonialism, racism, or poverty are often passed over in favour of 'psychological' causes even if not related to indigeneity, therefore bypassing community and colonization contexts for mental health solutions (Weaver & Brave Heart, 1999).

Characteristics of indigeneity. A third major topic found in the Indigenous Australian mental health literature focuses on 'indigeneity' in mental health, and is probably the substitute for the many DSM-based studies in the last chapter (Cawte, 1996; Janca & Bullen, 2003; Spencer, 2000; Vicary & Westerman, 2004; Ypinazar, Margolis, Haswell-Elkins, & Tsey, 2007). That is, in many cases, the specific causes, consequences, necessary treatments, or presentation of mental illness are said to be something essential to Indigenous Australians—something about them that is different to other Australians. This might be a type of mental 'disorder' or syndrome that is said to be specific only to Indigenous Australians (that is, not in DSM). In some cases, the diversity among Indigenous Australians is acknowledged, but in many cases, Indigenous Australians are all lumped together within a single category based on their indigeneity.

The main point here is that this is usually an outcome when hidden contexts—especially kin-based family and community contexts and effects of colonization—have failed to be adequately documented. Documenting the role of these contexts is difficult and time-consuming, and so it is simpler to explain mental distress through a combination of internal universal and indigenous elements. But almost all these impugned effects on mental health from 'indigeneity' arise from complexities and conflicts in the difficult-to-see family and community relationships and effects of colonization.

None of this is to say that there are no differences based on indigeneity, but that this attribution is very often made too quickly without consideration of the diversity within Indigenous Australians and non-Australians, and without any knowledge of contexts. My point here is that indigeneity commonly seems to be resorted to as an explanation *because* the community and colonization contexts have not been properly explored as a source of external determinants.

The real answer to the question of whether Indigenous Australians (and their 'mental health') are different or the same as other Australians is that the question itself is wrong. The real questions are: in what areas or domains of life are there differences; from what contexts do any differences arise; in what contexts are the differences important; are the differences more than the differences between any groups of people; and do we need to do something special because of what seems to be a difference? These are difficult questions to answer in general, and the real answer is that it will all depend upon spending time with the people and documenting specific cases and contexts (Waitoki, Nikora, Harris, & Levy, 2014).

Spirituality. Finally, spirituality is a common topic in the literature of Indigenous mental health and illness. Professionals cannot deal for long with Indigenous Australian mental illness without needing to consider both spirituality and the role of 'being on Country' (visiting or living on tribal lands; Grieves, 2009; Lock, 2007) as therapeutic or, at least, as an important consideration.

Despite this, there is remarkably little written systematically about Indigenous mental health and spirituality in its context, and much of what is written is misleading. For example, consider that traditional healers have often been referred to as 'witchdoctors' or 'sorcerers' in an attempt to help laypersons understand the concept (Cawte, 1996; Reid, 1983). But the term 'witchdoctor' gives a very wrong impression of what traditional healers do and who they are. It is like calling the local Christian church minister in your suburbs a 'witchdoctor'.

One difficulty is that Indigenous Australians, like many others, are frequently reticent to talk about or even mention spiritual matters. This comes from a long history of having spiritual matters involving secrets (Keen, 1994), from racism and discrimination directed against them for anything non-Western, from Christian missionaries dissuading talk about extra-Christian spiritual matters, and from a general reticence to divulge. This means that a process of informal yarning and a good relationship is required before anything much is learned (e.g. Panzironi, 2013).

I will give an example below of finding more concrete context about one aspect of spirituality—that of 'being on Country'. But the point here is that one will not learn much about these apart from superficial and exotic pseudo-facts without spending the time to observe, experience, and describe the Indigenous contexts more, especially the social and community relationships over history and the effects of colonization. For example, the power of the traditional healing techniques depends on the contexts within the community and social relationships, not on something exotic or magical that is 'indigenous'.

What else we know from other literatures

There is some good news, however. For many years, some practitioners and others treating the 'mental health' or well-being of Indigenous communities have moved away from individual pathologies and looked more into contexts of social relationships, community processes, politics, and effects of colonization (Heil, 2006). This has appeared in different ways which, although not all are aimed at Indigenous community mental health, might be utilized in our analyses:

- *community-specific mental health and well-being approaches*, and for Indigenous communities this usually emphasizes the contexts of family, land, traditions, whole-of-life, spirituality, and community involvement in 'mental health' (Anderson, 2004; Atkinson, 2002; Dudgeon, Garvey, & Pickett, 2000; Guerin & Guerin, 2012; Hunter, 2004; Trudgen, 2000; Trzepacz, Guerin, & Thomas, 2014; Vicary & Westerman, 2004)
- *transcultural mental health and well-being approaches* (Burr, 2002; Dossa, 2002; Ferguson & Pittaway, 1999; Giosan, Glovsky, & Haslam, 2001; Guerin, Guerin, Diiriye, & Yates, 2004b; Guerin, Elmi, & Guerin, 2006; Hodes, 2002; Holzinger, Kilian, Lindenbach, Petscheleit, & Angermeyer, 2003; Ryan, Elmi, Guerin, & Guerin, 2005; Tew, 2005; Wagner, Duveen, Themel, & Verma, 1999)
- *studying the role of racism and other discriminations in Indigenous mental health* (e.g. Ferdinand, Paradies, & Kelaher, 2012; Jasinskaja-Lahti, Liebkind, & Perhoniemi, 2006; Kelaher, Ferdinand, & Paradies, 2014; Paradies, 2006, 2016; Paradies & Cunningham, 2010; Taylor & Guerin, 2010).

These, plus the four generic areas given earlier, are the main currents of most current mental health thinking for Australian Indigenous communities, although I cannot summarize it all. There are many similarities around the world, so you should be able to take the main points, find out the contextual differences to where you live, and adapt the main points accordingly in line with your local literatures and talking to the people themselves (Agee, McIntosh, Culbertson, & 'Ofa Makasiale, 2012; Atkinson, 2002; Brave Heart, 1988, 2003; Bristow, 2003; Coronado, 2005; Deloria, 1999; Dudgeon et al., 2000; Durie, 1997, 1999; Fenton, 2000; Friedli, 2009; Grieves, 2009; Hunter, 2004; Incayawar & Maldonado-Bouchard, 2009; Lapsley, Nikora, & Black, 2002; Lock, 2007; Mead, 2003; Ngaanyatjarra Pitjantjatjara Yankunytjatjra Women's Council Aboriginal Corporation, 2003; Phillips, 2003; Purdie, Dudgeon, & Walker, 2010; Reid, 1983; Smith, 1999; Waldram, 2004; Wilson, 2008; Wilson & Yellow Bird, 2005; Zacharias, 2006).

The main message is to work *with* your local Indigenous communities to learn about the contexts in which they live, and in which their ancestors lived, to seek understanding of their 'mental health' issues.

The hidden contexts for Indigenous mental health

I have now gone quickly through four ways the literature treats Australian Indigenous mental health, and talked briefly about contexts of community/ family and colonization. I will now say a little more about these two and then give some more detailed examples to flesh this out and provide ideas for better working with your own local communities, if they wish.

Kin-based communities as hidden determinants of mental health. I have suggested that while the brief review found four main areas of research, and these are common for Indigenous mental health literatures elsewhere around the world, they were each mostly focused on individuals and on the status of being 'Indigenous' people. My review of the research literature also showed that there are places in the research where community-context-as-determinant has been hidden because finding those determinants is difficult and takes time. Determinants of mental health have therefore been attributed to individual causes, and especially indigeneity as a cause, and assessment and intervention have followed suit and usually failed.

Examples of these hidden kin-based family and community contexts were:

• the diversity of community contexts and the strategies for taking these contexts into account is removed and written instead into the bureaucratic form of rigid rules about protocol and 'cultural awareness'
• indigeneity is resorted to as an attribution of mental health and illness because the community context has not been properly explored as a source of external determinants
• underlying external social causes such as the impact of colonialism, racism, or poverty on family and community are often passed over in favour of 'psychological' or indigeneity causes
• the power of traditional healing techniques depends on community and social relationships, and the failure to see these external community contexts of healing leads to attributions to individual powers and to indigeneity.

The reader needs to explore more family and community contexts which are hidden because they need time and patience to explore and because the detailed cases will be unique across different groups of people. This requires a change in methodology to be able even to find out about subtle community and kin-based family relationships.

What I think this leads us to is that *the contextual analysis of mental health behaviours, talking, and thinking for Indigenous people has really only begun.* Social anthropologists have had the methods for this but have not often focused directly on mental health. These methods need to be included more because the contexts for the appearance of any 'mental health' behaviours (as seen in Chapter 4) will come from these.

Colonization effects as hidden determinants of mental health. Like community and family, the contextual effects of colonization are frequently hidden contexts from which the 'mental health' behaviours arise (Trudgen, 2000). Following colonization, these were the sorts of things forced upon Indigenous peoples:

- getting things done by paying money (rather than using familial obligation)
- interacting primarily with strangers in most settings
- keeping in regular contact with only a few kin
- employment having overriding importance (more than family, certainly more than community)
- time management being more important than family.

All the effects of capitalism and enforced bureaucracy can be seen (Chapters 2 and 5; Cowlishaw, 1999). In one case study further in this chapter, I will outline how these were found to be major stressors and hence 'mental health' issues for one Australian Indigenous community.

To finish I will give just one brief example here of the effects of colonization as a hidden context, to get the reader thinking and exploring more. This example occurred commonly for Aboriginal and Torres Strait Islanders in Australia, when the term 'walkabout' was used to refer to them. This meant that (once again) they were unreliable and whatever they were doing, at work or at school, they had an 'indigenous characteristic' to walk away or just leave suddenly—to go walkabout. This was sometimes referred to as either a cognitive/mental issue or as an essential part of their race, that they would periodically 'feel the need' to be mobile. In earlier times, this was particularly in reference to walking off a job for extended periods and then returning. While it has been used as a sometimes pejorative term, it has generally meant something intrinsic to the whole race that could not be changed and was part of their mental health problems.

More recently (Peterson, 2004), it has been noted how the term really arose when Aboriginal and Torres Strait Islanders working on cattle stations were not given time off when a family member passed away even though they were strongly expected by their communities to be at the ceremonies. Their solution to this conflict (Table 4.1) was to exit because family was more important than money (like 'irrational' and 'non-functional' behaviours in Chapter 6). In this case, we see that this is actually about *cultural or family events having a higher priority in their social worlds than keeping a job* or being punished when returning from a walk-off. The problem, then, is that referring to such events in essentialistic terms about a person or a whole race meant that it could be used as a reason to exclude them from work altogether when this suited—'they are unreliable and usually do not even show up'.

Some Australian contextual examples

While I will focus on examples from the contexts of Australian Indigenous groups, it must be stressed again that I know how little I really know and that what I will write is more a spur for more research and descriptions of mental health contexts with specific detail (Pere, 2009; Waitoki et al., 2014).

Much of this has been written up by the different teams I have worked with, and more context can be found in those papers for those who wish to follow up. So, what I have learned, and the research that has been done, was done in different ways with these teams. I will not list the all names but mentioning the team is not just gratuitous—it is a demonstration that this sort of community-based research to pursue proper contextual details from the people themselves in Indigenous communities cannot be done alone—research methods must adapt (see Fromene & Guerin, 2014; Fromene, Guerin, & Krieg, 2014; Guerin, 2010, 2012; Guerin & Guerin, 2008a, 2008b, 2010a, 2010b, 2011, 2012, 2014; Guerin, Guerin, & Seemann, 2011; P. Guerin & B. Guerin, 2009; Guerin, Guerin, & Tedmanson, 2011; Guerin, Guerin, Tedmanson, & Clark, 2009, 2011; Tedmanson, Guerin, Guerin, & Clark, 2011; Trzepacz et al., 2014).

APY Lands

To look at the contexts for 'Indigenous mental health' closer, a research team worked with different groups on the APY Lands in South Australia. The *Anangu Pitjantjatjara Yankunytjatjra Lands* is a large tract of land in the South Australian desert region ('the Lands') in which the Indigenous people have lived more or less in traditional ways without interruption. This is very different to most of Australia in which the Indigenous people were killed or forced to move. In the APY Lands they were certainly not left alone—most of their land was made into pastoral leases for cattle grazers, capitalism was foisted upon them, missionaries arrived, and parts of the land were even used as a testing ground for British nuclear weapons (still radioactive to this day). They were also affected in the 'Stolen Generations' when thousands of babies and young children were taken under government 'care' to be 'civilized' but most were left instead in abusive and poor conditions in orphanages and elsewhere (Atkinson, 2005; Pilkington, 1996). So, they were not ignored or left alone, but neither were they explicitly taken off their lands as happened with most other groups—they have been living continuously on their land (even if the pastoralists 'owned' them) for 60,000 years.

To give readers an idea on how one goes about such a research project, the methodology, I will say a bit more but skip ahead if this is not of interest. I am arguing, however, that this should be a method for any professionals working with 'mental health' and not just for researchers. Luckily, I have met a few psychologists and at least one psychiatrist who do this extra hard work.

We made contacts through our networking with some of the key people in the APY Lands and then visited (with permits) *for about a year before doing any research*—community-based research done with contextual sensitivity is not for those in a rush to get their career moving. We (the team, not just me) combined this with helping people out (not in a paternalistic way we hoped), and also hosting a few people when they had to visit the city for various reasons. In doing all this we were also being checked out, since there were many researchers who only wanted to get quick and dirty answers (and quick DSM correlations), and there were many people coming into the Lands who were not particularly trustworthy. If it had looked like we would only help until our research was finished and then disappear, we probably would not have got too far. If it had appeared that we were not there to listen, observe, and learn we would not have got far either—many researchers arrive thinking they know the answers already and just want confirmation from Indigenous people, to give their ideas some authority or 'authenticity'.

We must have seemed okay because after a year we were able to start talking about 'mental health' issues, helped by one of our research team who had done good things there previously with other research. The main topic was mental health but what we observed and talked about went way beyond this, for three main reasons. First, in community-based research you let the people involved set at least some of the research agenda, and tell you about things they need to be researched or documented, so we helped research a lot of other topics. Second, we were doing a contextual approach for mental health, meaning that we did not assume to know already what parts of life in the APY Lands would be relevant to mental health—we tried to take in everything that might be relevant, including the politics and administration, luckily. Third, we knew from our literature review and talking to others in preparation that mental health would likely be 'holistic' in many of the meanings of that word (Lock, 2007), so we needed to look widely.

The research did not consist of interviews but totally informal chatting (all with ethics and consent of course). We participated in events, got to know people, lived in the community for one or two weeks at a time, and basically 'hung out' and 'yarned' with people. These methods are aimed to get the best descriptions of what people actually do and the many contexts from which those behaviours arise. They are not particularly original, combining some of the best of social anthropology's methods and other social science methods.

While these methods are time-intensive, compared to questionnaires and 30-minute structured interviews with set questions, there are many advantages for what we were trying to do in this sort of contextual research. Spending a lot of time means many things:

- increased trust so people tell you more
- more chances to observe and participate in what is really going on
- chances to speak many times to people to clarify earlier conversations, see if they have thought of more since, or to finish off any bits you could not cover the first time
- not be rushed into getting through in a set time and so sending bad messages to the people
- ask about things thrown up in conversations with others since the earlier conversation
- ask about things you have observed in the meanwhile
- be there when things are happening rather than ask retrospectively
- cross-check things you have heard from one person only
- have lots of time for the participants to tell you about things they think are important but for which you had no idea and were not going to raise.

I have found across work with many communities that this extra time is worth it for the valuable things you learn and the better sense that you are learning what people are actually like rather than learning only rushed, superficially acquiescing responses. If you are seeking the contextual bases from which 'mental health' behaviours arise à la Chapter 4, this is how you have to do the hard work.

The contexts for mental health issues in remote Indigenous communities. With these sorts of methods, a lot of observing and talking over many years, and a lot of learning from other people, we got some good ideas of 'mental health' on the APY Lands. As explained earlier, there are many social and cultural contexts which can lead to the behaviours that become seen as a mental illness, but these contexts are usually difficult to observe. From our research there were three main hidden influences of communities on mental health and illness:

- community and family relationships affected by colonization
- how communities are governed and the impact of government bureaucracies on people's everyday lives
- how communities are governed and the impact of government social policy changes and reversals.

From a Western, DSM, or psychiatric perspective, these do not really seem 'proper' origins for mental health issues, especially if those are still considered brain problems, chemical imbalances, or miswirings of the brain. But we found them to be the major mental health influences in the context of people living in remote communities.

Family and community as contexts of mental health and illness. There are a whole realm of ways that Indigenous families and communities have been changed or destroyed by colonization and the imposition of capitalism and bureaucracy. We must avoid placing the blame on these victims, and stop trying to address the mental health issues by focusing on just the individuals exhibiting the behaviours.

Indigenous families have conflicts now over money and other issues that were never part of their lives, and for which *the communities do not have historically cultural ways of easily resolving.* (Some traditional healers, *Ngangkari,* even told us that there were modern problems they could not solve.) As we saw in the last chapter for refugee families, parents are very stressed typically over their children and the ways that modern Western culture is influencing them and reducing the cultural ways of learning. They are fearful over losing their culture and all that their ancestors had built to help face life.

So, when we asked people in remote Indigenous communities about mental health, or more usually about social and spiritual well-being, their responses were often couched in terms of how families in the communities are now interacting. This is something that is not normally considered in 'Western' mental health since the mental health system underemphasizes relationships in communities (Guerin & Guerin, 2008a, 2008b).

However, it is difficult to overestimate how much the lives of people in remote communities have been centred on their communities for generations—for both good and ill. From our fieldwork it is entirely inappropriate, in our view, to assess the mental health of someone in a remote Indigenous community without knowing about their wide family history, current community issues, as well as the historical, economic, and political concerns for the community (Hunter, 2004). This is often hard to conceive for those not involved in the communities and who are raised on the DSM conceptualizations.

There is a need here to go back to Chapter 2 and remember that another hallmark of 'Westernized' relationships is a tendency to become compartmentalized (Bailey, 1971, p. 144; Guerin, 2004) and people who are important in one area of a person's life (like work settings) may not be prominent in other areas (home). This was not the case for the communities we studied, and this is likely to be the case also for many other Indigenous communities. And Indigenous communities never had to deal with so many strangers in their lives, and certainly not strangers who interfere in their lives and say that they have the authority (backed by force) to do so (Guerin & Guerin, 2008a).

Community governance and government bureaucracy as contexts of mental health and illness. The second important issue identified in our conversations with people in remote Indigenous communities relates to governance: the extent to which 'mental health' issues are a result of the way federal government bureaucracies interact with people, rather than anything individual (due to their 'personality') or cultural (due to their 'indigeneity'). We and our colleagues have elsewhere called this the 'Bureaucratic Stress Syndrome' or *BS Syndrome* (P. Guerin et al., 2011a), where the 'syndrome' originates outside of the person and in the community and colonization contexts.

In remote locations when being forced to be Western, there is widespread poverty and few services available, compared with urban settings, and usually there is limited or no choice of service providers (Guerin & Guerin, 2008a, 2008b). This can cause a great deal of stress when everyday services—water, fuel, health, food, schools, electricity—consistently need attention and require dealing with bureaucracies. Remember that these are all interactions dealing with strangers, since the government runs these services and employs almost all non-Indigenous people.

For people to make something happen—the basic idea of self-efficacy—it requires a great deal of effort in highly regulated and bureaucratized remote Indigenous communities. Talking with people in the field has convinced us that this produces a form of helplessness directly related to this bureaucratic stress that would affect anyone adversely. That is, it is not about their indigeneity *per se*. Similar chronic bureaucratic stressors are evident, for example, in refugee communities (Chapter 7; Guerin et al., 2004a, 2004b).

Government policy as contexts of mental health and illness. Related to the 'BS Syndrome' is what we and our colleagues called the 'Policy Dis-Stress Syndrome' (Tedmanson et al., 2011). While everyone's lives in modernity are determined by government policies to some extent (Chapter 5), our talking and participating with people in remote communities suggests that far-reaching policy changes directly affect those living in remote Indigenous communities to a much greater degree. The problem is more than this, however; policy and its implementation for Indigenous communities gets changed extremely frequently (Dillon & Westbury, 2007). We have noted, for example, that on almost every field trip we have made there has been some turmoil because a government policy has been changed, usually without any warning to the people affected.

Overall, most people in such communities cannot simply 'get on with life' in a policy environment that is constantly changing, not determined by themselves, and when each policy change has huge effects on everyday life. So, rapid and radical policy changes are very real key contexts for mental health behaviours in remote Indigenous Australian communities, and all the determinants mentioned may be key factors in fostering what gets interpreted as 'depression' by psychiatrists.

Once again, for mental health professionals working in these communities, a lack of knowledge about these continual policy changes would, understandably, lead to thinking that the 'problem' lies within the individual—that is, they are depressed or anxious and require personal intervention of some sort, when in fact the intervention more appropriately would be to intervene on the government policy changes to find stable ways to improve the poverty, lack of appropriate service provision, and other contextual elements.

There were, then, three main sources for 'mental health' behaviours, each of which was exacerbated or brought about from a context of colonization and forced assimilation. Even the family and community problems, which are a normal part of everyone's lives (Table 4.1), were exacerbated by colonization and ignorance of the family and community structures.

Nukunu and the context of 'being on Country' for Indigenous mental health

> The simple proposition that Indians love nature and embrace it does not really tell you why different tribes manifest their relationships to the land in different ways. If you talk to tribal people in those particular lands, you will get a better insight into why their religion and their culture developed in certain ways . . . They do not abstract from that experience to a universal religion or set of universal concepts.
>
> *(Deloria, 1999, p. 224)*

> Land thus plays a crucial role in the culture of indigenous peoples. Even indigenous city dwellers—whether they are indigenous Australians or Mapuche in Chile—remain determined to retain their links to the land. Losing access to their lands and territories, on the other hand, makes indigenous peoples feel deprived of their material and spiritual sustenance. Traditional livelihoods are discontinued, traditional knowledge lost, rituals linked to the land or ancestral spirits can no longer take place, and social disintegration is often a result.
>
> *(United Nations, 2009, p. 57)*

It is often mentioned that Australian Indigenous people have a strong attachment to their Country which leads to better health outcomes, but it is unclear how these are concretely linked (Bishop, Vicary, Mitchell, & Pearson, 2012; Kingsley, Townsend, Philips, & Aldous, 2009). We know that their Land is important but as the two quotes above say, we do not know much about the concrete specific contexts for this. The second quote lists some that are not necessarily very obvious, but clearly, the Land also provided all the life resources for pre-colonized peoples.

In terms of the themes in this book, this make a relation between mental health behaviours and being 'on Country' likely, since they are hidden contexts that are not obvious when observing Indigenous people, and going out on Country for no apparent reason seems both dysfunctional in terms of regular employment and non-normal in terms of doing 'normal' Western activities. So, the relationship seems a likely ingredient in Indigenous mental health.

The other main hidden context for Indigenous mental health—subtle and long-lasting effects of colonization (Guerin, 2004, chapter 6)—is also relevant here. Colonization has ruined much of the Indigenous Country in terms of ecology and topography, wrecked their existence on Country in terms of an economic source of resources, and it has also taken it away from the people or restricted their access to their own Country.

There is research linking Country to social well-being and mental health, for example, evidence for the social and mental health benefits of attachment to Country (Bishop et al., 2012; Ganesharajah & Australian Institute of Aboriginal and Torres Strait Islander Studies, 2009; Guerin & Guerin, 2012; P. Guerin et al., 2011b). There are also bad consequences to mental health (that is, increased suffering) of being removed from Country, with findings, for example, that Indigenous people who spent large amounts of time away from their Country reporting experiencing episodes of depression (Vicary & Bishop, 2005; also Bishop et al., 2012).

For mental health, however, we still need to know a lot more about specific groups around the world, and how their Land or Country helps their mental health behaviours or how the ruination of the Land leads to poor outcomes for them which are difficult to trace and hence called 'psychological problems' or 'mental health issues'. This will be more common in the future, in fact, with ecological disasters in many Indigenous Lands and increased plundering by capitalists for mining and wealth (Klare, 2012).

For the APY Lands communities outlined earlier, they had been allowed to stay on their Country despite having pastoral leases and cattle in places. Being on their Country was important but it was taken for granted, unlike degradation of their lands and disappearance of flora and fauna which were frequently mentioned as stressors.

To look further at the context of being (and not being) on Country, myself and two colleagues (one Nukunu) worked alongside the Nukunu people to find out more about the importance and uses of their Country (Trzepacz et al., 2014). This was a small Indigenous group who had been very badly affected by colonization and most of whom now lived in cities and worked in Western occupations—again, a very different context to the APY Lands. It was a chance to find out how much Country still meant to them and in what more specific ways it was important, with a group for very different contexts.

For a brief context, Nukunu Country is about 250 km north of Adelaide in South Australia, encompassing Crystal Brook, Pt Pirie, Quorn, Wilmington and Pt Augusta, the upper-eastern Spencer Gulf and the Flinders Ranges. The Nukunu people experienced much trauma as a direct result of colonization and the removal of children from their families due to Australian Government policies that were in place up to the 1970s. Like many groups in the region (Andyamathanha, Banggarla, Kokatha, Kaurna, Narangga, Ngadjuri), their Country lay on the route out of Adelaide to the northern pastoral regions that skirted the Flinders Ranges, so during colonization they had land taken away, were attacked brutally, and later had children removed from the groups that survived. Stories of massacres are told.

Like many of the surrounding groups, the Nukunu people were taken off their Country, and made to live in missions (Point Pearce in particular) or on the outskirts of rural towns (if they had useful skills), and put under strict behavioural control by governments. For example, those in the Point Pearce Mission were forbidden by law to talk to their relatives still living on the outskirts of Port Augusta, and the police would arrest them if found. Of course, many stories are told of how they evaded the police and had family meetings together in Port Augusta under the cover of darkness.

All Nukunu now live a Western way of life and almost all are employed in various locations around South Australia, many in professional jobs. Many live in the towns which were built on their Country, in Port Augusta, Port Germein and Port Pirie, but none are living on the land in the bush, as they once had prior to the arrival of Europeans. So, some are living on Country but not living 'off the Country' for shelter and food.

In the 1980s some Nukunu traditional lands were returned, and so the group were looking at ways to redevelop their community. There were plans to create a Nukunu economy on Country in a culturally and environmentally sensitive way (Mascall, 2009). Although no one wished to live permanently on their Country in the bush, Nukunu wish to maintain it for visiting, respite, camping, and reviving their cultural practices for their children and future generations.

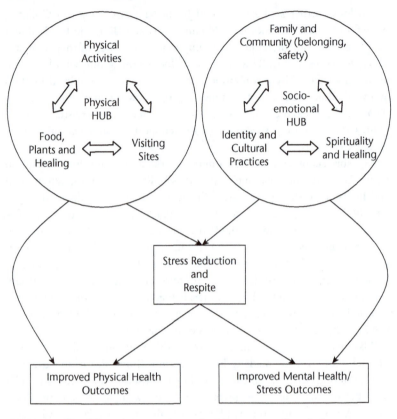

FIGURE 8.1 Possible pathways to better health outcomes from being on Country

Some of the Nukunu leaders and community members aged between 30 and 60 years (six men, four women) were asked in informal focus groups and repeated informal interviews about their attachment to Country. This research was done in a very relaxed way and the people knew all about the research. For instance, one 'focus group' was done around a barbeque and drinks, where everyone joined in and told stories, and built on points others had made in ways they would not have done in a more formal interview.

I will not go through all the detailed findings here, but the main themes that emerged from many talks and stories suggested strongly that:

- their Country brings Nukunu an identity and sense of belonging
- that it is a place with nurturing qualities
- people feel unhappy and unfulfilled away from their Land

- people return to Country to recover from illness (including what would be called 'mental illness')
- activities conducted on Country such as natural resource management could provide Nukunu with group cohesiveness and empowerment.

To try and get this across better we produced an illustration, here given as Figure 8.1. There were two main ideas: that being on Country improved physical health and that being on Country also improved 'well-being'. Both of these were thought to *directly* help physical and mental health outcomes for Nukunu, and to also *indirectly* help because they also reduced stress of all sorts when on Country. So, a clear mental health intervention for Nukunu is to let them have time to go and live on Country. They already were doing this, however, by themselves.

To give the ideas a bit better for readers, a few examples of quotes are also given below to conclude.

Box 8.1

One 40-year-old male participant claimed he did not own the country, it owned him:

> Nukunu people have been removed from Country only by a physical nature not spiritual. For us today the hills, trees, animals, and ocean remain a strong and spiritual connection. We as individuals experience different and similar emotions upon our visits. I have heard of a saying 'the hills are alive', as a Nukunu person, I truly understand what is meant by this statement. My connection to land reminds me that I do not own it, it owns me. I have a responsibility to ensure that it is no longer taken for granted and its riches are preserved for future generations.

One 31-year-old female participant described the experience of being away from Country and losing this foundation, which for her meant losing a sense of who she was, and her identity:

> People have built a home (the Country), however they may continue to travel a journey without this foundation. The experiences they have are the bricks, however if the bricks are loose and they are without their foundation (the Country) they experience emptiness as they don't have the resilience and strength to keep going.

(continued)

(continued)

One participant discussed driving over the hill on the highway and seeing the Flinders Ranges, comparing this to having a *'hot bath or putting on a pair of fluffy socks'*. They felt the weight lifted off their shoulders; it was a relief to get there.

One 50-year-old female participant spoke of the uplifting feeling she had when on Country:

> *Country is a powerful place and by being there you absorb this energy. This energy is our ancestors talking to us and teaching us about Country.*

> *Losing Country is like losing an arm or a leg, it's a part of you; you have to have it.*

The Nukunu spoke of returning to Country when they experienced illness. This was not only for 'physical' illnesses but when they became sad or depressed:

> *When burnout or rundown from work life the Country is somewhere where I can recharge my batteries and regather myself and be replenished.*

One participant claimed their job was highly stressful and being on Country allowed them to get their thoughts back. They reported feeling normal, and at peace when on Country.

Indigenous Australians and contextualizing 'Borderline Personality Disorder'

The final very brief outline of research on more detailed contexts for Indigenous Australian and mental health issues was an Honours research project by Robyn Fromene, supervised by myself and Anthea Krieg (also see Guerin, 2016, pp. 121–126). It focused on five participants who at some point had an official DSM diagnosis of Borderline Personality Disorder. They were listened to as they talked about their lives and their history, their stories and events; once again, over repeated informal talks. Most of it was very sad, and I still get tears reading the original full transcripts.

The difference here from the previous two examples is that these people had lived away from communities in cities most or all of their lives, and for many this was the result of the 'Stolen Generations' policy of taking children from their mothers and raising them in orphanages. They had, therefore, less context of a traditional Indigenous Australian community but, as we will see, this still deeply affected them and led to many of their 'mental health' behaviours which were given a BPD diagnosis in each case.

What we focused on that is relevant here were (1) the *historical contexts* of colonization and community destruction for Indigenous Australians (Fromene et al., 2014), and (2) the *personal contexts* of their own social and cultural contexts as Indigenous Australians trying to live in a white person's modernity (Fromene & Guerin, 2014). The first was really about how colonization and all the brutality affected these people here and now in their lives but in very non-obvious ways, while the second showed hidden effects from the completely changed family and community relationships which hugely affected their lives for the worse, especially during childhood. There were many more direct contexts for their 'mental health' issues and BPD diagnosis as well that I will leave out. But the point will be that to understand the contexts from which their behaviours arose—especially those which led them to being labelled as BPD—you need to have found out the historical community and more personal social and family contexts.

What we started doing in this project, and have continued in other projects since, is getting the list of behaviours from the DSM diagnosis and listening to the people talk about these behaviours as they occurred in their lives—how they saw these DSM symptoms in their world. BPD has nine main 'symptoms' associated with it in the DSM diagnosis (see Table 8.1). We found (see the papers for details) that those symptoms or complaints became much more understandable when related to their historical and personal social contexts.

Table 8.1 presents both the historical and the social-cultural personal contexts for the nine symptoms, as given by our participants.

I will only mention here one example of how we can rethink these symptoms in terms of the external contexts in which these people lived. The first 'symptom' of the DSM diagnosis is: 'Frantic efforts to avoid real or imagined abandonment.'

Historically (the second column), the people talked to us about each having three generations from which babies had been taken from mothers by the government (the Stolen Generations) and put in homes or orphanages. That is, for three generations these people had direct relatives taken away as babies from their mothers, grandmothers, and great-grandmothers. That was just one context in which you would likely have recurring thoughts of being abandoned or not wanting to form strong attachments to anyone.

TABLE 8.1 Alternative contexts of BPD symptoms from the DSM given by research participants

DSM IV-TR symptoms of BPD	Historical context from participants	Indigenous social and community perspectives from participants
Frantic efforts to avoid real or imagined abandonment.	Ongoing culture of forced separation from care-givers as children, Stolen Generation, loss of community and family structures.	Removal from birth families. Violence, neglect. Mistrust for self and others.
Unstable and intense interpersonal relationships.	Alternative care as children, unable to form appropriate attachment relationships, cycles of learned hopelessness, abusive relationships.	Histories of abuse, neglect, violence.
Identity disturbance.	Loss of cultural direction, walking in two worlds, racism.	Racism, walking in two worlds, removal from culture.
Impulsivity in at least two areas that are potentially self-damaging.	Social disadvantage, social isolation, loss of connectedness.	Stress relief, able to focus on something other than their life, environment.
Recurrent suicidal behaviour, gestures, or threats, or self-mutilating behaviour.	Traditionally uncommon, powerful symbolic statements, distraction from life, constant 'sorry business'.	Threats to loved ones, temporary measures, to sleep, to end it all. Stress relief.
Affective instability due to a marked reactivity of mood.	Loss of community, no stable point of reference on how they should feel.	Labile moods, up and down. Can be scary.
Chronic feelings of emptiness.	Apathy, 'vital depression', grief and loss, increased personal trauma, existential crises.	Emptiness of energy. Emptiness from achievement. Emptiness from emotions. Unsure of origins of emptiness, and what empty of, just knowing there is emptiness. Lack of culture.

Inappropriate, intense anger, or difficulty controlling anger.	Unjustified hurt, anger at loss of culture, government policy, indication of group membership, anger at institutions.	Internalized anger and anger at loved ones. Anger at disadvantage and racism.
Transient, stress-related paranoid ideation or severe dissociative symptoms.	Detachment from experience, communal trauma leading to feelings of disconnectedness. Lapses in reality testing.	Place of safety when disassociating, some experience of severe disassociating, disassociating related to past trauma and sexual abuse. Paranoia associated with past trauma.

In terms of their *personal social contexts* (the third column), their homes were a chaotic environment for many of the same reasons, and their parents either left them alone or did not tend to them since they were dealing with their own similar issues in their lives. They also had any possible cultural channels of safety ruined by effects of colonization.

> P2: I get scared as hell [I am going to be abandoned], yeah. When I am by myself, I don't like it. Yeah, I am scared they are gonna abandon me, but I think maybe it's my fault why they do it . . . because I don't want to get too close to them, a bit like, come here, go away. I confuse myself . . . It scares me. I know what I can do when I'm alone. I can harm myself when I am by myself.

> P5: I was always left alone . . . I feel I have been left to my own devices for too long, and that hasn't really helped me.

Each of these participants had been placed in alternative care as children, with one having been actually abandoned by the mother in a hospital. The constant feeling that they did not have a stable reference point in their early lives appeared to impact upon their associated feelings of abandonment and fears of being left alone, and also affected their ability to form loving and stable relationships (Clark, 2000).

So, the point is that we traced two types of hidden external contexts for these DSM symptoms and there were many more, and these made more sense of what was happening in their lives. More importantly, though, tracing these to these hidden contexts really changes the way you think about treatments and interventions, since most of the standard clinical methods will have little effect despite being 'proved' in clean, clinical trials. And placing the 'cause' as a disorder or from 'having' a borderline personality helps no one.

It was in this paper that we first used the motto of this current book, which I have used at the very start of the book and now at the end of the book:

> We conclude that practitioners need to explore a greater range of contexts for any symptoms, and that rather than thinking of individuals in terms of *having* a 'borderline personality', we suggest rethinking of them in terms of *having had* 'borderline socializing environments'.
>
> *(Fromene & Guerin, 2014, p. 569)*

Summary

- There is found an almost universal attribution of problems for Indigenous peoples to something essentialistic about the people themselves—they are weak, lazy, old-fashioned, unable to learn, uncivilized, resistant, inflexible, unappreciative, etc.

- Coupled with this has been the colonizers' fascination for the salient 'cultural' features of Indigenous peoples—an overemphasis on the bits of their lives that stand out as different or exotic.

- We must carefully explore the contexts of colonization if we want to understand and describe how the 'mental health' behaviours arise for Indigenous people, not just explore the salient 'culture' and impugned 'essentialistic characteristics' of those people.

- If you are working with Indigenous people you really need:

  o to know all about the colonization of their country with specific, local contexts

  o to know about their everyday ordinary lives and practices and not just the salient ones which seem exotic

  o to know about their family and community relationships in the many different forms and complexities (usually not the same as Western social relationships)

  o to learn this from the people themselves and their stories, not from books or me or policy-makers.

- We have learned in earlier chapters that (1) mental health focuses on behaviours for which a lot of context is hidden, and that (2) mental health focuses on behaviours that look non-normal, irrational, or dysfunctional compared to Western ways; the Indigenous situations around the world have serious issues in the extreme with both these points.

- In analyses of Indigenous mental health there are major blind-spots where in lieu of describing contextual details of the specific community and kin-based relationships or the effects of colonization as the contexts for the behaviours, abstract verbal substitutions are made; in particular:

  o the dynamics of kin-based communities are hidden contexts for 'mental health' behaviours not explored so 'internal' or group attributions are made
  o colonization effects are hidden contexts for 'mental health' behaviours not explored so 'internal' or group attributions are made.

- From our research there were three main hidden influences of communities for Indigenous mental health and illness at least for these particular groups:

  o how community and family relationships have been drastically affected by colonization
  o how communities are governed and the huge impact of government bureaucracies on people's everyday lives and 'mental health'
  o how communities are governed and the impact of government social policy changes and reversals.

References

Agee, M., McIntosh, T., Culbertson, P., & 'Ofa Makasiale, C. (Eds.). (2012). *Pacific identities and well-being: Cross-cultural perspectives.* London: Routledge.

Alexander, C. (1984). Aboriginals in capitalist Australia: What it means to become civilized. *Australian and New Zealand Journal of Sociology, 20,* 233–242.

Anderson, I. (2004). Aboriginal well-being. In C. Grbich (Ed.), *Health in Australia: Sociological concepts and issues* (3rd Ed., pp. 75–100). Sydney: Longman.

Atkinson, J. (2002). *Trauma trails, recreating song lines: The transgenerational effects of trauma in Indigenous Australia.* Melbourne: Spinifex Press.

Atkinson, R. (2005). Denial and loss: The removal of Indigenous Australian children from their families and culture. *QUT Law & Justice Journal, 5*(1), 71–88.

Bailey, F. G. (1971). *Gifts and poison: The politics of reputation.* Oxford: Basil Blackwell.

Bishop, B. J., Vicary, D. A., Andrews, H., & Pearson, G. (2006). Towards a culturally appropriate mental health research process for indigenous Australians. *The Australian Community Psychologist, 18,* 31–41.

Bishop, B. J., Vicary, D. A., Mitchell, J. R., & Pearson, G. (2012). Aboriginal concepts of place and Country and their meaning in mental health. *The Australian Community Psychologist, 24,* 26–42.

Brady, M. (2004). *Indigenous Australia and alcohol policy: Meeting difference with indifference.* Sydney: University of New South Wales Press.

Brave Heart, M. Y. H. (1988). The return to the Sacred Path: Healing the historical grief response among the Lakota through a psychoeducational group intervention. *Smith College Studies in Social Work, 68,* 287–305.

Brave Heart, M. Y. H. (2003). The historical trauma response among natives and its relationship with substance abuse: A Lakota illustration. *Journal of Psychoactive Drugs, 35*, 7–13.

Bristow, F. (Ed.). (2003). *Utz' Wach'il: Health and well being among indigenous peoples*. London: Health Unlimited.

Burr, J. (2002). Cultural stereotypes of women from South Asian communities: Mental health care professionals' explanations for patterns of suicide and depression. *Social Science & Medicine, 55*, 835–845.

Cawte, J. (1996). *Healers of Arnhem Land*. Sydney: University of New South Wales Press.

Clark, Y. (2000). The construction of Aboriginal identity in people separated from their families, community and culture: Pieces of a jigsaw. *Australian Psychologist, 35*(2), 150–157.

Coronado, G. (2005). Competing health models in Mexico: An ideological dialogue between Indian and hegemonic views. *Anthropology & Medicine, 12*, 165–177.

Cowlishaw, G. (1999). Black modernity and bureaucratic culture. *Australian Aboriginal Studies, 2*, 15–24.

D'Abbs, P. H., & Brady, M. (2004). Other people, other drugs: The policy response to petrol sniffing among Indigenous Australians. *Drug and Alcohol Review, 23*, 253–260.

Deloria, V. (1999). *Spirit and reason: The Vine Deloria Jr reader*. Golden, CO: Fulcrum Publishing.

Dillon, M. C., & Westbury, N. D. (2007). *Beyond humbug: Transforming government engagement with Indigenous Australia*. West Lakes, SA: Seaview Press.

Dossa, P. (2002). Narrative mediation of conventional and new 'mental health' paradigms: Reading the stories of immigrant Iranian women. *Medical Anthropology Quarterly, 16*, 341–359.

Dudgeon, P., Garvey, D., & Pickett, H. (2000). *Working with Indigenous Australians: A handbook for psychologists*. Perth, WA: Gunada Press.

Durie, M. (1997). *Puahou: A five point plan for improving Māori mental health*. Wellington, NZ: Māori Mental Health Summit.

Durie, M. (1999). Mental health and Māori development. *Australian and New Zealand Journal of Psychiatry, 33*, 5–12.

Fanon, F. (1963). *The wretched of the earth*. Ringwood, Vic.: Penguin Books.

Fenton, L. (2000). *Four Māori korero about their experience of mental illness*. Wellington, NZ: Mental Health Commission.

Ferdinand, A., Paradies, Y., & Kelaher, M. (2012). *Mental health impacts of racial discrimination in Victorian Aboriginal communities: The Localities Embracing and Accepting Diversity (LEAD) Experiences of Racism Survey*. Melbourne: The Lowitja Institute.

Ferguson, B., & E. Pittaway, E. (Eds.). (1999). *Nobody wants to talk about it: Refugee women's mental health* (pp. 31–39). Sydney: Transcultural Mental Health Centre.

Friedli, L. (2009). *Mental health, resilience and inequalities*. Geneva: World Health Organization, accessed at: www.euro.who.int/__data/assets/pdf_file/0012/100821/E92227.pdf.

Fromene, R., & Guerin, B. (2014). Talking to Australian Indigenous clients with Borderline Personality Disorder labels: Finding the context behind the diagnosis. *The Psychological Record, 64*, 569–579.

Fromene, R., Guerin, B., & Krieg, A. (2014). Australian Indigenous clients with a Borderline Personality Disorder diagnosis: A contextual review of the literature. *The Psychological Record, 64*, 559–567.

Ganesharajah, C., & Australian Institute of Aboriginal and Torres Strait Islander Studies. (2009). *Indigenous health and wellbeing: The importance of country*: Acton, ACT: Native Title Research Unit, Australian Institute for Aboriginal and Torres Strait Islander Studies.

Giosan, C., Glovsky, V., & Haslam, N. (2001). Lay concepts of 'mental disorder': A cross-cultural study. *Transcultural Psychology, 38*, 317–332.

Grieves, V. (2009). *Aboriginal spirituality: Aboriginal philosophy, the basis of Aboriginal social and emotional wellbeing*. Discussion Paper No. 9, Cooperative Research Centre for Aboriginal Health, Darwin, NT.

Guerin, B. (2004). *Handbook for analyzing the social strategies of everyday life*. Reno, NV: Context Press.

Guerin, B. (2010). A framework for decolonization interventions: Broadening the focus for improving the health and wellbeing of Indigenous communities. *Pimatisiwin: A Journal of Indigenous and Aboriginal Community Health, 8*, 61–83.

Guerin, B. (2012). Making psychology more relevant to Indigenous students (and others): Moving causes to context and expanding social relationships to the real world. In S. McCarthy, K. L. Dickson, J. Cranney, A. Trapp, & V. Karandashev (Eds.), *Teaching psychology around the world: Volume 3* (pp. 105–115). Newcastle upon Tyne: Cambridge Scholars Publishing.

Guerin, B. (2016). *How to rethink human behavior: A practical guide to social contextual analysis*. London: Routledge.

Guerin, B., & Guerin, P. B. (2008a). Relationships in remote communities: Implications for living in remote Australia. *The Australian Community Psychologist, 20*, 74–86.

Guerin, B., & Guerin, P. (2008b). 17 ways that 'community talk' misguides research. In R. DeSouza & A. Williams (Eds), *Researching with communities: Grounded perspectives on engaging communities in research* (pp. 263–274). Auckland: Muddy Creek Press.

Guerin, B., & Guerin, P. (2010a). Sustainability of remote communities: Population size and youth dynamics. *Journal of Economic and Social Policy, 13*, 49–79.

Guerin, B., & Guerin, P. (2010b). *Sustainability: A case study of Nepabunna and its environs*. DKCRC Working Paper 66, Desert Knowledge CRC, Alice Springs.

Guerin, B., & Guerin, P. (2011). *Pukatja/Ernabella and its environs*. DKCRC Working Paper 65, Desert Knowledge CRC, Alice Springs.

Guerin, B., & Guerin, P. (2012). Re-thinking mental health for indigenous Australian communities: Communities as context for mental health. *Community Development Journal, 47*(4), 555–570.

Guerin, B., & Guerin, P. (2014). 'Mental illness' symptoms as extensions of strategic social behaviour: The case of multicultural mental health. *Rivista di Psicologia Clinica, 1*, 67–81.

Guerin, B., Guerin, P. B., Diiriye, R. O., & Abdi, A. (2004a). Living in a close community: The everyday life of Somali refugees. *Network: Journal of the Australian College of Community Psychologists, 16*, 7–17.

Guerin, B., Guerin, P. B., Diiriye, R. O., & Yates, S. (2004b). Somali conceptions and expectations of mental health: Some guidelines for mental health professionals. *New Zealand Journal of Psychology, 33*, 59–67.

Guerin, B., Guerin, P., & Seemann, K. (2011). *Seeds of sustainability: Growing your desert communities*. Alice Springs, NT: Ninti One Limited.

Guerin, P. B., Elmi, F. H., & Guerin, B. (2006). Weddings and parties: Cultural healing in one community of Somali women. *The Australian e-Journal for the Advancement of Mental Health, 5*(2), www.auseinet.com/journal/vol5iss2/guerin.pdf.

Guerin, P., & Guerin, B. (2009). Social effects of fly-in-fly-out and drive-in-drive-out services for remote Indigenous communities. *The Australian Community Psychologist, 20*, 8–23.

Guerin, P., Guerin, B., & Tedmanson, D. (2011a). *Bureaucratic stress syndrome and remote Aboriginal communities*. Paper presented at the International Society of Critical Health Psychology 7th Biennial Conference, Adelaide, South Australia.

Guerin, P., Guerin, B., Tedmanson, D., & Clark, Y. (2009). How do we think about Indigenous mental health in rural and remote communities? *STATEing Women's Health*, 8–13.

Guerin, P., Guerin, B., Tedmanson, D., & Clark, Y. (2011b). How can Country, spirituality, music and arts contribute to Indigenous mental health and well-being? *Australasian Psychiatry, 19*, 38–41.

Heil, D. (2006). Shifting expectations of treatment: From 'patient as individual' to 'patient as social person'. *Australian Aboriginal Studies, 2*, 98–110.

Henderson, R., Simmons, D. S., Bourke, L. et al. (2002). Development of guidelines for non-Indigenous people undertaking research among the Indigenous population of north-east Victoria. *Medical Journal of Australia, 176*, 482–485.

Hodes, M. (2002). Three key issues for young refugees' mental health. *Transcultural Psychiatry, 39*, 196–213.

Holzinger, A., Kilian, R., Lindenbach, I., Petscheleit, A., & Angermeyer, M. (2003). Patients' and their relatives' causal explanations of schizophrenia. *Social Psychiatry Epidemiology, 38*, 155–162.

Hunter, E. (2004). Commonality, difference and confusion: Changing constructions of Indigenous mental health. *Australian e-Journal for the Advancement of Mental Health, 3*, www.auseinet.com/journal/vol3iss3/huntereditorial.pdf.

Incayawr, M., & Maldonado-Bouchard, S. (2009). The forsaken mental health of the Indigenous Peoples: A moral case of outrageous exclusion in Latin America. *BMC International Health and Human Rights, 9*, 1–5.

Janca, A., & Bullen, C. (2003). The Aboriginal concept of time and its mental health implications. *Australasian Psychiatry, 11*, S40–S44.

Jasinskaja-Lahti, I., Liebkind, K., & Perhoniemi, R. (2006). Perceived discrimination and well-being: A victim study of different immigrant groups. *Journal of Community & Applied Social Psychology, 16*, 267–284.

Keen, I. (1994). *Knowledge and secrecy in an Aboriginal religion*. Oxford: Clarendon Press.

Kelaher, M., Ferdinand, A., & Paradies, Y. (2014). Experiencing racism in health care: The mental health impacts for Victorian aboriginal communities. *Medical Journal of Australia, 201*, 44–47.

Kingsley, J., Townsend, M., Philips, R., & Aldous, D. (2009). If the land is healthy it makes the people healthy: The relationship between caring for country and health for the Yorta Yorta nation, Boonwurrunga and Bangerang tribes. *Health and Place, 15*, 291–299.

Klare, M. T. (2012). *The race for what's left: The global scramble for the world's last resources*. New York: Picador.

Lapsley, H., Nikora, L. W., & Black, R. (2002). "*Kia Mauri Tau!*" *Narratives of recovery from disabling mental health problems*. Wellington, NZ: Mental Health Commission.

Lawson, C. W., & Saltmarshe, D. K. (2002). The psychology of economic trans-formation: The impact of the market on social institutions, status and values in a northern Albanian village. *Journal of Economic Psychology, 23*, 487–500.

Lee, W. M. L. (2007). *Introduction to multicultural counseling for helping professionals*. New York: Routledge.

Lock, M. (2007). *Aboriginal holistic health: A critical review*. Discussion Paper No. 2, Cooperative Research Centre for Aboriginal Health, Darwin, NT.

Mascall, S. (2009, April 3). Culture not colour. Television broadcast, BBC World Service Documentaries. Retrieved May 17, 2009, from www.bbc.co.uk/worldservice/documentaries/2009/04/090403_culture_not_colour.shtml.

Mead, H. M. (2003). *Tikanga Māori: Living by Māori values*. Wellington, NZ: Huia Publishers.

Moeke-Pickering, T. (1998). *Evaluation of the effectiveness of a decolonization/anti-oppression and liberation workshop as an intervention strategy*. Hamilton, NZ: University of Waikato.

Moody, R. (1988). *The indigenous voice: Visions and realities* (Vol. 1 & Vol. 2). London: Zed Books.

Nagel, T. (2006). The need for relapse prevention strategies in Top End remote indigenous mental health. *Advances in Mental Health, 1*, www.auseinet.com/journal/vol5iss3/nagel.pdf (accessed 29 August 2012).

Nelson, A., & Allison, H. (2007). Relationships: The key to effective occupational therapy practice with urban Australian Indigenous children. *Occupational Therapy International, 14*(1), 57–70.

Ngaanyatjarra Pitjantjatjara Yankunytjatjra Women's Council Aboriginal Corporation. (2003). *Ngangkari work—Anangu way: Traditional healers of Central Australia*. Alice Springs, NT: Ngaanyatjarra Pitjantjatjara Yankunytjatjra Women's Council Aboriginal Corporation/Black Point, NS: Fernwood Publishing.

Panzironi, F. (2013). *Hand-in-hand: Report on Aboriginal traditional medicine*. Fregon, SA: Anangu Ngangkari Tjutaku Aboriginal Corporation (www.antac.org.au).

Paradies, Y. (2006). A systematic review of empirical research on self-reported racism and health. *International Journal of Epidemiology, 35*, 888–901.

Paradies, Y. (2016). Colonisation, racism and indigenous health. *Journal of Population Research, 33*, 83–96.

Paradies, Y. C., & Cunningham, J. (2010). The DRUID study: Exploring medi-ating pathways between racism and depressive symptoms among Indigenous Australians. *Social Psychiatry and Psychiatric Epidemiology, 47*, 165–173.

Pere, L. (2009). Creating better futures: When the theory fails and the future is no more. *Australasian Psychiatry, 17S*, 12–14.

Petchkovsky, L., San Roque, C., Jurra, R., & Butler, S. (2004). Indigenous maps of subjectivity and attacks on linking: Forced separation and its psychiatric sequelae in Australia's Stolen Generation. *Australian Journal for the Advancement of Mental Health, 3*(3).

Peterson, N. (2004). Myth of the 'walkabout': Movement in the Aboriginal domain. In J. Taylor & M. Bell (Eds.), *Population mobility and Indigenous peoples in Australasia and North America* (pp. 223–238). London: Routledge.

Phillips, G. (2003). *Addictions and healing in Aboriginal country.* Canberra, ACT: Aboriginal Studies Press.

Pilkington, D. (Nugi Garimara). (1996). *Follow the rabbit proof fence.* Brisbane: University of Queensland Press.

Powell, M. B. (2000). PRIDE: The essential elements of a forensic interview with an Aboriginal person. *The Australian Psychologist, 35,* 186–192.

Purdie, N., Dudgeon, P., & Walker, R. (2010). *Working together: Aboriginal and Torres Strait Islander mental health and wellbeing principles and practice.* Canberra, ACT: Australian Government Printers.

Reid, J. (1983). *Sorcerers and healing spirits: Continuity and change in an Aboriginal medical system.* Sydney: Pergamon Press.

Ryan, J., Elmi, F. H., Guerin, P. B., & Guerin, B. (2005). *Going 'Walli' and having 'Jinni': Considerations in the evaluation and treatment of Somali refugees.* Paper given at the Mental Health Services Conference, Adelaide, October 2005. Available from: http://psychology.waikato.ac.nz/people/bguerin/.

Scott, J. C. (1985). *Weapons of the weak: Everyday forms of peasant resistance.* New Haven, CT: Yale University Press.

Smith, L. T. (1999). *Decolonizing methodologies: Research and Indigenous Peoples.* Dunedin, NZ: University of Otago Press.

Spencer, D. J. (2000). Anomie and demoralization in transitional cultures: The Australian Aboriginal model. *Transcultural Psychiatry, 37,* 5–10.

Street, J., Baum, F., & Anderson, I. (2007). Developing a collaborative research system for Aboriginal health. *Australian New Zealand Journal of Public Health, 31*(4), 372–378.

Taylor, K., & Guerin, P. (2010). *Health care and Indigenous Australians: Cultural safety in practice.* Sydney: Palgrave-Macmillan.

Tedmanson, D., Guerin, B., Guerin, P., & Clark, Y. (2011). *Policy Dis-Stress: The unbearable 'whiteness' of being (Indigenous and remote).* Paper presented at the International Society of Critical Health Psychology 7th Biennial Conference, Adelaide, South Australia.

Tew, J. (Ed.). (2005). *Social perspectives in mental health: Developing social models to understand and work with mental distress.* London: Jessica Kingsley.

Trudgen, R. (2000). *Why warriors lie down and die: Towards an understanding of why the Aboriginal people of Arnhem Land face the greatest crisis in health and education since European contact.* Darwin, NT: Aboriginal Resource and Development Services.

Trzepacz, D., Guerin, B., & Thomas, J. (2014). Indigenous Country as a context for mental and physical health: Yarning with the Nukunu Community. *The Australian Community Psychologist, 26,* 38–53.

United Nations. (2009). *The state of the world's Indigenous peoples.* New York: United Nations, Department of Economic and Social Affairs.

Vicary, D. A., & Bishop, B. J. (2005). Western psychotherapeutic practice: Engaging Aboriginal people in culturally appropriate and respectful ways. *Australian Psychologist, 40,* 8–19.

Vicary, D., & Westerman, T. (2004). 'That's just the way he is': Some implications of Aboriginal mental health beliefs. *Australian e-Journal for the Advancement of Mental Health, 3*, www.auseinet.com/journal/vol3iss3/vicarywesterman.pdf.

Wagner, W., Duveen, G., Themel, M., & Verma, J. (1999). The modernization of tradition: Thinking about madness in Patna, India. *Culture and Psychology, 5*, 413–445.

Waitoki, W., Nikora, L. M., Harris, P., & Levy, M. (2014). *Māori experiences of bipolar disorder: Pathways to recovery.* Auckland, NZ: Te Pou o te Whakaaro Nui.

Waldram, J. B. (2004). *Revenge of the Windigo: The construction of the mind and mental health of North American Aboriginal peoples.* Toronto: University of Toronto Press.

Wanganeen, R. (2001). Spiritual healing using loss and grief. *Aboriginal and Islander Health Worker Journal, 25*, 12–14.

Wanganeen, R. (2011). Integrating personal and professional experiences: Seven phases to integrating loss and grief. *Grief Matters: The Australian Journal of Grief and Bereavement, 14*, 78–88.

Weaver, H. N., & Brave Heart, M. Y. H. (1999). Examining two facets of American Indian identity: Exposure to other cultures and the influence of historical trauma. *Journal of Human Behavior in the Social Environment, 2*, 19–33.

Westerman, T. (2004). Engagement of indigenous clients in mental health services: What do cultural differences play? *Australian e-Journal for the Advancement of Mental Health, 3*, 1–7.

Wilson, S. (2008). *Research is ceremony: Indigenous research methods.* Black Point, NS: Fernwood.

Wilson, W. A., & Yellow Bird, M. (2005). *For Indigenous eyes only: A decolonization handbook.* Santa Fe, NM: School of American Research Press.

Ypinazar, V., Margolis, S., Haswell-Elkins, M., & Tsey, K. (2007). Indigenous Australians' understandings regarding mental health and disorders. *Australian and New Zealand Journal of Psychiatry, 41*(6), 467–487.

Zacharias, S. (2006). Mexican *Curanderismo* as ethnopsychotherapy: A qualitative study on treatment practices, effectiveness, and mechanisms of change. *International Journal of Disability, Development and Education, 53*, 381–400.

INDEX

Stolen Generations 204, 210, 221–222
stories 6, 39, 64, 67, 73, 80, 97–98; *see also* speakable
strangers 14, 43, 44, 129, 153; properties of 45–46
strategic usurpation 54, 109, 110
stratification 51; *see also* opportunity contexts
stress 53, 97–99, 141–145, 151, 185, 214–215
substrate (physical) 13, 17, 19, 22; *see also* bodily substrate
substitution 59, 139
suffering 2, 23, 31, 121, 96–98, 97–98t4.1
supernatural 11, 13
symbols 85–86, 95
systems theories 10; *see also* ecological thinking

taxonomy 19–20
tedious academic referencing xiii, xiv; *see also* obsession, analysis of
theories xi, xii, 1, 2, 3, 6, 17, 18, 25, 29, 35, 37, 40, 41, 62, 73, 74, 94, 100, 121; *see also* abstractions as discursive strategies; essentialisms
therapies 15, 39, 65
thinking 63–67; and context 12, 42, 63, 67; disorders 65, 69, 88, 155, 162–163; is like 'talking with your audiences about events but not out loud' 68, 89; thinking is not like 'talking-to-yourself about events' 68, 89
thinklings 12, 63
thought 'repression' *see* escape, avoidance

thoughts: do not control actions 36, 42 *see also* controlling actions by thoughts; are external 12, 27, 42, 68; are social 67, 68, 80; not in conflict *see* contradictions not in world but in audiences; as readiness to speak 42, 68; 'rehearsed' 67
transcultural 12, 207
trauma 9, 52–53, 190, 222–223; *see also* post-traumatic stress disorder
trust 38, 47, 55, 71, 102, 113, 119, 160, 190, 212, 222
truth 65, 70
two systems of cognition 79–80

unconscious 42, 63, 79
uncontrollable behaviour 110, 163
understanding behaviour 38, 42
unwanted behaviour 110, 163
usurpation *see* strategic usurpation

verbal reports, paucity of 8, 69, 74, 75
virtual reality 71–73

walking contingencies 80
Weber, M. 138–139, 140
weird, strange behaviours 48, 77, 94, 109
western relationships 13, 16, 39, 45–46, 47; *see also* stranger relationships
'witchcraft' 14, 206
women, see gender inequalities; *see also* essentialisms
words versus world 69–70, 75; *see also* Zen
work colleague relationships 49, 88, 131, 132, 144

Zen 69, 72, 165, 169

Taylor & Francis eBooks

Helping you to choose the right eBooks for your Library

Add Routledge titles to your library's digital collection today. Taylor and Francis ebooks contains over 50,000 titles in the Humanities, Social Sciences, Behavioural Sciences, Built Environment and Law.

Choose from a range of subject packages or create your own!

Benefits for you

» Free MARC records
» COUNTER-compliant usage statistics
» Flexible purchase and pricing options
» All titles DRM-free.

Benefits for your user

» Off-site, anytime access via Athens or referring URL
» Print or copy pages or chapters
» Full content search
» Bookmark, highlight and annotate text
» Access to thousands of pages of quality research at the click of a button.

REQUEST YOUR **FREE** INSTITUTIONAL TRIAL TODAY

Free Trials Available
We offer free trials to qualifying academic, corporate and government customers.

eCollections – Choose from over 30 subject eCollections, including:

Archaeology	Language Learning
Architecture	Law
Asian Studies	Literature
Business & Management	Media & Communication
Classical Studies	Middle East Studies
Construction	Music
Creative & Media Arts	Philosophy
Criminology & Criminal Justice	Planning
Economics	Politics
Education	Psychology & Mental Health
Energy	Religion
Engineering	Security
English Language & Linguistics	Social Work
Environment & Sustainability	Sociology
Geography	Sport
Health Studies	Theatre & Performance
History	Tourism, Hospitality & Events

For more information, pricing enquiries or to order a free trial, please contact your local sales team:
www.tandfebooks.com/page/sales

R Routledge
Taylor & Francis Group | The home of Routledge books

www.tandfebooks.com

PROPERTY OF
SENECA COLLEGE
LIBRARIES
KING CAMPUS